D0116148

TRANSGENERATIONAL

DESIGN Products for an Aging Population

JAMES J. PIRKL

VAN NOSTRAND REINHOLD VNR
New York

Library of Congress Catalog Card Number 93-9870
ISBN 0-442-01065-6

I(T)P   Van Nostrand Reinhold is an International Thomson Publishing company.
          ITP logo is a trademark under license.

Printed in Hong Kong.

Van Nostrand Reinhold
115 Fifth Avenue
New York, NY 10003

International Thomson Publishing Germany
Königswinterer Str. 418
53227 Bonn
Germany

International Thomson Publishing
Berkshire House, 168-173
High Holborn, London WC1V 7AA
England

International Thomson Publishing Asia
221 Henderson Building #05-10
Singapore 0315

Thomas Nelson Australia
102 Dodds Street
South Melbourne 3205
Victoria, Australia

International Thomson Publishing Japan
Kyowa Building, 3F
2-2-1 Hirakawacho
Chiyoda-Ku, Tokyo 102
Japan

Nelson Canada
1120 Birchmount Road
Scarborough, Ontario
M1K 5G4, Canada

CP 16 15 14 13 12 11 10 9 8 7 6 5 4 3 2 1

Library of Congress Cataloging-in-Publication Data

Pirkl, James Joseph, 1930–
    Transgenerational design : products for an aging population /
  James Joseph Pirkl.
        p.   cm.
    Includes bibliographical references and index.
    ISBN 0-442-01065-6
    1. Aged as consumers—United States.   2. Aging—United States.
  I. Title.
HC110.C6P57   1993
658.8'348—dc20   93-9870
                                          CIP

To Sarah, my wife, and our children,
Theo, Jay, and Philip

J.J.P.

Contents

PART 4: THE TRIUMPH OF CONSCIENCE

Foreword
At the Heart of It All

Arthur J. Pulos, FIDSA *

We have been so conditioned by depersonalized knowledge—by the reality that facts are facts—that we tend to forget that people, everyone, you and I, are at the heart of it all. Recognizing and accepting our common obligation to one another is the first step toward putting a human face on science and technology, communications, and our personal and shared places on this planet. Transgenerational design is finding its place between the physicist and psychologist, between engineer and huckster, between print and electronic images, and between us and our environment. Transgenerational design is our alter ego—our confidential representative—offering a "neutral field" as James Pirkl proposes, for a harmonization of different philosophies and professional specializations.

Transgenerational design establishes a common ground for those who are committed to an integrated rather than a divided society. It is possible that the fragmentation of society into targets for study or sales has contributed to a decline of empathy and social responsibility that permits exploitation without pangs of conscience. However, with the cooperation of scientists and planners as well as industrial and mercantile establishments, transgenerational design promises that our aging citizens may be brought back into the mainstream of society. Its underlying principle is that human beings, including those who are aged, have an equal right to live in a unified society. Fundamental to this principle is the fact that there must be sympathetic accord among those professions responsible for the quality of products and the environment.

It was once conventional wisdom that services and products could be provided in a home that met the physical, social, and cultural needs of all

---

*Chairman Emeritus of the department of design at Syracuse University, a Fellow, past president and board chairman of the Industrial Designers Society of America (IDSA) and the International Council of Societies of Industrial Design (ICSID)

age groups from infants and toddlers, through teenagers, college students, and newlyweds to homemakers, mature adults, and senior citizens. This multigenerational structure depended on its members to share the burdens and pleasures of communal living. There was a time when the young, the mature, and the aging lived in harmony, with each administering to the needs and comforts of the others. However, since then, as various age groups have spun away to form separate households, each has become a distinct marketing target for independent professionals, builders, and manufacturers. At first glance one might presume that this practice would lead to better services and products meeting the unique needs of each targeted group. Yet, this well-intended specialization with its attendant fragmentation, whatever the immediate benefits might be, may also work against the general public good. There is now increasing competition as each age group insists on having its own needs met first.

Present marketing programs are aimed directly at the consumer group expected to purchase the product. The target may be a prospective bride or new homemakers who are expected to either buy the product themselves or have it bought for them. Yet many of these products may continue to be used by the original recipients whose reflexes and acuity have changed over the years since the product was acquired. As a result they may become victims of their own acquisitions in later years.

Manufacturers, understandably, develop and manufacture products following certain physical, performance, and aesthetic criteria that promise to be attractive to a carefully researched market. We might, for example, describe one such market as comprised of men and women in their twenties and thirties whose sense perceptions and physical abilities are at their peak and who are in the process of acquiring and equipping a home enriched with the pleasures and promises of technology for themselves or their family.

The majority of people may not see any reason to concern themselves with changes and social segregation that will penalize them as they become older and less able to cope with their own earlier idyllic environment. They believe that the American dream will one day carry them to a higher life style where technological advances will provide them with new products commensurate with their new status. If, however, they do not move up and their products are not replaced, they and others who follow may find themselves in an environment whose architectural features are now inhospitable, equipped with furnishings that are falling apart and undependable appliances with worn controls and faded labeling which are becoming more difficult to use and increasingly threatening to their health and welfare.

It is logical to expect manufacturers and promoters to direct products to those most likely to purchase them. It is not realistic in a conventional sense to expect them to consider those not included in the targeted market. Nor are they obligated to take into account the fact that purchasers will move from one stage of living to another. However, it is evident that new technologies and more conscientious manufacturing can provide longer product life in harmony with the fact that people themselves are living longer. It is increasingly shortsighted and may even be humanistically and environmentally irresponsible to consider products as fragile acquisitions to be consumed and discarded in a relatively short time. As an aside there is a growing rebellion of sorts among collectors of "modern antiques" (there's an oxymoron for you) who are rescuing and even returning to service products that were made years earlier. Such products were manufactured at a time before the now questionable principle that shorter product life and disposability were good for business.

Most designers are still trying to live down the era when planned obsolescence was the catchword of clever marketing. All that this accomplished was to create a vast marketing and promotional establishment that was presumably more important than the quality of the product itself. Echoes from that era still reverberate in the current focus on peripheral aspects of design management that appear to be less concerned with public service and product accountability than they are with the world of marketing as an end in itself. Too often what is ON the package seems to be more important than what is IN it.

One hopes that a reawakened social conscience will help manufacturers turn their attention to more humane products better able to serve the public welfare over a longer period of time. There is no virtue in a product whose deliberate obsolescence for marketing reasons jeopardizes a human being whether or not he or she happens to be elderly.

It is also evident that attractive products can be designed to meet the needs of a broader spectrum of users without diminishing their value to those who purchase them. This should not be confused with the "styling" that employs superficial implications of value and relevance that can be extolled by promotional media. Such misguided energy might be better put to searching out and refining the real values and meaning of a product's typeform. In fact, this policy would enhance the end value of products by increasing quality and reducing the present impact of psychological and physical obsolescence on society and the environment. A more enlightened philosophy on the part of manufacturers would help redirect those institutions and industries that now support and even encourage the widening of the social chasm between various adult age groups in our society.

A more rational and sensitive approach to architectural and product design would better serve consumers as well as builders and manufacturers. Broadening design criteria to bring the aging back into the fold would make homes, furnishings, and products more useful and safe for everyone.

Product forms that communicate their function and means of operation should be the first order of importance to designers and manufacturers. Such simple changes as larger typefaces on product controls, labels, and instructional literature would convey their meaning to everyone with increased efficiency and safety. By some peculiar twist of design logic it is still presumed that smaller markings and instructions (referred to as "jewelry" in the trade) connote quality. Another curious aspect of applied aesthetics dictates that product elements and controls must be designed to serve style equally with utility and safety. Every whim of the art world is also immediately reflected in the form and configuration of products. Note the awards for design given by designers to designers. And witness the irresponsible configuration of such simple daily necessities as "designer" telephones and kettles as well as the amorphous form (another oxymoron) of automobiles. These are evidence of a baroque era of product aesthetics that may now, it is to be hoped, give way to the more intelligent functionality of computer-driven form.

There also appears to be a lapse in communication between the makers and users of products. Manufacturers listen to their corporate boards and stockholders while focusing attention on the "bottom line" where there are no human beings. Merchandisers seem to be enthralled with performances in the marketplace. Advertisers wave print and electronic images flagrantly at professional buyers. Designers aspire for the star system approbation of their own colleagues. And parents purchase products for their children in the same way adults do for their aging parents. All of these trends tend to contribute to the stereotypes for various consumer groups that are established to further isolate them from one another.

Today's products and furnishings are being developed to match what is considered to be public taste with the planned parameters of price, durability, and service. In the process quality control is taken into account as a means of eliminating waste of energy and materials. Yet, despite its friendly implications, it may also serve to reduce product quality to the lowest level acceptable in the marketplace that promises a stronger marketing position and/or a greater financial return to the maker. It is also believed to be essential to the survival and growth of industry that the public be encouraged to make successive purchases to replace worn-out or outmoded products with others that have been upgraded functionally and technologically or are more fashionable.

One would expect that the elderly, who may be bypassed by product planners, would be especially receptive to those products and services attuned to their capabilities and needs. As a result the "graying" of America has stimulated the establishment of industries to serve this growing market area. Some have found a lucrative market in the production of accessories that supplement the capabilities or rectify the shortcomings of original products. Other companies are engaged in the research, development, and marketing of special appliances, furnishings, and clothing to serve an aging population.

Again, despite the goodwill and conscientiousness that attract manufacturers to this area of public service, such products often stigmatize rather than dignify the aging. An environmental otherworld now seems to exist, as manifested in the paradox that, in a society that prides itself on eternal youth, its elder citizens are obliged to retire from public view to seek a safer place for themselves. One suspects that those who promote retirement homes and villages at various economic levels, no matter how conscientious they may be, are perhaps inadvertently creating isolated retreats for the elderly that blemish the social fabric of America. Once a society provides such well-meaning havens, often at an inordinate cost to the residents, it presumes that its familial and social responsibilities to them have been discharged.

We should acknowledge that all humans have similar needs and desires and that, therefore, no one should be discriminated against by an environment conceived to suit narrower social and economic norms. There remains the final disturbing vision of a democracy shredding itself by endorsing segregation rather than encouraging integration.

Intergenerational design is a very small step in the right direction. Nevertheless, it represents a large leap toward a future that may begin to mend the American social fabric.

The search goes on, with human beings AT THE HEART OF IT ALL.

Preface

Transgenerational Design is a book with two purposes: first, to sensitize the reader to the aging process by exploring those physical and sensory changes that occur throughout one's life span; and second, to help people make intelligent decisions connected with designing, producing, marketing, specifying, or buying consumer products and environments for use by our aging population. It is intended for use by those who may not have specialized knowledge about the aging process and whose uninformed decisions may unwittingly discriminate against older as well as younger people.

- ▶ *Designers:* industrial designers, interior designers, graphic designers, architects, planners and engineers

- ▶ *Producers:* manufacturers, builders, and contractors

- ▶ *Marketers:* buyers, advertisers, packagers, wholesalers, and retailers

- ▶ *Managers* of nursing homes, retirement communities, housing developments, hotels and motels, and city governments

- ▶ *Health care professionals:* physicians, nurses, social workers, and elder care personnel

- ▶ *Consumers of our artifact environment:* particularly middle-aged, elderly, and people with disabilities

Such a book is long overdue. Although I offer its message to a multi-disciplinary audience, I do not presume a matching set of expertise. Rather, I seek expertise in sources beyond my field, link and present their data and opinions, create new patterns of understanding, and offer a unique perspective. While specialists within a variety of professional disciplines may probe this book seeking definitive answers to particular problems, I offer it as a neutral field, a meeting place for disparate points of view. In this sense the book is meant to be *generic* rather than *scientific*—an inquiry into the human factor called aging, providing a workable strategy for accommodating the sensory and physical challenges faced by many throughout our transgenerational population.

Some may argue that a book attempting to weave together so many multidisciplinary threads can have little "scientific" validity. Notwithstanding, the question of whether any human factor investigation is a science at all, is, according to Chapanis (1992), irrelevant. He suggests that the real question is whether human factors information is ultimately useful to design. "If it is properly defined and circumscribed and correctly applied," he argues, "the answer is an unequivocal 'yes'." This is my goal.

The book also has a peripheral purpose. It broadens the conventional idea of "environmental support" to include the microenvironmental level—those singular products and artifacts on which all of us depend to maintain our independence as we undertake the activities of daily living. It explores a timely set of conceptual opposites—the "young" and the "old"—a relationship whose essence is at the heart of design discrimination.

Many of us remain blind to those struggling to maintain their precious independence, forced to cope with products and environments once desirable and helpful but now hostile and unyielding. Unfortunately, we tend to associate decreased physical capabilities with growing old. But many of these same conditions also affect the younger generations. Indeed, a great number of conditions that limit the freedom and independence of many older people also affect those who are considered "young." I want to make that connection clear by presenting data supporting another view of age accommodation; a *transgenerational* view that removes the barriers between young and old, and erases the artificial distinctions that have discriminated against so many for so long.

Throughout the book I will be promoting the concept of transgenerational design as a strategy for eliminating design discrimination against older members of the population. The premise behind the transgenerational design idea demands that we expand the range of product and environmental usability to include elderly people as well as younger generations—*without penalty to either group.* Transgenerational design is based on the fact that many physical limitations normally associated with older people are also found in many younger members of the population.

I am not interested in providing quick-fix formulas for designing or selling "elderly" products—I am interested in changing perceptions about growing old and eliminating design discrimination toward all, regardless of age. Moreover, I will present ideas and facts that can penetrate the outdated mental structures we have built around us, and shatter the false distinctions that limit our perceptions and understanding about what is "young" and what is "old."

It would be foolhardy for me to suggest that the book's content offers more than an overview of the subject's complex knowledge base. It does not. Moving from part to part, it touches many professional specialities. It will explore the impact of an aging society on a variety of issues ranging from consumer products to life care communities; from managing the environment to communicating with persons with hearing and hearing and sight impairments. I will address the issue of design discrimination of elderly people from the point of view of an industrial design educator, offering some observations about the impact of technology on an aging society and how the elderly have become the victims of discrimination by design. I will conclude with a collection of designs that succeed in accommodating a transgenerational population while, at the same time, maintaining their appeal to younger generations. These may offer an insight or two that may prove useful to your own area of specialization as, together, we explore the challenge of creating a humane environment that appeals to all and discriminates against none.

Acknowledgments

My appreciation goes to the many people who have helped make this book a reality:

To those who reviewed the final manuscript and offered valuable advice and suggestions: Arthur J. Pulos, Chairman Emeritus of Syracuse University's Department of Design, who helped me grow as a designer, educator, and human being during our 28-year association; Walter M. Beattie, Jr., Professor Emeritus and founder of Syracuse University's All-University Gerontology Center, who introduced me to the field of gerontology over two decades ago; Richard Hollerith, industrial design colleague and member of the President's Committee on the Employment of People with Disabilities, whose suggestions shaped the book's outline and clarified its intended message.

To Gershon Vincow, vice-chancellor of Syracuse University, and Donald M. Lantzy, dean of the College of Visual and Performing Arts, for the research sabbatical that granted me the time to write this book.

To Syracuse University colleagues whose collaboration on past projects conferred many useful insights: Neal S. Bellos, professor of social work; Robert M. Diamond, assistant vice-chancellor for instructional development; gerontologist Anna L. Babic.

My gratitude also extends to others for their helpful information and advice, especially: Jean M. Coyle, Ph.D., director of the Institute for Gerontological Research and Education (TIGRE), New Mexico State University; Health Educator, Theo M.P. Gilmore, R.N., B.S.N.; Vernon I. Greene, Ph.D., director of the All-University Gerontology Center, Syracuse University; Richard J. Ham, M.D., Distinguished Chair in Geriatric Medicine, State University of New York Health Science Center; and Mark A. Stratton, Pharm.D., director of the Center for Aging, University of New Mexico.

Special thanks go to the following colleagues and organizations for contributing information and providing the photographic illustrations without which Part 4 would not have been possible:

Colleagues Bradford W. Agry, Andrew Alger, Douglas J. Birkholz, Daniel Blitzer, Douglas Cleminshaw, Deborah S. Coffee, Morison Cousins, Todd

Dannenberg, Alberto Delser, Larry Eisenbach, Frank Ferreri, Robert Graeff, David Hodge, Geoff Hollington, John T. Houlihan, David W. Kaiser, Kevin W. Jameson, Scott A. Johnstone, Joseph L. Kemme, Stephen B. Leonard, David Levy, Robert L. Marvin, Jr., Pascal Malassigne, Sue Manfred, R. Kathy McCain, Michael McCue, Patricia A. Moore, Joseph C. Moro, David Muyers, James A. Odom, Lee Payne, James Roediger, Ward Sanders, Len Singer, Edward P. Stevens, Joseph L. Ungari, Tucker Viemeister, Jennifer Ward, Gianfranco Zaccai, Adele Zeller.

Organizations Advance Retail Technologies, Advanced Technology Labs, American Foundation for the Blind, AMSCO International, Inc., Anderson Design Associates, Arthritis Foundation, AT&T, Baxter Healthcare Corporation, Novocor Division, Better Living Products, Inc., California Medical Products, Inc., Clement Clarke International, Cleminshaw Design Group, David Hodge Design, Inc., DeFelsko Corporation, Department of Health and Human Services, Geriatric Initiatives Branch, Design Continuum Inc., The Design Management Institute, Diversified Fiberglass Fabricators, Doron Precision Systems, Inc., Fiskars, Inc., Guynes Design Incorporated, Goldsmith Yamasaki Specht, Inc., Guardian Medical Sunrise, Inc., Henry Dreyfuss Associates, Herman Miller Corporation, Hollington Associates, Honeywell, IDEO Product Development, Kangaroo Motocaddies, Kohler Company, La Grange Memorial Hospital, Kevcor Limited, Lee Payne Associates, Inc., Lightolier, Machen Montague, Inc., McGaw, Inc., META-FORM design, Moore Design Associates, Moro Design, National Association of Retired Persons, National Institute on Aging, Omron Healthcare, Inc., Oxo International, Polaroid Corporation, Prince Corporation, Robins Industries, Inc., Kitchen Art Division, Smart Design, Inc., Timex Corporation, Tucker Housewares, Inc., a Mobil Company, Tupperware, University of Wisconsin–Stout, Virginia Polytechnic Institute, Wheaton Medical Technologies, Division of Wheaton Industries, Inc., William Stumpf & Associates, Virginia Polytechnic Institute and State University, Zanussi/Zeltron, Zelco Industries, Inc.

My students also deserve special acknowledgment. Over the past three decades, many have pursued the deeper meanings of design activities and succeeded in enlarging the concept of professional service to the benefit of us all. Many examples of their sensitive design contributions are represented in this book.

I am indebted to Amanda Miller, my editor at Van Nostrand Reinhold, for her early, enthusiastic support; her guidance, patience, understanding, and professionalism.

Finally, I want to thank my wife, Sarah, for her constant belief, encouragement, and support; for deflecting the many distractions; for her valuable insights and suggestions; and for countless hours of editing the drafts. I will always be grateful.

THE NEW CENTURIONS

*"There is as much difference
between us and ourselves as
between us and others."*
—MICHEL DE MONTAIGNE
(1533–1592)

How Young is Old? A Problem of Perception

▶ A DESIGN PARADOX

Most of us are familiar with a variety of opposite concepts. Obvious examples are dark/light, good/bad, large/small, and birth/death. Years of education and experience have molded our perception and understanding of these concepts. We feel comfortable manipulating their distinctions and applying them in a wide range of daily situations. Yet their normal use is at variance with another notion expressed by Zukav (1989) who labels such opposite concepts "false distinctions." They are, he writes, "self-maintained illusions that we create . . . the sole cause of paradoxes."

To understand paradoxes, Zen Buddhist monks learn to abandon their dependence on reason and gain sudden intuitive enlightenment by exploring the *koan,* a puzzle which cannot be answered in ordinary ways because it is paradoxical. A *koan* changes our perceptions and understanding of such false distinctions. "What is the sound of one hand clapping?" is a Zen koan (Zukav 1989).

Today, another pair of opposites—*young* and *old*—challenges our perception and understanding, demanding we acquire a new sense of intuitive enlightenment. These "false distinctions" present us with a design puzzle we cannot solve with yesterday's preconceptions based on biased distortions of intellect. Each of us carries baggage weighted with conceptual limitations that prevent us from seeing the environmental realities encountered daily by the older generations as they pursue the activities of daily living (ADL).[1] "Only by penetrating the confines of our conceptual limitations," says Zukav, "can we hear the sound of one clapping hand." And only by dismantling our preconceptions of age can we be free to understand the paradox: *How young are the old?*

1. The term "activities of daily living" (ADL) normally refers to the six basic ADLs on the Index of Independence in Activities of Daily Living developed by Katz (1970). They include bathing, dressing, toileting, transferring, continence, and feeding. Additional ADLs include communication, grooming, visual capability, walking, and use of the upper extremities (Ham 1991).

► MYTHS OF AGING

Whatever our age, someone thinks of us as old, and, indeed we will always be older than someone else. To a teenager, someone who is "thirty something" is almost elderly. Centenarians regard octogenarians as youthful. A 5-year-old feels grown up when viewing a newborn brother or sister.

Today, it is commonplace to acknowledge the greying of America and declare one's sensitivity to the "problems of the elderly." But this, like the explosive growth of the elderly population, is a recent phenomenon. We tend to believe that today's values and attitudes have always existed. But the ebb and flow of our cultural transformation tends over time to erode societal attitudes, forming new ones that evolve, develop, and flourish. The problem of course, stated clearly by Achenbaum and Kusnerz (1978) is that "we must continually question whether we are addressing real needs or figments of our imagination." Yet, this is not an easy distinction to make.

It seems to be characteristic of attitudes and images that they echo the same forces that induced them—particularly those that mold our perceptions and crystalize our concept of growing old. We have realized only recently that the flow of changes over the past 200 years has affected our attitudes about the elderly, forcing us to reevaluate our image of those we call "old."

Gerontologists generally accept the idea that the condition of older Americans has improved significantly during the past half-century. Yet, despite fairly significant gains in income, health care, employment opportunities, and life style, "most Americans," according to Achenbaum and Kusnerz (1978) "subscribe to negative ideas of older people which once seemed to make sense, but which no longer have any basis in fact." While many people, old as well as young, still believe the myth that all old people are either infirm, senile, or warehoused in nursing homes, the facts present a dramatically different picture. Such "stereotypes," say Achenbaum and Kusnerz (1978), "are not simply distortions of current 'facts': they sometimes represent the persistence of earlier 'truths,' which subsequently have been invalidated." Such "earlier truths" about growing old, fossilized by time and preserved by older persons as well as the young, still persist. Here are some examples:

The Myth of Senility

MYTH: *Older persons "naturally" grow more confused, child-like, forgetful, and lose contact with reality. They become "senile."*
REALITY: Senility is an outdated term referring to abnormal deterioration in the mental functions of some old people, linking the process of

growing old to symptoms of forgetfulness, confusion, and changes in behavior and personality. Such an image is false, stereotypical, and is neither a normal sign of aging nor even a disease (Fiber and Neurath 1985). The word "senility" implies an assumption about the elderly that, because they are old, they are also mentally deficient. This insidious myth, still perpetuated by society and reinforced by the media, discriminates against the elderly by causing or promoting social isolation, dependency, and loss of independence.

The Myth of Disability

MYTH: *Older persons with severe functional disabilities experience a greater number of associated diseases than those with less severe disabilities.*
REALITY: Researchers have found no correlation between the severity of a functional disability and the number of associated diseases. While incidences of both increase with age, the number of diseases affecting a person does not equate with either the severity of a disability or the magnitude of functional loss. Vigorous older people can acquire several diseases and remain independent. Conversely, many older people with severe functional disabilities remain otherwise healthy (Besdine 1990).

The Myth of Asexuality

MYTH: *Older people lack interest in and capacity for sexual activity.*
REALITY: Considerable sociological and medical evidence has established that our need for intimacy, its quality and capacity, need not diminish with age. In one study, over half the men and women between the ages of 60 and 93 indicated that they were sexually active overall, with "no significant decline from past activity under the age of 75" (Comfort 1990).

The Myth of Homogeneity

MYTH: *As we age, we lose our individual differences and become progressively more alike.*
REALITY: Aging does not affect us as a person; our personality remains fairly constant. Not only do we retain our individual differences throughout our lives, these differences become even more pronounced as we get older. We generally become more like our youthful self; i.e., a talkative teenager, for example, becoming a talkative older person and a stubborn youngster carrying the trait of stubbornness into old age (Pirkl and Babic 1988). Except for changes in our physical appearance and experiencing more physical problems, being "old" feels no different from how we feel now or when we were young (Comfort 1990). In reality, an old person is a young person who has just lived longer.

The Myth of Poverty

MYTH: *Older people are generally poor with little economic clout.*
REALITY: Older persons receive income from diverse sources, and their assets and net worth range from poverty to great wealth. Those over the age of 50 control over 50 percent of America's discretionary spending funds (Ostroff 1989), and those over 65 control 77 percent of all assets (Pirkl and Babic 1988). Home ownership is enjoyed by 75 percent of older Americans. In terms of net worth, 18 percent have less than $5000 while 13 percent show over $250,000. Significantly, one third of all millionaires in America are over the age of 65 (Pirkl and Babic 1988).

The Myth of Lonely Isolation

MYTH: *Older persons are abandoned by their families and forced to live out their lives in isolation, loneliness, and despondency.*
REALITY: Most older people do not live alone. Over half of those age 65 and over live with a spouse or with other relatives, while less than one in five live alone. Most of these, however, are women, who account for 14.8 percent compared to only 4.6 percent of older men who live alone (U.S. Bureau of the Census[2]).

The Myth of Dependency

MYTH: *The elderly become helpless and cannot take care of themselves.*
REALITY: The overwhelming majority of older people are not helpless and for the most part can and do take care of themselves. Ninety-four percent of those over 65 live independently and enjoy many of the same activities as do younger people. It is important to understand that very few older persons require *specialized* products. Most want—and use—the same kinds of consumer products enjoyed by younger generations. Many, however, have demonstrated remarkable ingenuity in modifying such products to accommodate their functional limitations. Yet, relatively few require assistance with their daily living activities; that is, one quarter of those under age 85 and less than half of those over age 85. Furthermore, only 4 to 6 percent of all older people are institutionalized at any one time (Pirkl and Babic 1988).

The Myth of the Rocking Chair

MYTH: *As age increases we withdraw, become inactive, and cease being productive.*

2. U.S. Bureau of the Census, *Current Population Reports*, series P-20, No. 445.

REALITY: Healthy aging covers the spectrum from introspective disengagement to staying active for a long as possible. Diminished capabilities and personal preferences also tend to affect our level of activity. These factors, coupled with personality differences, result in some of us staying active while others disengage. "The goal," according to Sloane (1992), "is that the older adult lives a personally satisfying and socially satisfactory life."

The Myth of Inability

MYTH: *Older persons are forgetful, incapable of learning, and refuse to adopt new way.*

REALITY: Aging does not affect our ability to learn. The information processing literature does not support the idea that cognitive functioning declines with age (Bikson and Goodchilds 1978). While we may experience some difficulty with short-term memory as we get older, our long-term memory generally remains sound. Older persons do, however, tend to solve problems differently than younger persons, preferring to "think things out" rather than relying on "trial and error." And while our reaction time increases with age and correlates with the complexity of a task, this increase is only measured in milliseconds (Pirkl and Babic 1988).

The Myth of Retirement

MYTH: *Most persons retire between ages 65 and 70.*

REALITY: Although the 1978 amendments to the Age Discrimination in Employment Act raised the mandatory retirement age to 70 for most workers, today, over 60 percent choose to retire early (Smedley 1976). In fact, early retirement before the age of 65 has become a pattern ingrained in our society. Indeed, all indications point to this trend continuing; but this does not mean that people will stop working.

▶ CHANGING IMAGES[3]

Throughout the centuries the basic qualities inherent in human aging, including cognitive capabilities and emotional sensibilities, have remained demonstrably unchanged. Yet, our *perception* of older people reflects the ebb and flow of roles and values accorded them by society. Over the years,

---

3. This section was developed from historical information contained in Achenbaum, W. Andrew, and Peggy Ann Kusnerz, 1978. *Images of Old Age in America: 1790 to Present.* Ann Arbor, MI: Institute of Gerontology.

various age-related myths and stereotypes form and replace the realities of aging. Dychtwald (1985) tells us, "These myths obscure the truth about the later years of life and ultimately undermine our images and expectations of our potential for vigor and health as we grow older." But what are the earlier truths? From where and how do the myths of age originate?

It should be apparent that our elders have not always been associated with low status. Indeed, the past offers numerous examples in which older persons enjoyed exalted positions. Gray and Wilcox (1981) note that most societies at some point in their history have been a gerontocracy (a society ruled by elders): "the Aztec, the Inca, the Maya, the major tribes of Oceania and Africa, the Aborigines."

Ancient writings and words record the exaltation and deep respect accorded our elder ancestors. Praising old age in his essay *De Senectute* written in 50 B.C., Cicero, at age 63, declared, "If there were no old men there would be no civilized states. Old age is far from being deprived of good council; on the contrary, it has these qualities in the highest degree. States have always been ruined by young men socially, and restored by the old" (Gray and Wilcox 1981).

Familiar words can also hold deeper meanings. The patriarch of an Anglo-Saxon clan was called the *aldor* or *ealdor,* which appeared as "elder" during the Dark Ages. These terms, according to Gray and Wilcox (1981), evolved into the political title, *aldorman,* adopted by the magistrates of trade guilds long before the term became "alderman" and entered the modern system of local government.

Gray and Wilcox (1981) offer two reasons why earlier societies held old people in high regard. Both reveal factors that set us apart from earlier times. One reason for their high status is that older people were society's repository of knowledge and wisdom acquired from a lifetime of experiences. Their deep understanding of traditional customs and rituals, tool-making and crafts, and politics and warfare, assured their continued respect and adulation. The second reason that old people were honored is simply because they were rare. Not many lived to an old age. Today, telecommunication systems dispense knowledge and information to anyone, anywhere, instantaneously; and reaching age 80, 90, or even 100 is no longer remarkable.

Thus, it is not surprising to find that America's 200-year legacy of growth and change should echo centuries of evolving images and values, and mold them into our current perception of aging.

The Young Republic

The period from the American Revolution to the Civil War saw most older Americans treated with deference and respect. Their lifelong contributions were not only recognized but, in fact, "venerated" by fellow citizens.

Achenbaum and Kusnerz (1978) point out that Noah Webster illustrated the meaning of "to venerate" in the 1828 first edition of his famous dictionary with terms familiar to readers of his day: "We venerate parents and elders . . . we venerate old age or grey hairs . . . we venerate . . . the Gospel."

The virtuous life, valued highly during the birth of our nation, was exemplified by the elderly. Prior to 1860, these older men and women were considered "custodians of virtue" and were respected for their age, wisdom, and experience. They enjoyed a place of importance within the family and the community. Their business experience—like that of Benjamin Franklin, whose advice continued after his death—was widely sought.

As the republic grew, the elderly remained influential. "America relied on the experience of its elder statesmen," Achenbaum and Kusnerz state that "countless federal, state, and local laws disqualified young men from voting or holding office but for the most part older men could—and did—play an active role in government." This kind of elder involvement was not unusual. John Quincy Adams, elected to the House of Representatives at age 61 after leaving the presidency in 1829, continued to serve his constituency and wielded considerable influence until his death at 81.

A Time of Transition

American's favorable view of old age endured through the Civil War and beyond. The country's respected artists and poets of the time portrayed the elderly's usefulness with admiration, affection, and respect. "For age is opportunity no less than youth itself, though in another dress" wrote Henry Wadsworth Longfellow in his *Morituri Salutamus* of 1875. But the seeds of change had already begun to germinate; American culture and society was beginning to change, and a new picture of the elderly was beginning to emerge. "Longfellow's good friend, Ralph Waldo Emerson," Achenbaum and Kusnerz note, "never could have predicted that the dark liabilities rather than the dazzling assets of old age would come to dominate images of the elderly."

The industrial revolution magnified the changes America experienced by the shock of the Civil War. As the world raced toward industrialization the experience of age, with its sage advice previously sought by the young and passed from the old, became less valued. Youthful attributes—strength, endurance, agility, and stamina—became increasingly valued. Moreover, the competitive pressures of reconstruction fueled the need for American industry to increase production, and one way to do this was to eliminate workers who were "slow." Those over 40 quickly became less desirable—those over 60, expendable. The friction of America's first round of discrimination by age sparked the country's first mandatory industrial retirement systems.

The Birth of Technology

At the turn of the century, medical science, with help from improved public sanitation, extended the lives of young people but failed to cure what Dr. Elie Metchnikkoff, a leading medical researcher of the era, called the "infectious, chronic disease" of old age. Scientific wisdom of the day doubted seriously that old people led "normal" lives. In fact, Achenbaum informs us that "the 'authoritative' research of the day led to the conclusion that sex after 50 was both unnatural and risky," proclaimed by doctors to be "medically and morally reprehensible." The myth of "the dirty old man," he notes, "took on more sinister implications."[4]

An emerging dynamo of youth generated the energy that charged the roaring twenties. "Work was not just a part of life, explains Neary (1990a), "it was life itself, relinquished only by death or illness." Yet, many "old dogs," ignored or excluded by their age, were forced to "learn new tricks." Others chose, instead, isolation and inactivity. Sensing keenly the new negative roles assigned to them, the elderly endured the prejudice of an insensitive society by turning inward. They frequently "shut their eyes to other possibilities," notes Achenbaum, thus, "they themselves contributed to the process of social isolation in old age."

The Rise of Dependency

The changes sweeping American life between 1865 and 1935 altered the dimensions of old-age dependency. The elderly's earlier self-reliance, sharpened and honed by the natural forces that governed a life style based on agriculture, could not be easily maintained in the city. Very few could maintain their independence after their working days ended without peddling their wares or selling off their belongings. Increasing financial hardship eroded their independence. Public assistance under freedmen's and veterans' programs was available—but only to the few who qualified. According to Achenbaum and Kusnerz (1978), "as late as 1929, 80% of all those over 65 who had any type of public assistance were only eligible because they were veterans or veterans' widows, not because they were needy." Providing special relief measures for those in need was deemed "socialistic, too expensive, and a threat to family stability." Consequently, county poor-houses and old age homes became the alternatives for those without family support or alternative means for public assistance.

The Depths of Despair

Of those traumatized by the Great Depression, few suffered more or carried their scars longer than America's older people. Soaring unemployment,

---

4. Today's bumper stickers that proclaim, "I'm not a dirty old man—I'm a sexy senior citizen," are contemporary attempts to erase this lingering derogatory image.

bank closings, exhausted savings, and bankrupted pension funds brought the country to its knees. The tragic social and human conditions spotlighted the fragility of unsupported old age, shocking the national conscience into providing the elderly with a greater form of future security than simple self-sufficiency. Older people had become a social responsibility and burden. The once-venerable elderly were now reviled.

A New Dignity

In his message to Congress, June 8, 1934, President Franklin Delano Roosevelt declared, "I am looking for a sound means which I can recommend to provide at once security against several of the great disturbing factors in life—especially those which relate to unemployment and old age." Within 2 years, at 3:30 p.m., on August 14, 1935, the Social Security Act was signed into law. The country was committed to helping America's elderly citizens cope with financial adversity.

Since then, our federal, state, and local governments have created many new, imaginative programs to help elderly persons maintain a dignified life style and image: the Older Americans Act (OAA) and Medicare legislation approved in 1965 have been followed by various housing programs and other elder services offering educational, nutritional, and social benefits. The dramatic increase in our elderly population has demanded increasing program effectiveness and, together with the affluence generated in the last 40 years, signals a shift in societal perceptions of old age. As new realities become evident, fresh, vital images of aging are slowly replacing the old stereotypes.

But stereotypes die hard—their roots flourish in the soils of prejudice and ignorance. Indeed, it is not surprising to find that a survey by Harris (1975) indicated, according to Neary (1990b), "that old people were generally viewed as useless and inactive members of society." Such "negative attitudes, myths, and stereotyping of elderly people," claims Neary (1990b), "have perpetuated the public image of the aged."

Thus, the younger public's view of older people generally reflects a more negative image than that which older persons have of themselves. Comfort (1990) points to two troubling views of aging in America. "One is generated by thoughtless ageism and the other by overstating the injustices inflicted on the old in order to reform them." Both views, he concludes, can be remedied by changing attitudes:

> Once an older person comes to be seen, not as old first and provisionally a person second, but as a person who happens to be old, and who is still as he or she always was, plus experience and minus the consequences of certain physical accidents of time—only then will social gerontology have made its point.

The Tilting Balance

▶ THE NEW DEMOGRAPHICS

The Numbers Game

At the heart of the transgenerational design issue is the dramatic rise in the numbers of older people.

Consider these facts:

- ▶ There are more people age 65 and older living in the United States today than the combined populations of Canada (24,070,000) and Ireland (3,401,000).[5]

- ▶ By the year 2000, the U.S. population of those 65 years and older will have risen to over 34 million people.[6] That equals the present combined populations of New York (14,622,000), London (9,170,000) and Moscow (10,367,000).[7]

- ▶ By the year 2000, the world population of those 65 and above will be over 419 million people—a number larger than today's combined populations of Japan (123,642,000), Brazil (152,505,000), France (56,358,000), and Germany (78,475,000).[8]

5. Source: U.S. Bureau of the Census. 1991. Table No. 1434. Population and Area, by Region and Country, 1980 and 1990, and Projections, 2000 and 2010, pp. 830–832. In *Statistical Abstract of the United States: 1991.* (111th edition.) Washington, DC, 1991.

6. Source: U.S. Bureau of the Census. 1991. Current Population Reports, series P-25, Nos. 519, 917, 1018, and 1057. Table No. 41. Population 65 Years Old and Over, by Age Group and Sex, 1960 to 1989, and projections, 2000, p. 37. In *Statistical Abstract of the United States: 1991.* (111th edition.) Washington, DC, 1991.

7. Source: U.S. Bureau of the Census, World Population Profile: 1989. Table No. 1437. Population and Average Annual Rates of Growth for World's 94 Largest Cities: 1989 to 2000. pp. 835–836. In *Statistical Abstract of the United States: 1991.* (111th edition.) Washington, DC, 1991.

8. Source: U.S. Bureau of the Census. 1991. Table No. 1434. Population and Area, by Region and Country, 1980 and 1990, and Projections, 2000 and 2010, pp. 830–832; Table No. 1437. Population and Average Annual Rates of Growth for World's 94 Largest Cities: 1989 to 2000, pp. 835–836; and Table No. 1435. World Population by Age Group, 1990 and Projections, 2000, p. 833. In *Statistical Abstract of the United States: 1991.* (111th edition.) Washington, DC, 1991.

We are living in a unique period. Never before has the world contained so many older people—or such a large percentage of them. In vivid contrast to the past, these large numbers of older people are a new phenomenon with profound implications.

Most of us are not used to dealing with such huge numbers and find them difficult to conceptualize. Numbers, however, can be useful in a variety of ways to illustrate conditions and illuminate trends. Some numbers become, in effect, what Brotman (1976) labels, "artificial rulers." They describe averages, ranges, or relationships. Others describe the *differences* between age groups. Still others describe the differences *within* age groups.

But caution is in order. It seems characteristic that statisticians present numbers for accuracy rather than for clarity. And a statistician, says Brotman (1976), is "someone who uses numbers like a drunk uses a lamp post, for support rather than illumination." I will try not to fall into this trap.

The Swelling Elder Population

For the first time in the history of our planet the generational epicenter of advanced societies is shifting from youth to age—from adolescence to maturity. For the first time in U.S. history there are more Americans over 65 than under 25 (Abrams and Berkow 1990). Moreover, the median age in the United States, now 33, is expected to rise to about 44 by the year 2080 (Greene, Monahan, and Coleman 1991).

Today, 50 million middle-aged baby boomers, the driving force behind yesterday's youth culture, are approaching the threshold of senior citizenship. Between 2010 and 2030, they will pass through the portal of longevity, join the ranks of "the elderly," and swell our country's older population from about 12 percent today to 20 percent when they reach retirement age (Abrams and Berkow 1990).

The upward trend of the age distribution pattern shows a startling increase in the numbers of older persons when compared with the growth of our population. The U.S. Bureau of the Census projects that between 1990 and 2050 the U.S. population will increase by 19.8 percent, growing from 250.4 to 299.9 million. In contrast, the population of those 65 years or older will increase by 117 percent, more than doubling from 31.6 million to 68.5 million.[9]

Not only is the age structure of the population changing, a dramatic change in the age structure *within* the older population is also occurring. The fastest growing subgroup among the elderly are the "old-old"—those

9. U.S. Bureau of the Census, U.S. Department of Commerce. Projections of the Population of the United States by Age, Sex, and Race: 1988–2080. Current Population Reports, Series P-25, No. 1018. In *Statistical Abstract of the United States: 1991.* (111th edition.) Washington, DC, 1991.

85 years and older. This group alone will more than quadruple from 3.25 million to 15.3 million, climbing from 10 percent of the over 65 population in 1990 to 22 percent in 2050 (Greene, Monahan, and Coleman 1991).

Similar changes are occurring in other parts of the world. Data indicate that the aging populations of Western societies have also been increasing over the last 85 years. Consider by way of comparison that this increase in Western European countries is about 20 years ahead of the United States. Moreover, by the mid 1970s, the population of those age 65 and older in England, Germany, France, and Sweden was already at 14 to 15 percent.

In contrast, the United States is not expected to reach the 14 percent level before the year 2000. At that time, in all likelihood, Western Europe will have hit the 20 to 25 percent mark (Neumann and Boldy 1982). But even before then, projections show that some nations such as Sweden and Japan can expect their 65 and older populations to swell to over 25 percent (Chellis and Grayson, 1990).

It is widely believed that from 1980 to the year 2020 the number of elderly persons throughout the world will have doubled. The segment of those age 75 and over alone will swell from 40 percent in 1980 to 50 percent at the turn of the century (Struyk 1987). The rising numbers of the world's elderly is expected to increase sharply in the late 1990s, cresting again between the years 2030 and 2050. Beyond this point, expectations point to a leveling off followed by a slow decline.

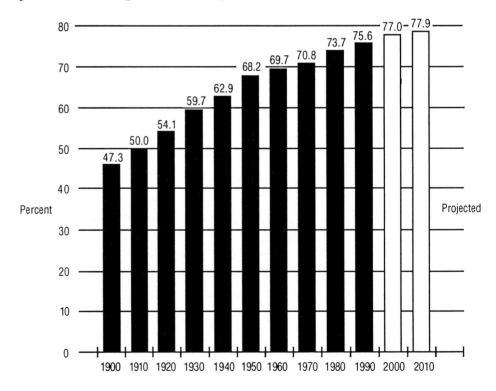

Figure 2–1. Life expectancy at birth.

Source: U.S. Department of Health and Human Services, *Vital Statistics of the United States, 1988.* Volume II, Part A, Table 6.5. Washington, DC. U.S. Bureau of the Census, *Historical Statistics of the United States, Colonial Times to 1970,* Series B 107–115; *Current Population Reports,* Series P-25, No. 1018; and *Statistical Abstract of the United States: 1991* (111th edition), Table No. 105. Washington, DC, 1991.

Increasing Life Expectancy

Not only are the numbers of older people increasing, but they are also living longer as life expectancy increases dramatically. Two thousand years ago the average Roman could expect to live 22 years (Katchadourian 1987). A person born in 1900 could only expect to live 47.3 years; in 1930, 59.7 years; and in 1960, 69.7 years. Today, according to the National Center for Health Statistics, a newborn infant has a life expectancy of 75.6 years. In the year 2000, it will be 77.0 years (Figure 2-1).

This dramatic increase is not accidental. Its substantial and pleasing rise resulted from infectious disease control, public health initiatives, and new surgical and rehabilitation techniques (Wallin 1965). Put in perspective, life expectancy at age 65 has increased more during the last 30 years than during the entire 200-year period from 1750 to 1950 (Mellström 1989). A person age 62 can expect to live another 25 years. A man of 75 has a 50-50 chance of reaching 84; a woman, 86. The longer you live, the longer you're likely to live.

That said, however, it is also important to remember that older people are not the only beneficiaries of increased longevity. This dramatic increase in life expectancy has also occurred for those in infancy, childhood, and even early adulthood due to improved medical breakthroughs in solving problems with birth, early infancy disorders, and contagious diseases. Add to this improvements in nutrition and sanitation and we can see the reasons why most children today reach adulthood and why most adults reach old age (Brotman 1976).

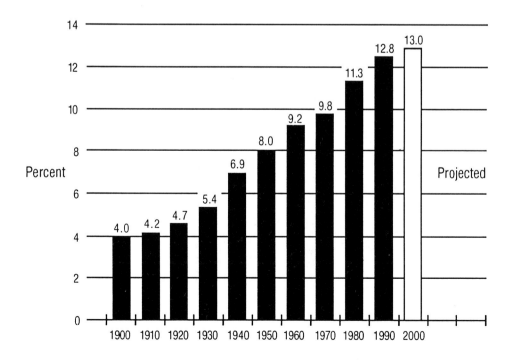

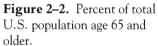

Figure 2–2. Percent of total U.S. population age 65 and older.

Source: U.S. Bureau of the Census, *Historical Statistics of the United States, Colonial Times to 1970,* Series B 107–115; *Current Population Reports,* Series P-23, No. 59; and *Statistical Abstract of the United States: 1991* (111th edition), Tables No. 13, 18, 22, and 41. Washington, DC.

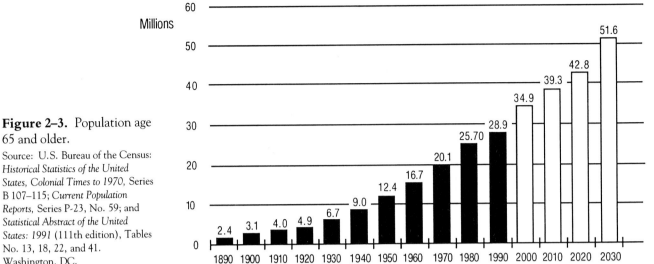

Figure 2–3. Population age 65 and older.

Source: U.S. Bureau of the Census: *Historical Statistics of the United States, Colonial Times to 1970*, Series B 107–115; *Current Population Reports*, Series P-23, No. 59; and *Statistical Abstract of the United States: 1991* (111th edition), Tables No. 13, 18, 22, and 41. Washington, DC.

But the numbers attached to life expectancy also reveal interesting conclusions. In 1900, the life expectancy at birth of about 48 years was a projection based on the death rate in the year 1900, not a forecast of survivorship. If this projection had been correct, virtually no one 92 or over would be alive today, which is simply not the case. While great progress has been made in lengthening the life expectancy, the *rate* of improvement slows and drops off sharply in the older years—the time when chronic health conditions set in. Unfortunately, this is also the area of medical research where less progress has been made. Notwithstanding the number of people reaching older ages, once having reached these high age levels, they are not as likely to live as long thereafter than did earlier, perhaps heartier, generations (Brotman 1976).

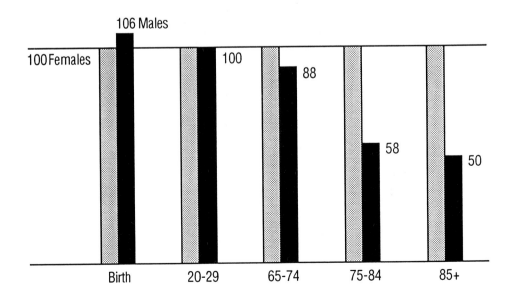

Figure 2–4. Sex ratio over the life span.

Source: Department of Health and Human Services, *Vital Statistics of the United States, 1988*, Volume I, Table 1-20, Washington, DC; and U.S. Bureau of the Census, *Statistical Abstract of the United States: 1991* (111th edition), Table No. 20. Washington, DC.

Sex Ratio

The sex ratio (the number of men per 100 women) changes over the human life span (Figure 2-4). As we grow older, women begin to outnumber men and the older population becomes predominantly more female.

The sex ratio for male and female births slightly favors males: there are 105 male births for every 100 female births. Men continue to exceed women until the third decade (age 20 to 29) when the number of males and females equalize. From then on, women increasingly outnumber men, with the difference becoming more pronounced as we approach the "old-old" group, those age 85 and over (Figure 2-5). By the time we reach 85 the sex ratio is almost 50 men to every 100 women, or about one male for every two females (U.S. Department of Health and Human Services 1988).

Thus, as the population gets older, it also becomes predominantly more female. This has important implications for designers and marketers. Clearly, designing and marketing products for an older population means accommodating the particular needs of older females. This fact amplifies the growing need for anthropometric and behavioral research among this group. Designers and human factors specialists need additional data for the older population in general and older women in particular.

▶ EVOLVING COHORTS[10]

Cohorts of Age

Gerontologists recognize that each generation grows up in its own era and is influenced by a unique set of events and values. Each generation views

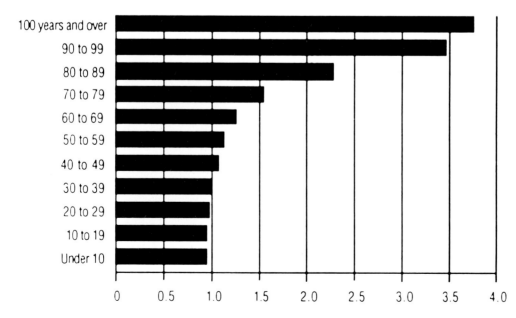

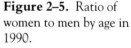

Figure 2–5. Ratio of women to men by age in 1990.

Source: Department of Health and Human Services, *Vital Statistics of the United States, 1988.* Volume I. Table 1-20. Washington, DC. Adopted from Figure 1-3, Ratio of women to men by age in 1990. In *Primary Care Geriatrics: A Case-Based Approach,* Richard J. Ham, and Philip D. Sloane (eds.). 1991. St. Louis: Mosby Year Book. Reproduced by permission.

the present through eyes screened by a unique set of temporal and cultural filters (Figure 2-6). This is known as the "cohort effect." Common values shared by individuals born of common experiences follow each cohort group through their life span and color their views as they pass from one age to the next. Gradually, with the passage of time society's perception of age also changes, the critical mass of society's values adjusting to a new, collective equilibrium.

Today, fifty million baby boomers approaching retirement are putting a new "spin" on society's concept of growing old. These almost-elderly are helping to tilt society's traditional views of aging with a more transgenerational perception. Growing old is now becoming OK—albeit with resistance, according to one cosmetic ad that proclaims, "I'll fight it every step of the way." The media is also beginning to recognize the commercial value of elder appeal: television's "Golden Palace" competes with "Designing Women" and "Matlock" argues his case opposite "The Young Riders."

As the arbitrary line once separating youth from age becomes blurred and faded, 65 no longer remains a relevant passage marker. Dychtwald (1988) suggests a new set of aging designations:

▶ 40 to 60 middle age

▶ 60 to 80 late adult

▶ 80+ old age

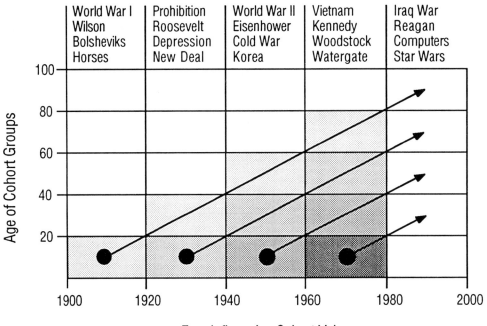

Figure 2–6. The cohort effect.

Such transgenerational overlapping, according to Dychtwald, will change our view of life span from a linear progression of education-work-retirement to a series of cyclical activities spread throughout our lives and extending well into old age (Figure 2-7).

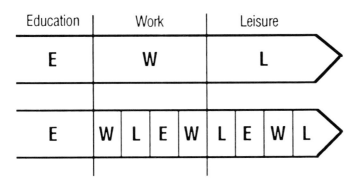

Figure 2–7. Changing views of life span.

These longer life experiences will permit today's energetic life styles to continue to the point where most of us can expect to live 20 to 25 percent of our lives in active retirement. Today's physically and intellectually active younger cohorts suggest that tomorrow's elderly population will be better educated, healthier, culturally literate and, as individuals, more discerning consumers. They will demand and respond to flexible schedules, leaves-of-absence, continuing education, intellectual stimulation, travel, and other enriching experiences. And, as they begin to experience declines in their own physical capabilities, they will demand products that help them maintain their active lifestyles and activities.

Moreover, today's younger cohort groups have environmental expectations that are more elaborate than pre-Depression generations. This is a prime factor in their growing preference for ecologically responsible design, environmental stewardship, exercise, fitness and health programs, as well as a desire for self-governance. Such advocacy is also powering change within professional organizations. Broadly worded principles developed by an environmental task force of the American Design Council are being recommended for adoption by U.S. design associations as "a forceful statement of commitment representing 120,000 U.S. designers" (Industrial Designers Society of America 1992).

In the wake of society's move toward new, energetic life styles, an increasing number of middle- to higher-income older persons are skewing the trend in traditional retirement housing expectations. A decade ago studio or one-bedroom units were the most popular. Now, according to Regnier (1987b), "two-bedroom and even three-bedroom units are becoming increasingly popular for affluent retirees over the age of 75."

Age and Disability

The full impact of 35 million people in the United States reaching age 65 by the year 2000 cannot be assessed adequately without also talking about disabilities. Both topics are congruent transgenerational issues. Significant and perhaps far more profound is the realization that 58 percent of these older persons will acquire some form of disability. This should not, however, imply that disabilities occur only within the older generations. In fact, more than one in five Americans aged 15 and over have some type of disability; problems with walking and lifting are the most common (Raschko 1987). Part 3 will explore the issue of disability in more detail, linking it to the need for environmental assistance.

10. This section was developed from an article originally published in Pirkl, James J. 1991. "Transgenerational Design: A design strategy whose time has arrived." *Design Management Journal* 2(4) 55–60, courtesy of Design Management Institute, Boston, MA.

A Market of Silver

▶ THE COMPETITIVE CHALLENGE

The trend is crystal clear. Americans are aging—and with increasing numbers. Decades of demographic data siphoned from every tributary of society continue to accumulate, its documentation filtered, churned, and analyzed. The results are inducing a swelling pressure on today's volatile markets—global as well as domestic—to acknowledge the legitimate product needs of our aging population.

According to Anita Shalit (1987) a specialist on aging issues at the U.S. Department of Health and Human Services' Administration on Aging, "Business is just beginning to realize that it is both reasonable and profitable to adopt and develop products that are suitable to an older person's mature physical characteristics and lifestyle preferences."

Until recently, however, with the exception of housing and drugs, little marketing action relating to the elderly was in evidence (Wallin 1965). But this is changing. According to Allan (1981), "marketers—ranging from such giants in the cosmetics industry as Estée Lauder and Elizabeth Arden to travel companies such as American Express, Amtrak and Greyhound, from food manufacturers such as General Foods to manufacturers of sporting goods such as Wilson and a myriad of other companies including Proctor & Gamble, Colgate-Palmolive, Bristol-Myers and the like," have been quietly shedding old conceptions and exploring the demographic realities of this age-skewed market.

Such companies have recognized the growing dimensions of a new, emerging elderly market of consumers coalescing on a global scale. Even cable television recognizes this new market. *Modern Maturity* (April-May 1992) reports "a network that caters to the interests and concerns of people 50 and older. Topics on the Golden American Network include everything from healthy lifestyles to women's issues. There are also programs giving news and information about social security and medicare."

Many products traditionally thought of as youth-oriented (i.e., sporting goods and housewares) easily penetrate the elderly market by accommodating declining physical and sensory abilities normally attributed to the aging process. Many companies also associated with the youth market such as Levi Strauss & Company and McDonalds, now target the older consumer. Even infant-care companies court the elderly. Gerber Foods, over a decade ago, discarded its slogan, "Babies are our business, our only business," and expanded its product line to include insurance and health care products for older people (Allan 1981).

As the physical and economic status of older consumers improves, aging becomes more and more acceptable. Furthermore, the collective strength of the growing number of older people will undoubtedly convince reluctant companies that products and environments that respond by compensating for sensory and physical impairments may, indeed, have a marketing edge. Designers, too, must respond and, as they do, predicts Hiatt (1987), "designs that accommodate and overcome sensory (and physical) impairments will become more acceptable."

But "marketing" means many things to many people: sales; advertising; design; or research. It is, in fact, none of these, yet all of these. Hambrook (1990) describes marketing as, "the overall strategy that launches all these parts into motion, and then monitors and adjusts them as the project succeeds on time and on budget."

Yet, with all its potential, the elderly market is not easily defined; it resists easy identification and classification. Moreover, capturing this older market demands new management policies and strategies. But these can best be formulated only if the old myths are dispelled and the new facts become clear. This is starting to happen. Enlightened companies are realizing that the old policy of "make it and peddle it" cannot continue if market share is to be maintained. (The Japanese have described American marketing strategy as "ready, fire, aim.") Many acknowledge the validity of target-market "understanding," inserting it into their marketing equation (Figure 3-1). And the keys to understanding the new transgenerational market are (1) *product choice* and (2) *transgenerational accommodation.* I'll review both concepts.

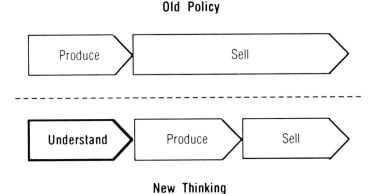

Figure 3–1. The marketing equation.

▶ A MATTER OF CHOICE

Today, professionals in most fields are familiar with such terms as market segmentation, product differentiation, marketing mix, price, promotion, distribution and aftersales service. The historic philosophy behind these words was popularized by Levitt (1986) who introduced the idea that "corporate survival depends on doing everything necessary to satisfy the needs and wants of the customer." This may be even more true today as industry's new focus on ergonomic design promises to humanize the exploding output of technological innovation, a process which is powering the development of such exotic new electronic product systems as computer/telecommunication integration, virtual reality, and "smart" houses—as different from the present as our present differs from the industrial revolution.

In matters pertaining to social and human services, however, Americans tend to react rather than taking the initiative. We wait for problems to develop rather than planning for and preventing them. We do not easily accept old age or disabilities. Our youth-oriented society filters out the realities of growing old, shielding our eyes and minds from the elderly and those with disabilities (Chellis and Grayson 1990). Yet those who are young and without disabilities often forget that they also are vulnerable to the disabling conditions of chronic health disorders, sickness, or accidents (Weisgerber 1991). Indeed, the facts support this claim. Storck and Thompson-Hoffman (1991) report that "most persons with a functional limitation are under 65, with over 14 million of the more than 37 million functionally limited persons under 55 years of age."

The key issue, however, is how designers, manufacturers, and care providers can best (1) help us remain active and independent as we grow older; (2) provide an environment that adapts to our changing sensory and physical needs; and (3) enable us to choose the means by which we accomplish our activities of daily living (ADL).

I see four options: First, we can *do nothing*. This, of course, will only perpetuate the problem by ensuring that our artifact environment continues to ignore and alienate those with age-related functional limitations.

Second, we can design specialized products for the elderly and target those with "mature needs." Experience, however, has shown that such products often quickly become stigmatized and are rejected by those for whom they were intended. No one, including the elderly, wants to be labeled "old" or use products that imply any negative connotation.

Third, we can continue to devise more "geriatric gadgets" and "assistive devices" to compensate for the lack of sensory and physical accommodation found today in most consumer products. Notwithstanding the availability of "a wide range of ingenious aids," which, according to Hale (1979), "extend the horizons of millions of disabled people," most assistive devices exist to fill the vacuum created when existing products or environments fail to accommodate a particular impairment. They tend to address factitious problems by inserting additional layers of technology between the user and the required accommodation.

Thus, jars and bottles designed with tight lids and caps require opening devices to help those with a weak grip remove them; eating utensils designed with thin, flat handles require large-diameter slip-on handles to help those with diminished grip and muscle control hold and manipulate them; and rotary doorknobs require add-on lever-action doorknob turners to increase the twisting leverage required by those with arthritic hands and wrists. Unquestionably, many with severe disabilities benefit from such supplementary products. Nevertheless, many of these products, frequently marketed as "aids to independent living," mask their questionable benefits behind cruel, demeaning, and unattractive facades.

Finally, most products can be designed at the outset for use by a transgenerational population. Such products can accommodate and appeal to all, including the aged as well as the young and able-bodied—and *without penalty to any group.* I believe this last option offers the greatest benefit to our aging population and those experiencing declines in functional ability while offering a *better* product to younger generations. Shouldn't a fire extinguisher or a television set be equally usable by a teenager with a sprained wrist and a septuagenarian with an arthritic hand?

Beattie (1978) clarifies the answer: "Because the processes of aging are processes of individualization and differentiation, there is a need to design supportive environments which offer choice and options." "Our goal," he insists, "must be to support the unique identities and capacities of older persons in order that our elders can continue to participate in and contribute to the family, neighborhood, and community as long as possible."

The transgenerational design idea promises the availability of products and environments flexible enough to extend our independence by supporting the changing physical and sensory needs we encounter as we grow older. Such products serve similar needs of younger cohorts whose disabilitites may also limit *their* independence. This shift in bias, says Glenn (1989), signifies the need for a transition from the mechanical to the organic; from the imposed to the adaptive. He calls for a "conscious technology" that represents the merger of humans and their technologies; a co-evolution of mind and machine.

Understanding people, of course, is at the heart of transgenerational design. Its essence is part of a growing trend to place human need above the constraints of technology. Others have underscored this point of view. John Thackara (1988) sees it as signaling the dawning of "the human age," a new era for our artifact environment. Arthur Pulos (1988) eloquently argues that "a new morality is emerging by which the tyranny of runaway production may be displaced by a democracy of quantity and quality that will be more sensitively and humanely matched to human need and desires."

▶ TRANSGENERATIONAL ACCOMMODATION

Transgenerational design is the practice of making products and environments compatible with those physical and sensory impairments associated with human aging, which limit major life activities. With all of its cold logic, however, it creates a warm and humane accommodation between products and their users; between product components and users' impairments.

The characteristics of transgenerational design stem from the same roots as "universal" design, seeking to shift the priorities of product development from aesthetics to suitability; from sales to service; from discrimination to accommodation. The transgeneration design doctrine rejects, as discriminatory, specialized "elderly" products or devices targeted directly at older consumers. Studies show that such products usually acquire the stigma of "old age" and are either rejected outright or used only reluctantly by those who feel the threat of embarrassment or diminished social status. Unfortunately, many abasing appliance-like devices designed for functional expediency instead of human service infect the "elderly market" and erode their users' dignity and self-respect (see Figure 3-2).

But despite the substantial and functional efficiency of such products, the negative appearance repels one's desire to use them in normal social settings. Conventional wisdom suggests that even the private use of such awkward, offensive implements underscores the maladaptive quality of the disability and gnaws at one's self-image. How difficult must it be, then, to maintain one's dignity and self-respect.

In stark contrast, transgenerational products are attractive and accommodate instead of discriminate, serving needs that change continually as all of us grow older. Of equal importance, transgenerational products also benefit those of any age and ability with disabilities by providing normal, useful—and usable—products that are not demeaning, embarrassing, or stigmatized.

Transgeneration design extends the traditional boundaries of "barrier-free accessibility" to embrace the various functional limitations we may acquire as we grow older. Such limitations, generally brought on by chronic conditions, are likely to diminish our level of activity. They become what Storck and Thompson-Hoffman (1991) call "the most general indicator of disability . . . markedly correlated with age." Weisgerber

(1991) reminds us, however, that "barrier-free" must also mean free from the barrier of *attitude*.

The transgenerational design outreach benefits younger people who also experience disabilities congruent with normal impairments of age. It recognizes that many disabilities, normally associated with the elderly, frequently occur much earlier in life due to sickness or accident. Such impairments limit the life activities of the young no less than the old. Many young people, for example, including children, develop vision or hearing impairments requiring eyeglasses or specialized hearing devices. Others, suffering from arthritis, sprains, burns, broken bones, or lower back problems, experience similar limitations to their freedom and independence as do older people fighting the effects of degenerative, orthopedic, or neurological impairments. Designs that accommodate temporary impairments serve those afflicted no less than those with permanent or progressive disabilities. This is the message of transgenerational design.

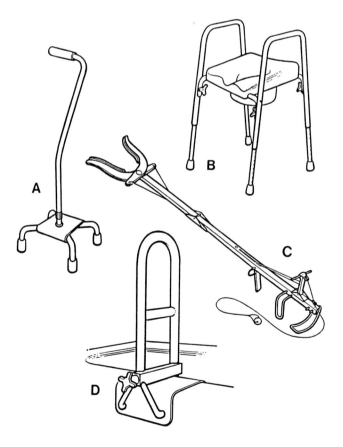

Figure 3–2. Examples of stigmatizing assistive devices and apparatuses: (A) quad cane, (B) transportable toilet seat and frame, (C) wrist-supported reacher, (D) bath tub grip bar.

Summary of Part 1

Clearly, designers, manufacturers, health care providers, and elderly consumers need to think about older people in new ways. Conceptual limitations, reinforced by erroneous myths and stereotyped images, would have us concentrate on the differences that separate the young and the old, rather than the similarities that bring us together. Centuries of social and economic changes, shaped by successive waves of science and technology, have eroded the once venerated image of age into today's tarnished preconceptions of "young" and "old."

Older Americans, treated with deference and respect at the birth of our republic, became less valued as industrialization transformed our early agrarian society into a young nation. The image of age, once viewed as a valued asset, changed with time to represent dependent liabilities. Reversing decades of decline and neglect, the Social Security Act of 1935 offered dignity to countless old people caught in the currents of financial hardship and despair and increased the quality of our lives. Life expectancy was 47 years in 1900 and surged to almost 72 in 1965 when the *Older Americans Act* provided additional medical, nutritional, and social benefits to elderly people.

Today, not only are we living longer, there are more of us. By the year 2000, 35 million elderly people will live in the United States with the 85 and over group growing the fastest. Tomorrow's elder population, however, will differ from those of past decades. Enjoying health and active life styles, they will demand products that offer continued enjoyment and stimulation while, at the same time, supporting functional limitations and maintaining independence. Refusing to be stigmatized by specialized "elderly" devices, tomorrow's older adults will seek transgenerational products that accommodate rather than discriminate, and appeal to users of all ages.

Designing, developing, and providing transgenerational products, however, requires knowledge about the aging process and an understanding of those sensory and physical limitations associated with growing old. Toward this end, part 2 explores the characteristics of human aging and describes a variety of common conditions associated with age that can inhibit our pursuit of independence.

HUMAN AGING

A LIFETIME OF CHANGE

*"The ultimate value of life
depends upon awareness,
and the power of
contemplation rather than
upon mere survival."*
—ARISTOTLE
(384–322 B.C.)

A Spectrum of Capabilities

▶ WHAT IS AGING?

Gerontologists perceive human aging as a continuous, complex, and dynamic process starting with birth and ending with death. Despite the fact that we all experience the aging process, many remain unaware of its effects. Even as dramatic changes take place, their reasons and results are often not understood. Yet, unless we die in our early years, we will all experience the effects of the aging process. (Pirkl and Babic 1988).

While much empirical data about the changes associated with aging have been amassed, Sloane (1992) reports that "the basic mechanisms of aging are poorly understood." This is not to suggest, however, that researchers are without explanations. To be sure, Neary (1990b) reminds us that "no single theory adequately describes the aging population." Nevertheless, several unproven theories based on observations in laboratory animals and human subjects seek to unravel the physiological keys to the aging phenomenon.

According to Sloane (1992) researchers commonly believe that "aging occurs at the biochemical and cellular levels." One theory, he says, affirms that "aging results from gradual cellular damage through gene mutation, protein degradation, or autoimmune processes." Such mutation may occur by exposure to radiation and other environmental toxins. Another investigation concludes that "aging results from the accumulation of toxic substances, possibly from cell metabolism." Sloane points to this theory's relevance to brain cells, which cannot replicate like the cells of most bodily organs. Still another theory is based on cell senescence—the belief that cells are genetically programmed to age. Sloane argues that "genetically programmed decrements . . . could contribute to age-associated declines in T-cell function, to degenerative vascular disease, and to producing a finite limit to the human life span."

In the last 20 years, much of what was considered normal aging was attributed to be the result of disease or disuse. This view is changing. Sloane suggests a useful rule of thirds for considering functional declines in older people: 1/3 due to disease, 1/3 to inactivity (disuse), and 1/3 caused by the aging process itself (senescence) (Figure 4-1).

According to Lovering (1985), "No matter how well your body and mind work at your present age, 20, 30, or 50, if you should be fortunate (or unfortunate) to live long enough, you will become a victim of the aging process. You will be forced to cope with and adjust to this prognosis that says that tomorrow will most likely be a little worse."

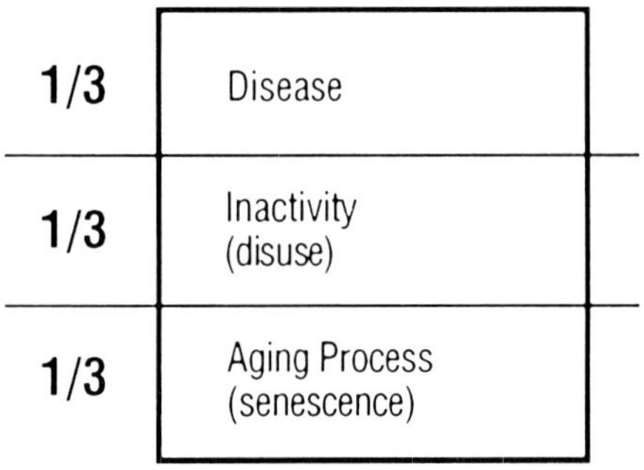

1/3	Disease
1/3	Inactivity (disuse)
1/3	Aging Process (senescence)

Figure 4–1. Rule of thirds for considering functional declines in older people.

▶ THE FOUR SEASONS

The dynamics of our life span should arouse our attention no less than the exigencies of our disabilities. One, in fact, does not exclude the other. But caution and reason are in order. If we perceive life as a process spanning a continuum stretching from birth to death, a variety of possible trajectories emerge, each patterned by our particular understanding of the aging process.

Popular wisdom suggests that most people perceive a pattern of aging similar to the one shown in Figure 4-2.

This pattern presumes that our functional capacity climbs steadily from birth until we retire, at which time we become old, our functional capacity declines, and we die. This simplistic and erroneous analysis serves only to reinforce the old myths and stereotypes; it disregards the realities of the aging process and the individual variances that emerge between individuals as age increases.

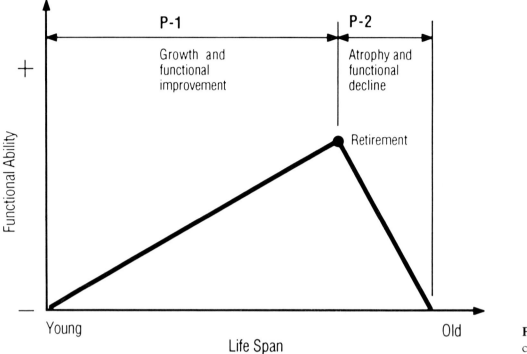

Figure 4–2. Popular conception of life span.

A more sophisticated but similar model proposed by Svanborg (1985) and cited by Weisgerber (1991) acknowledges the various biomedical and environmental influences on aging by offering the notion that life proceeds in two phases: phase one consists of growth and functional improvement; phase two continues with atrophy and functional decline (Figure 4-3).

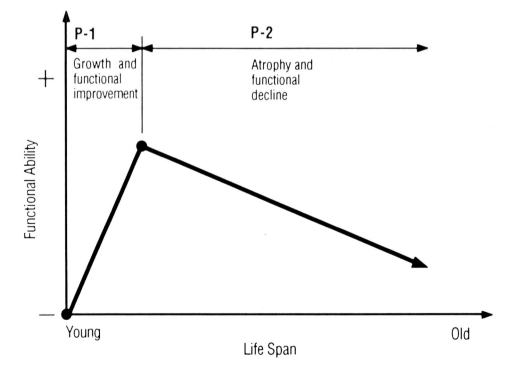

Figure 4–3. Model of two-phase life span.

A third, perhaps more convincing, model is offered by Weisgerber (1991). He reports evidence that points to life proceeding in four phases:

1. Growing and functional improvement

2. A constant, nearly level period

3. A period of functional decline

4. A rapid decline following the onset of aging manifestations

Figure 4-4 illustrates the relationship of these phases.

Phase one, *growing and functional improvement,* is represented by line A-B. It spans the years of our infancy, childhood, and formal education. This is a time of measured growth, rapid skill development, socialization, and structured learning; a period that defines our unique characteristics. During this phase both mind and body develop to prepare us for the challenges awaiting us in our adult years.

Phase two, represented by line B-C, consists of a *constant, nearly level period* of adult productivity. It is underscored by responsibility and accomplishment, and characterized by freedom of choice, independence, and self-sufficiency, often lasting well into retirement (Weisgerber 1991). This period, which normally encompasses our working years, is influenced by a gradual decline in vital body functions "at a rate of approximately 1% per year starting from the age retrogression begins" (Mellström 1989).

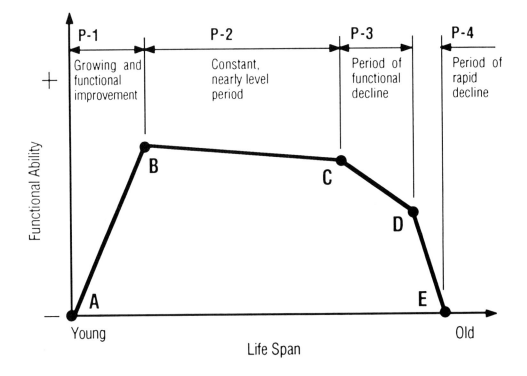

Figure 4-4. Model of four-phase life span.

Phase three starts at point C and is characterized by a period of *functional decline* represented by line C-D. As the mechanisms of biological aging assail our body's physical and sensory health, the restorative faculties progressively decline. Accordingly, functional declines induced by impairments in our motor capacity and perception produce a corresponding loss in our ability to perform the activities of daily living (ADL).

Phase four starts at point D and marks the onset of a *rapid decline* of our vital functions. Changes induced by the decline compound our already diminished capacity to remain active and maintain independence. It is important to note that the location of point D, varies with each individual, occurring within a wide range of ages and a wide range of functional abilities. Individual differences increase with age due largely to nongenetic factors, such as environment and life style influences (Dahlman 1989). As our activity level drops, our bodily systems begin to atrophy, accelerating the deterioration of our biological processes until death occurs. The location of point E also varies widely between individuals.

The Critical Support Point

After reaching Phase 3, we depend more and more on environmental support to compensate for the progressive decline of our functional ability. Such support, however, becomes increasingly critical during this phase, enabling many persons to remain independent and perform their normal ADL.

A wide range of specialized "supportive devices" intended for this purpose are marketed for use during Phase 3. They include a variety of walkers, grippers, writers, dressers, squeezers, holders, supporters, clippers, turners, and openers. Most, however, exhibit prosthetic-like appearances, adding to the stigma of being different or less competent, which many older people already feel. This causes "negative self-labeling," which, according to Moos, Lemke, and David (1987), "leads older persons to view themselves as sick or frail," and exposes them to such psychological and social stresses as frustration, lack of self confidence, excessive stimulation, and lack of stimulation.

Many designs intended to address the physical limitations of the elderly, instead present and reinforce a stereotyped image. Some products are designed with an institutional image, associating them with a disability or nursing home environments. Such discriminating designs are rejected by all except those whose condition demands that which is immediately available (Regnier 1987).

Parsons and Felton (1990) point out that an individual's inability to cope with environmental stresses can trigger the body's defense mechanism and expose one to such stress-induced problems as diabetes mellitus. This, of course, compounds one's condition and induces the premature arrival of critical support point (CSP) (Figure 4-5).

Transgenerational products, on the other hand, extend the range of usability to include elderly people and those with reduced functional abilities, as well as the young and able-bodied. Such products pay greater attention to human performance and accommodation throughout our life span and offer features that contribute to optimizing health in later life (Hiatt 1987). More importantly, such products can extend the CSP (see Figure 4-5), thus lengthening the period of one's independence—and life.

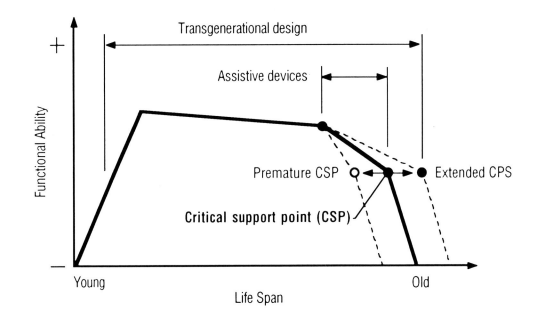

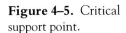 **Figure 4–5.** Critical support point.

▶ CHARACTERISTICS OF THE AGING

The topic of aging is not particularly popular among many of the young or those at the height of their careers, who prefer the stereotypes that reinforce their comfortable self-image. The contemporary values of youthful cohorts tend to insulate them from vicarious sensitivity, and their sense of immortality blunts any suggestion that their own capabilities may one day decline. Because of mistaken assumptions, many stereotypes and generalizations about older people continue and defy reality. Chapanis (1992) suggests several reasons for rejecting such generalizations: people differ, people change, and the world changes.

The Heinz company learned this lesson the hard way over a decade ago. The company targeted the elderly for a new, experimental food line marketed as "senior foods." Allan (1981) reports that "the Heinz experiment failed—the majority of older people do not need an easily digestible food akin to baby food, and the small number who do might not want to be labeled as such."

Many people—old as well as young—harbor another false notion; the idea that, as a group, older people become more alike. This simply is not the case. With increasing age, the elderly grow more *dissimilar*. In fact, diversity among the elderly is greater than between the young and the old. In most aspects, other than advanced chronological age, they are a diverse, heterogeneous group of older adults who *defy characterization*. This is readily understandable for a number of reasons.

First, age per se is not an infallible predictor of either personality or behavior. Despite popular images to the contrary, many in their nineties, like George Burns and Bob Hope, have more vitality and *joie de vivre* than many other persons half their age. Moreover, as a set, this group ranges in age from 50 to 100 and includes such diverse categories as full-time and part-time workers, the retired, middle-age couples, the elderly widow or widower living alone, the physically and socially active, and those with mild or severe disabilities (Allan 1981).

Second, there is no correlation between chronological age and physical age. We need not be chronologically old to be physically old. Each individual ages at his or her own pace as do an individual's abilities. One may be "old" at 75; another may be "old" at 40. Many older people experience physical limitations because of the sedentary life style they have chosen. In fact, many middle-aged people (and their children) are in worse physical condition than their older parents.

Finally, a variety of functional limitations associated with normal aging cause our usually benign product environment to become unyielding and hostile. Reduced eyesight, hearing, arthritis, sprains, burns, and broken bones can ignite within us feelings of helplessness and frustration. Such experiences and limitations, occurring at all ages, mold our personalities and carve unique features that characterize our individuality.

▶ MILESTONES OF AGE

The Twenties

The years of our twenties vibrate with confidence and self-indulgence. Reinforced by our sense of immortality, we discard our teenage image and climb the tree of life; assessing the dimensions, sampling the fruits, and often falling from limbs we've climbed out on too far. It's a time for defining the proportions of our values, our abilities, and our personality. The sobering tastes of family responsibilities soon replace the savory flavors of courtship and marriage.

It's also a time when the first signs of thinning hair and a noticeable decline in near vision can signal our first awareness of personal aging. Yet, of all the ages we pass through, our twenties are the years in which we least concern ourselves about health or survival. Tragically, our major threat comes, not from health-related causes, but from violent death. As an unintended consequence, motor vehicles, suicides, and homicides cause almost 68 deaths per 100,000 within this group alone (Parsons and Felton 1990). Thus, physical injuries frequently present many of us with disabilities that shatter our ambitions and aspirations.

The Thirties

Noticeable strands of grey hair and a changing hairline confirm our passage from earlier ages. Financial concerns about family, job, and home intensify one's involvement in work and career. Regular eating habits and lack of exercise add pounds, and pride energizes our resolve to sweat them away. Our hard-playing, intermittent role of "weekend warrior" invites injuries and erodes our youthful resistance to disease.

After 35 years of experiencing risks to life and health our sense of immortality fades, and we begin to recognize—and accept—our individual limitations. Many women, sensitized to each tick of the "biological clock," grow apprehensive about the end to their childbearing years.

More highly motivated and experienced than their younger counterparts, those in their thirties drive themselves to achieve higher performance (and economic) levels. The price is high. Such tenacity also brings about the start of a slowly diminishing sense of well-being. Injurious life style components like smoking, alcohol, drugs, and stress tend to undermine health and well-being. Furthermore, a number of chronic diseases, such as bronchitis and hypertension begin appearing, but tend to remain passive until the later years (Parsons and Felton 1990).

The Forties

The years of the forties bridge young-middle and middle adulthood. We become aware of life's finite limitations and, as friends and relatives become sick and die, we begin to acknowledge and accept our own mortality. It is a time of reappraisal and a period of adjustments; we begin to evaluate and compare past and future expectations. This frequently leads to the familiar "mid-life crisis," comparable only to that which occurs in our teens. We redirect our focus from pursuing specific goals to exploring our inner self. Internal unrest and frustration may bring dramatic life style turbulence, which can influence threats of cancer, heart disease, accidents, cirrhosis, cardiovascular diseases, and suicide (Parsons and Felton 1990). By age 40, most of us require glasses and "all have osteoarthritic changes visible in radiographs of the cervical spine" (Sloane 1992).

The Fifties

Fifty becomes a major age marker in our lives as we cross a key dividing line. We carry with us the emotions, feelings, and relationships we have come to accept during our thirties and forties. Meanwhile, our values undergo a reexamination, and our attitudes slowly change. We become less irritable and our outlook becomes more philosophical. Feelings of joy, sorrow, tenderness, and affection tend to supplant those of hatred, anger, and self-pity (Parsons and Felton 1990).

Health problems begin restricting some activities. One of the major problems is obesity. Another is the risk of heart disease, cancer, cardiovascular disease, accidents, and cirrhosis (Parsons and Felton 1990). The first signs of Alzheimer's and Parkinson's disease among our contemporaries jolt our complacency about our own future health.

A constellation of events, from the "empty nest" to menopause, begins, confirming our sense of growing older. We notice that an increasing number of younger friends and colleagues, as well as parents and relatives, die with greater frequency. Our children graduate from college, marry, and present us with grandchildren. Memberships in such organizations as the American Association of Retired Persons initiate us into the social world of the elderly (Sloane 1992).

The Sixties

Retirement is one of the most important events that occurs as we pass this milestone and characterizes the decade of our sixties. Its meaning, however, has changed dramatically since Otto von Bismarck, 19th-century chancellor of the German empire, set 65 as the retirement age, well aware that few workers lived beyond age 45. One by-product, of course, is that the U.S. Social Security Act of 1935 also adopted 65 as its year for "normal" retirement, which still continues today. Notwithstanding, the retirement age continues to drift lower with the passage of time.

Sloane (1992) citing Sheehy (1979) indicates that those between 65 and 70 years are happier than in any younger group of adults—this in spite of potential losses and limitations. And this happiness continues well into the seventies. Sloane offers several reasons, arguing that older adults enjoy certain advantages over younger persons: more independence, fewer responsibilities, less concern about daily inconveniences, and financial security.

The Seventies, Eighties, and Beyond

The older we live, the greater the chance we will live longer and the greater the chance of disruption in our ADL. A man of 75 has a 50-50 chance of reaching 84; a woman, 86. Moreover, Neary (1990b) confirms that "elderly people who survive their seventh, eighth, and ninth decades encounter variable losses in health, mobility, independence, material possessions, memory capacities, sensory capabilities, and especially loved ones through death." Yet many who survive these demanding tasks and challenges adjust to their losses and continue to live enriching lives despite their limited capabilities.

We are still likely to live independently beyond the age of 85, albeit with help from family and friends in care-giving settings. Yet, even at these advanced ages, less than 20 percent live in nursing homes (Sloane 1991). The frail elderly, however, are hampered by physical impairments and at least one chronic illness. Their limited mobility frustrates their natural desire for autonomy and choice in living accommodations. They neither anticipated their gradual decline in mobility nor appreciate their changing needs brought about over time by functional loss and disability.

Rare is the older person who has not experienced the death of a spouse, and is without a few disabilities or in need of care-giving. Bereavement and loneliness become common emotions. Sensory impairments, particularly loss of hearing, may interfere with social interaction and exacerbate the sense of isolation among the elderly, while physical impairments increasingly limit their ADL and diminish their sense of independence.

Sensory Changes

▶ DECLINES IN SENSITIVITY

Gradually, throughout our lifetime, all our senses—taste, touch, sight, smell, and hearing—undergo normal declines in sensitivity (Regnier 1987). These declines can take place over periods as long as 40 years. The slowness of this advance, however, suggests that many of us may not readily identify our changing needs (Hiatt 1987). Unfortunately, such changes often signal us with a jolting awareness of functional limitations as we confront unyielding environmental demands.

As we grow older, the majority of us will develop some form of sensory impairment—sight being one of the most common and demanding (Regnier 1987). About half of all visually impaired and blind persons and many hearing-impaired persons are elderly. Unfortunately, the common tendency for most people is to think in terms of absolutes and view the terms "blind" and "deaf" as total debilities. In reality, however, these are relative terms. Most people legally labeled "blind" have some sight, and most of those labeled "deaf" experience some hearing. Yet, many with some remaining sight or hearing ability do not seek available services, believing they are unqualified because they still retain some sight or hearing ability (Hiatt 1987). Others, believe that their acceptance of such services is a public admission of their disability.

Throughout our artifact environment, many design features echo the public's perception of "blind" as meaning "sightless." In some respects, this lets designers—and design standards—off the hook. In the past, both have tended to focus on small features that accommodate people at the extremes of sensory loss. For example, mandatory braille notations in elevators clearly provide help to the small percentage of sightless users who know braille. Those with some sight, however, who could benefit greatly from large, raised or recessed, well-contrasted, tactile letters and numerals have been largely ignored (Hiatt 1987).

Sensory losses and specialized training to offset such losses vary among individuals. Some of us develop vision or hearing problems early in life, while others retain sensory capacity well into the sixth, seventh, and eighth decades. Yet, individual sensory abilities can also vary: one can have poor eyesight and excellent hearing while another can have excellent eyesight and poor hearing. And this variation can occur at different ages for different people.

Most elderly persons with vision impairments also have impaired hearing, mobility, or agility (Hiatt 1987). We tend to compensate for the loss of one sense by relying more on the senses that remain. Persons with hearing loss, for example, unconsciously begin to sight-read lips. Consequently, we become acutely aware of any limitations to our remaining senses. Unfortunately, products and environments are usually directed toward only one disability, thereby failing to accommodate the combined effects of multiple losses.

Many professional providers of health care, living environments, and products for daily living still remain unfamiliar with the factors that play a key role in sensory deterioration: particularly such diseases and disorders as cataracts, glaucoma, diabetic retinopathy, presbyopia, presbycusis, and tinnitus.

▶ VISION

Among the conditions that restrict the daily activities of those 65 and older, vision impairment ranks fourth after orthopedic impairments, arthritis, and heart disease (LaPlante 1991a). And while 13 percent of older adults have some vision impairment, only 3 percent of all Americans 65 and over are totally blind (Kirchner and Lowman 1978).

But the term "visual impairment" does not mean "blindness." According to the American Foundation for the Blind (AFB), legal blindness refers to "central visual acuity of 20/200 or less in the better eye with best correction, or a visual field of 20 degrees of less" (American Foundation for the Blind 1993). On the other hand, severe visual impairment, as defined by the National Center for Health Statistics (NCHS), is "the self- or proxy-reported inability to see to read ordinary newspaper print even when wearing glasses or contact lenses" (Nelson and Dimitrova 1993).

Although the majority (68%) of severely impaired people are age 65 or older, "the rate of severe visual impairment," according to Nelson and Dimitrova (1993), "increases steadily and dramatically with age." Poor eyesight, however, is not an inevitable result of age. Most older people maintain good eyesight into their eighth decade and beyond (National Institute on Aging 1986). While the normal aging process may produce vision losses gradually over long periods of time, many older adults are not aware of the changes taking place. This effect is similar to sitting in a hot bath and not being aware that the water is gradually cooling (Osterburg 1987). Both effects suppress our normal reaction to environmental hostility.

As we grow older, most of us can expect to experience one or more moderate changes in our vision (Hiatt 1987).

▶ Increased sensitivity to glare

▶ Decreased ability to see objects clearly (visual acuity)

▶ Need for greater illumination

▶ Difficulty adapting to darkness and brightness

▶ Altered color perception

▶ Narrowing field of vision

TABLE 5–1. LEGAL BLINDNESS★

Age (years)	Total Population (in 1,000's)	Prevalence Rates (per 1,000)	Prevalence Estimates
All ages	248,710	2.51	623,930
0–17	63,604	.57	36,930
18–44	107,493	1.06	113,940
45–64	46,371	2.46	114,070
65–74	18,107	6.37	115,340
75 and over	13,135	18.60	244,320

★Legal blindness refers to central visual acuity of 20/200 or less in the better eye with best correction, or a visual field of 20 degrees or less. The National Society to Prevent Blindness (NSPB) calculated the rates based on 1970 data. The American Foundation for the Blind (AFB) slightly modified NSPS's childhood age categories to make them comparable to those available for severe visual impairment. Estimates were calculated using national rates applied to population data from the 1990 census. For additional technical information, contact AFB to obtain Statistical Brief No. 36, by Nelson and Dimitrova (1993).
Source: U.S. prevalence of legal blindness, by age; and Severe visual impairment, April 1992. *Social Research Department Typescript,* New York: American Foundation for the Blind, Inc. Reproduced by permission.

Glare

As we age, the lens and fluid in our eyes (vitreous humor) change and begin scattering incoming light rays (Kupfer 1990; Pynoos, Cohen, Davis, et al. 1987). Cataracts—cloudy or opaque areas in the lens—also contribute to glare. They usually develop gradually and without pain. As they form they disperse the passage of light rays, decrease the amount of light that enters the eye, and affect the eye's ability to focus (National Institute on Aging 1987). Seasonal and weather conditions can greatly affect this condition. If too little light is a problem, too much light can be a major problem (Regnier 1987). Such conditions as bright sunlight reflecting off snow or water can intensify the affect of glare and produce brilliant halos around each light source. Indoors, direct lighting, highly polished floors, reflective wall coverings, and uncovered windows can also produce the same effect (Osterburg 1987).

TABLE 5–2. SEVERE VISUAL IMPAIRMENT*

Age (years)	Total Population (in 1,000's)	Prevalence Rates (per 1,000)	Prevalence Estimates
All ages	248,710	17.3	4,293,360
0–17	63,604	1.5	95,410
18–44	107,493	3.2	349,350
45–54	24,838	13.5	340,510
55–64	21,533	28.4	600,600
65–74	18,107	59.0	1,068,290
75–84	10,055	118.4	1,190,520
85 and over	3,080	210.6	648,680

*Severe visual impairment is the self- or proxy-reported inability to read ordinary newsprint even with correction; caregivers of children under 6 report lack of useful vision. For persons under 65, the American Foundation for the Blind (AFB) increased the rates from the 1977 Health Interview Survey (HIS) by 74% to reflect procedural improvements in the Supplement on Aging (SOA) to the 1984 HIS. Rates for older persons come directly from the SOA. Estimates were calculated using national rates applied to population data from the 1990 census. For additional information, contact AFB to obtain Statistical Brief No. 36, by Nelson and Dimitrova (1993).

Source: U.S. prevalence of legal blindness, by age; and Severe visual impairment, April 1992. *Social Research Department Typescript,* New York: American Foundation for the Blind, Inc. Reproduced by permission.

Visual Acuity (Clarity)

Our eyes provide most of the information we receive about the environment. The term visual acuity refers to the accuracy or sharpness of our pattern vision which transmits this information (Kantowitz and Sorkin 1983). We commonly refer to this ability as 20/20 vision, i.e., "the ability to correctly perceive a letter three-quarters of an inch high from a distance of twenty feet. Those who can see, even with the best corrective lenses, no more at a distance of twenty feet than someone with normal sight can see at a distance of 200 feet, is considered legally blind" (National Center for Vision and Aging 1986).

Visual acuity peaks in our teens, remaining constant until the fifth decade, gradually declining until we reach age 60, and dropping off sharply after age 70 (Pirkl and Babic 1988). As we age, the cornea, iris, and lens change and permit less light to enter the eye. That which does, scatters and becomes less focused. Such changes increase our vulnerability to the environment (Pynoos, Cohen, Davis, et al. 1987). As visual acuity declines, the level of illumination required for "normal" viewing also increases. This means that as we grow older, we require more light in order for perception to occur (Wright 1980). For example, a 60-year-old with normal vision for this age needs twice the level of illumination as a normal 20-year-old (Wright 1980). Visual acuity increases in direct proportion to the quantity of light that falls on the viewed surface. Therefore, older people generally need brighter light for such tasks as reading, cooking, and driving a car. On the other hand, low light levels, coupled with poor figure-to-ground contrast, can cause us to perceive information inaccurately. Incandescent light, however, is better than fluorescent light for older eyes.

Visual Accommodation (Focus)

Visual accommodation refers to the eye's ability to focus on close or nearby objects. This ability peaks at age 10. At age 20, we can focus our eyes on objects as close as 4 inches (10 cm) (Pirkl and Babic 1988). As we age, however, the lens stiffens and loses its elasticity, thereby inhibiting us from changing its curvature and adjusting our focus. In time our eye muscles weaken and contract with increasing difficulty. These conditions reduce the refractive power of the cornea-lens system, extend our near-point of focus, and hamper our ability to read fine print (Kantowitz and Sorkin 1983). By age 70, our near-point of focus (without corrective lenses) reaches 40 inches (100 cm). This condition, termed "presbyopia," is common after the age of 40. And by age 55, there is almost a 100 percent chance that we will need corrective lenses (Sloane 1992).

Brightness Adaptation

As we reach the later years, our ability to adapt to rapid changes in lighting decreases. This happens whether such changes occur from dark to light or light to dark (Pynoos, Cohen, Davis, et al. 1987). As we grow older, the lens loses its ability to contract and the muscles of the iris become less effective. These changes affect the pupil's ability to constrict and exclude excessive light. With too much light entering the eye, adjustments to excessively bright light and shiny surfaces produce ever-longer periods of bright, intense glare, especially if cataracts exist. Moreover, as our eyes lose their ability to distinguish between dark and light surfaces, we require increasing contrast to maintain our perception level (Pirkl and Babic 1988).

Darkness Adaptation

Increasing age also diminishes our eye's ability to adjust to low light levels. We gradually experience increased difficulty seeing objects in dim light, requiring more and more light for us to see objects clearly. This is because our visual threshold for perceiving light increases, doubling each 13 years between age 20 and age 60. It's important to make that distinction clear: the light-gathering power of the cornea and lens at age 60 is only about one third that of 20-year-olds. Therefore, the older we get, the greater levels of illumination and higher contrasts we require. Consequently, night driving becomes increasingly more demanding. (Pirkl and Babic 1988).

Color Perception

The chromatic intensity (brightness and purity) of perceived colors seems to diminish with age. Our ability to see and differentiate colors depends on the optical quality (clarity) of the lens and its ability to accurately transmit the wave lengths of light entering the eye. Aging, however, causes the lens to lose its transparency. This "filtering" of the incoming light rays tends to dull our color sensitivity. Consequently, many older persons seem to prefer exuberant color combinations, often seen in their choice of clothing and interior furnishings, which to them may appear "OK" but to younger eyes may seem loud and garish. This amplified chromatic intensity provides increased stimulation that compensates for the diminished sensitivity of older eyes (Pirkl and Babic 1988). Elderly people also show strong color preferences. Interviews disclose that elderly residents rate warm colors high and cool colors rate medium to low. Blue was especially disliked (Osterburg 1987).

Our ability to distinguish between analogous (closely related) colors, especially blues and greens, also diminishes with age. This seems to be due partly to the gradual coloration of the aqueous humor (fluid within the eye), and partly because the lens, over time, becomes less transparent and assumes a yellowish tint. Such changes filter out the shorter wavelengths of light (greens, blues, and violets), thus reducing our ability to distinguish cool colors (blues and greens). We begin experiencing these changes beyond age 20 with noticeable declines after age 70 (Pirkl and Babic 1988).

Field of Vision

Our field of vision is the total circular area that we see when looking straight ahead at a fixed point. It is sometimes referred to as "the cone of vision." Until age 35 the angle of the eye's field of vision remains an almost constant 180° horizontal and 135° vertical. At age 40, this angle begins to decline slightly, becoming rapid after age 50. Commonly known as *tunnel vision*, this age-related condition is most acute above age 75. It is caused by changes in the retina and central nervous system which reduce the periphery of our field of vision and the eyeball sinking into the head due to changes in the skin and muscles around the eye (unrelated to the eye itself) (Pirkl and Babic 1988).

▶ HEARING

Hearing Impairments

Despite all the advantages of being sighted, many human behavior professionals believe that hearing loss can impact one's life more profoundly than can loss of sight. According to the American Association of Retired Persons (AARP), there are more people of all ages with hearing disorders than the combined totals of those with heart disease, cancer, blindness, kidney disease, tuberculosis, and multiple sclerosis. "Hearing, like seeing," says Lovering (1985), "requires a receptor (ear), a transmission line (nerve pathway), and a decoder (brain). Any defect in one of these produces a hearing impairment," which refers to "any degree of loss for the hearing of loudness, or pitch that is outside the range for normal."

It may be useful at this time to establish a clear distinction between hearing impairment and deafness. Hearing impairments, according to Lovering (1985), are caused by:

▶ Wax or bone growth blocking sound waves in route to the inner ear

▶ Damage to the inner ear mechanism (infection or the trauma of explosion or continual loud noises)

▶ Damage to the neural transmitters or decoding areas of the brain

The term "deaf" refers only to those hearing impairments of a profound degree (Laufer 1984). While about 60 percent of the 16 million Americans over age 55 have some form of hearing impairment, total deafness is not very common. The AARP reports that only 2 percent of those 55 and older are classified as legally deaf.

While hearing loss is common and considered by some the most prevalent impairment among older persons, it is not a normal condition (Laufer 1984). Sixteen million Americans are hearing impaired, with 60 percent of these being 55 years or older. Those between the ages of 25 and 55 will experience a gradual deterioration in hearing followed by a rapid decline. Studies indicate that among the elderly, 75 to 80 percent have some hearing impairment with up to 20 percent of those age 80 to 84 using hearing aids (Brody and Persky 1990; Hiatt 1987).

Our hearing system normally responds to frequencies from about 20 cycles per second (cps) to 20,000 cps. By way of comparison, piano notes range from 25 to 3,400 cps. As we age our sensitivity to sounds at the higher frequencies decreases. This explains why many older people seem to prefer low-frequency sound and set their radio's tone control on "bass" rather than "treble." It also explains why many people with hearing impairments are victims of emergency audio warnings, such as clock or appliance alarms, that went unheard because their frequency level was set too high.

Factors other than aging can also cause hearing impairment. Head injury or stroke may produce permanent damage in younger people as well. Moreover, according to Laufer (1984), "antibiotics such as streptomycin and erythromycin, diuretics, and large dosages of aspirin can be oto-toxic—a term used to describe medications that can damage the structures of the inner ear." Disrupted blood flow to the inner ear resulting from heart or kidney disease, diabetes, emphysema, or stroke can also cause permanent hearing loss (Laufer 1984).

Intensity

Sound intensity (loudness) is measured in decibels (dB). The threshold of normal hearing ranges from 0 to 3 dB hearing level (HL). A quiet house will measure 30 dB, and the level of conversational speech is about 50 dB (Parsons and Felton 1990). Prolonged exposure to noise at 85 dB can result in gradual hearing loss. Above 100 dB, the threshold of pain, even brief exposure can result in permanent damage. A jackhammer, a rock concert, and a portable cassette player with a headphone can all reach 110 dB. With the current preference for high-volume music by the young, it is easy to understand why hearing problems among this cohort group will occur, causing them to experience increasing difficulty interacting with their environment as they grow older. Dean Garstecki, head of the hearing impairment program at Northwestern University notes, "we've got 21-year-olds walking around with hearing-loss patterns of people 40 years their senior" (Toufexis 1991).

Over the years the products of industrial progress have inflicted its noise on us—and noise affects our hearing. Hazardous noise levels in the workplace affect about 15 million workers, causing approximately 6 million to lose their hearing. Occupational Safety and Health Administration (OSHA) regulations, however, permit higher levels of noise for limited periods. For each 5 dB increase in noise level one's allowable exposure time is cut in half. For example, in any 24-hour period one is allowed to endure 85 dB hearing level (HL) for 8 hours; 90 dB HL for 4 hours; and 110 dB HL for 15 minutes (Parsons and Felton 1990).

Presbycusis

It is not unusual to experience some degree of hearing loss by age 55. The most common diagnosis is *presbycusis* which means literally, "elder" (*presby*), "hearing" (*akousis*). Generally, this kind of hearing loss affects both ears equally and, because of degenerating changes to auditory nerve cells in the inner ear (cochlear mechanism), such loss remains permanent. More common and severe in men, the condition gradually worsens with age, particularly for high-pitched sounds (Laufer 1984).

Hearing Changes

While hearing loss can occur at any age, it is most common in older people. As we age, many of us will experience one or more of the following changes in our hearing (Pirkl and Babic 1988):

▶ Decreased hearing acuity

▶ Loss of pitch discrimination

▶ Reduced speech discrimination and comprehension

▶ Altered directional hearing

Hearing Acuity (Volume) *Hearing acuity* means the ability to hear sound of "normal" volume. As we age, our hearing changes, gradually reducing the vibrancy of our environment by muffling such sounds as flowing water or the placement of feet on wood or stone (Laufer 1984).

Frequency Discrimination (Pitch) Hearing loss caused by loud noise generally affects the higher frequencies first; the greatest damage occurring at 4,000 Hz. In comparison, normal speech ranges from 500 to 2,000 Hz. The first symptom of such loss is a ringing, hissing, or buzzing in the ear (Parsons and Felton 1990). This complaint, termed *tinnitus,* is "the perception of sound in one or both ears in the absence of an externally applied stimulus" (Gulya 1990). It can be brought about by a variety of bodily conditions including an obstruction of the external auditory canal (such as earwax), infections of the hearing mechanism, or a perforated eardrum (typanic membrane).

Speech Discrimination and Comprehension Our ability to hear and understand speech depends on how well our auditory and central nervous systems function. Changes to the mechanism of the inner ear can affect the transmission of sound waves generated by the spoken word, as can the loss or atrophy of cells of the central nervous system's specialized auditory cells. Such changes can alter our ability to hear and comprehend speech. While little change usually takes place between ages 20 and 60, a 25 percent loss can be expected from age 60 to 80 years.

Words containing the higher-pitched consonants, such as c, ch, f, s, sh, and z, which are normally spoken with less power than vowels, become increasingly more difficult to comprehend. Rapid speech also becomes increasingly more difficult to understand (Pirkl and Babic 1988).

Directional Hearing   Directional hearing gives us the ability to locate the source of sounds. It also provides us with an awareness of our spatial environment and helps orient our body within it. Both ears are required to accurately determine the direction of sound. Changes to either the inner ear or the central nervous system can affect the reception and analysis of the sound waves. Thus, locating the source of sounds becomes difficult, leading to confusion and disorientation.

▶ TOUCH

Many elderly people must interact with the environment using limited sensory information. Touch becomes an indispensable means of gathering environmental information and, in some cases like that of Helen Keller, it becomes the only means. We receive environmental clues through our sense of touch in three ways: *tactile sensitivity*, *pressure sensitivity*, and *thermal sensitivity*.

Tactile Sensitivity   Our skin provides us with an ability to "feel" objects and surfaces, allowing us to perceive forms, textures, and shapes with just our sense of touch. Our tactile sensitivity, however, depends on our skin's condition, its receptors, and the neurological condition of our central nervous system.

Our skin is made up of two layers. The surface layer (epidermis) consists of densely packed cells tightly bonded together. It becomes thicker where the body receives the most friction, such as the hands and feet. Calluses are an extreme example. Ridges (fingerprints and heelprints) and creases (wrinkles) anchor this outer layer to the underlying layer (dermis), which supports the various ridges and folds by elastic fibers. As we age, these fibers lose some of their elasticity, causing additional creases to occur (Beare and Myers 1990). Aging also causes the epidermis to become thin, which, in turn, reduces the number of receptors, and varies their size, shape, and distribution. Progressive decline of the oil-secreting (sebaceous) glands also affect the skin's sensitivity. This loss of sensitivity increases significantly with age, but with wide variability, affecting about 25 percent of the older population.

Pressure Sensitivity   Our ability to "feel" actions or movements through our sense of touch may decrease with age. For example, we "feel" when a typewriter key has been fully depressed and release it on receiving the proper stimuli. We also "feel" when the seat of a chair is hard or soft the moment we sit on it. Limited information suggests that pressure receptors deep within the underlying (subcutaneous) tissue, and decrements associated with other functions of the central nervous system, provide our sensitivity. Should this be the case, our sensitivity could be reduced with increasing age.

Thermal sensitivity   Our sensitivity to heat and cold depends on the condition of the skin and the status of the central nervous system. Two reflex centers in the brain control the body's temperature; one sensing an increase, the other sensing a decrease (Beare and Myers 1990). The skin's temperature is controlled involuntarily by mechanisms which pass more or less blood through the skin's superficial blood vessels. Specialized sensory nerve end organs receive sensations of temperature (and pain, and itch) and transmit them to the brain (Bullock and Rosendahl 1988), which causes us to react to the sensation.

As age increases, we tend to lose body fat and the skin gets thinner and is less able to insulate our body. Thus, older persons retain heat less efficiently and tend to compensate for heat loss with a sweater or a blanket. Moreover, the ability of our body's temperature regulating mechanism to transmit accurate information also decreases. The normal slowing down of our central nervous system intensifies both effects. Thus we may become less sensitive to dangerous temperature extremes commonly found in such environmental elements as hot bath water, radiators, hair dryers, irons, ranges, ovens, and freezers. This danger exists for the very young as well as the very old: the very young due to their lack of knowledge, experience, and sensory development, and the very old due to a lack of sensory capability.

Dysmobility

▶ MOVEMENT LIMITATIONS

Of all the factors that impact on our ability to remain independent, the most critical may be those that relate to bodily movements. All activities of daily living (ADL) (e.g., bathing, dressing, toileting, feeding, etc.) require some form of bodily movement: walking, sitting, lifting, reaching, grasping, stooping, or bending. Limitations in our ability to perform these movements, whether produced by disease, injury, or the aging process, change normally benign environments into hostile confrontations and block our access to the ADL.

It is a mistake, however, to believe that movement limitations are determined by chronology—they are not. Decreased dexterity and limited movement of the body and limbs can occur at any age. Sports-induced joint injuries, for example, can impair our abilities in ways similar to the functional limitations caused by arthritis. In both cases the impairment can impede our ability to freely move hands, arms, or legs. Many young people with hand or finger injuries are surprised to find that control knobs, appliance handles, and packages, once easily grasped, have become sources of painful frustration.

Our range of movements also decreases. As we age, the muscles and joints associated with large and small motor movements become less efficient and reduce our ability to perform complex tasks. Between ages 30 and 80 the number of muscle fibers and size of the motor units decrease, bringing about a linear decline. Moreover, changes in bodily subsystems can also affect our motor ability by reducing the required energy supply of oxygen and nutrients that go to our muscles.

By age 40, some form of joint deterioration, particularly in the weight-bearing parts of our bodies (hips and knees), is experienced by 90 percent of the adults in the United States. This is provoked by the loss of elasticity in the *collagen tissue*, the body's most prevalent protein (and a major factor causing wrinkles). As we age, cartilage separating the bone ends in the joints thins and loses its elasticity and protective ability. Consequently, joints become less flexible, and moving them becomes increasingly painful (Beare and Myers 1990; Pirkl and Babic 1988).

▶ ARTHRITIS

Arthritis is a generic term used to describe a variety of degenerative and inflammatory changes in our joints. This term applies to over 100 different diseases, many involving heat, swelling, redness, and severe aches and pains in the joints and connective tissue throughout the body. The pain and suffering associated with this affliction evolved over millennia; the roots of antiquity provide evidence of its Cro-Magnon existence (Pirkl and Babic 1988).

According to the Arthritis Foundation, the disease disables over 7 million individuals. And while not considered part of the aging process, arthritis interferes with the normal daily activities of about 4 percent of all young adults, 50 percent of those in middle age, and about 80 percent of those in their seventies. Of those over age 75, 85 percent have arthritis in one or more joints.

Related problems of stiffness or paralysis affect over 5 million households or about 60 percent of all elderly households (Struyk 1987). Most forms of arthritis are chronic, although proper treatment usually quiets some symptoms. Commonly found throughout the world, it is the major crippling disease in the United States today, affecting more women than men and more whites than nonwhites. While rarely fatal, there is, unfortunately, no cure (Pirkl and Babic 1988).

Losses in muscle strength, especially the grip, affect one's ability to perform the activities of daily living (ADL) (Neary 1990a). This can also dramatically affect independence by limiting a person's ability to climb and descend stairs, get in and out of bed, chairs, toilet, dress, bathe, eat, cook, wash clothes and dishes, and respond quickly in cases of emergency.

The common types of arthritis affecting older persons are *osteoarthritis* and *rheumatoid arthritis*.

Osteoarthritis

The most common form of degenerative joint disease, osteoarthritis, leads all other causes of disability in those over 65 years of age. Moreover, radiographic evidence suggest the presence of osteoarthritis in one third of those over 35, with its prevalence increasing well into the eighties. Contrary to popular belief, it is not an inevitable consequence of the aging process (Ettinger 1990). While its cause is unknown, it occurs in most people over 60.

Osteoarthritis is characterized by slowly progressing joint pain, which may be accompanied by deformity and limited joint movement. Changes provoked by the disease are cartilage deterioration and the development of bony spurs (osteophytes) at joint edges, which usually produce stiffness or pain in the fingers or stress-bearing joints (knees, hips, and lumbar spine). As the disease progresses, joint motion becomes restricted and weight-bearing joints may fail. Inflammation is rare (Neary 1990b). Generally, according to Murphy (1991), "women have a higher prevalence and severity of OA in the hands, knees, ankles, and feet; whereas men have a higher prevalence in the spine and hips." Over time, this disease, particularly in the hip or knee, reduces our physical activity and impedes our mobility, thus tending to increase the risk of coronary heart disease (Haan 1991).

Traumatic arthritis, another term for osteoarthritis, can prematurely result from overwork or trauma. It is common among bricklayers, tennis players, bowlers—even active persons in wheelchairs—who literally wear out their elbows, shoulders, wrists, etc. (Lovering 1985). According to DeLoach, Wilkins, and Walker (1983), it "may occur at a much earlier age in those with disabilities that force them to over-use certain areas of their bodies, such as the arms and shoulders in the case of paraplegics."

Rheumatoid Arthritis

This is the most frequent form of arthritis after osteoarthritis. Unlike osteoarthritis, however, the incidence of rheumatoid arthritis declines after 65. It occurs primarily in the small joints of the hands, feet, and wrists, later involving such larger joints as the elbow, shoulder, hip, knee, and cervical spine. Symptoms commonly include intense inflammation of the joint membrane (synovitis), which causes vascular congestion and leads to irreversible joint damage and deformities (Neary 1990b). There is no known cause or cure.

The disease commonly begins in youth or middle age and continues as an ongoing process into the older years. Unfortunately, most who are afflicted with the disease become progressively disabled, lowering their threshold of functional ability. Prolonged bed rest may cause temporary immobility to become irreversible (Ettinger 1990). In order to maintain independence, physical and occupational therapy are essential, along with exercise and assistive products.

Secondary physical disabilities erect serious obstacles to self-help care and independence. While assistive devices such as canes, walkers, braces, etc. may help overcome many environmental barriers, the present institutional appearance of most such devices tends to impose a sense of embarrassment and loss of dignity. Many persons are reluctant to use these devices, and their continued reluctance leads to a decline in independence.

A more humane alternative is to redesign such devices to offer a less intimidating appearance. Moreover, while hardly a substitute for transgenerational accommodation, such products can also offer more supportive, and humane environments and artifacts. These include bathtubs, shower stalls, and stairwells featuring soft, nonskid surfaces; hand rails and grab bars appropriately placed and attractively integrated into environmental settings; adequate, indirect glare-free lighting; easy-to-grasp controls and handles for ranges, ovens, washers, dryers, doors, and windows; and a thousand other objects used in the ADL and found throughout both public and private environments.

► TREMOR

Parkinsonism

Parkinson's disease is a chronic, progressive illness affecting about 1 percent of those over 50. Generally associated with the elderly and those with impaired motor function, it is rarely seen in those under 40 (Murphy 1991). Yahr and Pang (1990) describe parkinsonism as one of a number of "clinical disorders characterized primarily by abnormal involuntary movements (dyskinesias), alterations in muscle tone, and disturbances in bodily posture." Apparently caused by degenerating pigmented cells located in the brain stem (Bullock and Rosendahl 1988), the disease commonly results in the gradual stiffening and slowing of movement, a bent-over posture, and uncontrollable muscle spasms. It usually ends with deteriorated mental processes (Parker 1988).

Nearly 1 million persons in the United States are affected by the disease with 50,000 new cases developing each year. It affects both sexes and all races, appearing most frequently in those between ages 50 and 79. Its incidence increases with age. "Curative therapy," according to Yahr and Pang (1990), is presently unavailable.

About 70 percent of those with the disease display tremor, affecting mainly the upper extremities and commonly starting in one or both hands. The fingers often react with a familiar "pill-rolling"[11] motion. Tremor can also affect the leg, head, voice, lips, and tongue (Murphy 1991). Such tremors are characterized as *resting tremors*, which commonly occur during periods of rest; and *intentional tremors*, which occur as one attempts precise movements (Bullock and Rosendahl 1988), (e.g., dialing a telephone or setting the controls of a range or oven).

Instinctive and spontaneous movements, like swinging the arms while walking, decrease and eventually cease. Smooth-flowing motions are arrested by muscular rigidity. This chain of reactions, characterized as the "cogwheel effect," causes instead "a series of interrupted jerks." Slow, purposeful movements can also stop suddenly, "freezing" the motion in mid-sequence. Thus, such basic ADL, including walking, dressing, grooming, cooking and eating, and writing can be particularly frustrating, and at times, impossible.

As the disease progresses, walking becomes increasingly difficult and hazardous. The posture of the body becomes more stooped and the gait is reduced to a shuffle. Furthermore, the decreased speed of muscular movements makes it impossible to correct a missed step (Robinson and Conard 1986). Falls can also occur if the body is pushed from the back or front (Yahr and Pang 1990).

---

11. The motion caused by rolling a pill or other small, round object between the thumb and forefinger.

Balance and Falling

▶ BALANCE

Elderly people exhibit a unique set of behaviors brought about by the gradual decrease in their sensory functions. Such incremental losses blunt their awareness of hazardous environmental conditions that are either not perceived or do not register. Thus, as older people experience sensory losses, and changes in stature and spatial orientation, they tend to lose their balance more readily. Moreover, complex combinations of disabilities (vision, hearing, osteoporosis, osteoarthritis, etc.) and the use of medications tend to multiply their chance of falling (Parker, 1988).

While 85 percent of those age 65 and older live in residential situations used by people of all ages, those who have fallen—like those with impairments or disabilities—learn quickly to modify their environment according to their unique needs. Seventy-five percent own their own homes and are more likely to modify them to fit their own life styles and capabilities than younger occupants (Lawton 1989).

Postural Competence

Falls, according to Robinson and Conard (1986) are "a mismatch between environmental demand and postural competence." Stated another way, whenever aging or disease alters our ability to stand, walk, or navigate, we require compensating environmental responses. The goal is to reestablish this lost equilibrium with appropriate environmental support.

Behind this idea is the concept of postural competence (Figure 7-1), the quality that helps us maintain our stable upright posture. Falls occur when environmental demand (a continuous variable) exceeds postural competence (another continuous variable).

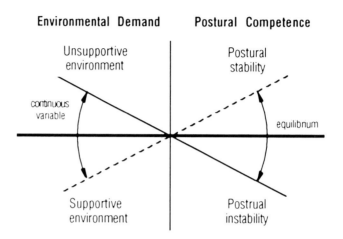

Figure 7–1. Model of postural competence.

A safe and stable upright posture requires the interaction of three unimpaired elements: senses, motor function, and central processing. Impairments to any one of these elements reduce safety and stability, and increase the risk of falling (Robinson and Conard 1986).

The Sensory Element

Our vision supplies us with the most accurate and sensitive information about the spatial position of our body, and contributes significantly to our postural competence. As other senses diminish with age or disease, we rely increasingly on our vision to determine our body positions. Studies link the incidence of disease-related visual impairments to age, and identify impaired vision as a major risk factor for falls (Robinson and Conard 1986).

Our ears' vestibular function signals changes in our head position caused by gravity (via the maculae) or acceleration (via the semicircular canals). Such input coordinates our balancing reflex as we respond to sudden bodily movements. This ability, however, decreases with age. As vestibular diseases diminish the accuracy of our sensory input, we receive inaccurate and conflicting input signals, which send inappropriate stimuli to the central processing system. One result is *vertigo,* defined as a hallucination of movement.

Moreover, proprioceptive information (stimuli produced in the tissues of the muscles and tendons and caused by movement of the body and its parts) expedites our stretch reflexes, which transform our flexible limbs into stable supports for standing or walking. Falls occur when we cannot place our limbs outside our body's balancing limits (center of gravity). The characteristic shuffling gait of older people increases their chance of falling. Their shorter step lengths and heights inhibit recovery once their body's center of gravity extends beyond this shorter step base (Figure 7-2).

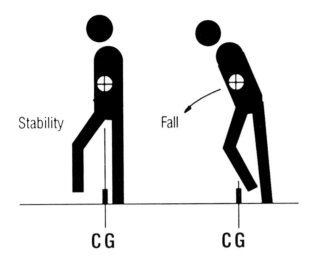

Stability   Fall

C G   C G

Figure 7–2. Influence of center of gravity (CG) on falling.

The Motor Element

Motor changes can also impair postural competence and cause chronic instability. In order to maintain our stable upright posture, we rely on (1) muscular strength and tone, and (2) joint stability. Studies indicate that the aging process reduces both of these requirements and contributes to early fatigue. Motor function is also impaired by degenerative joint disease (arthritis), soft tissue injury (bruises and lacerations), fractures, and bodily weakness caused by a sedentary life style (Robinson and Conard 1986). Proper exercise becomes an important element in maintaining postural competence and preserving our range of motions.

The Central Processing Element

The central processing system collects and processes the raw stimuli sent from the three sensory areas (visual, vestibular, and proprioceptive) and the various motor functions. Correct interpretation of this information is essential if we are to maintain postural stability. It is also widely believed that lowered performance and slower reaction times associated with some aging persons come from neural noise (spontaneous neural activity) and degenerative changes in the central processing system.

Chronic disease-related disorders affecting the central processing system, such as dementia, parkinsonism, and stroke, interfere with postural competence and increase one's chance of falling. Of these, dementia shows the strongest correlation to the probability of falls and fall-related injury among the elderly. Associated functional impairments, such as gait changes, judgmental errors, and reduced coordination are contributing factors. Stroke-induced paralysis, perceptual changes, and proprioceptive losses also affect postural competence by altering one's gait and balance (Robinson and Conard 1986).

Parkinsonism impedes one's gait and reduces the speed of muscular movement, preventing one from correcting a missed step. The disease greatly affects stability because the posture is flexed and forward-leaning. Those affected lift their feet only slightly above the ground and assume a shuffling gait. Walking surface irregularities (e.g., thresholds, curbs, thick carpets) cause them to trip and fall easily. Since postural stability is compromised, they tend to fall when turning and getting in and out of chairs (Kay and Tideiksaar 1990).

▶ FALLS

The issue of falls is a compelling topic. All of us have fallen sometime in our lives. Most of us, however, tend to dismiss the importance—particularly if we are young—and shrug off any serious suggestion that we "be careful" or "hold on to something." We remember falling as a child and conclude that accidental tumbles resulted from unpredictable childhood behavior—the price we paid to acquire ambulation and physical maturity.

Medical research is finding that a relationship exists between environmental demand and physical ability. An understanding of this relationship may help older people prevent falls and maintain their previous independence. Dr. Richard J. Ham, Distinguished Chair in Geriatric Medicine at the State University of New York Health Science Center, argues that "falling is an important syndrome in the elderly, since it may be a sign of specific or nonspecific disease and clearly puts the patient at risk, not only of injury but also of loss of confidence and potential institutionalization" (Ham 1986).

A surprisingly large percentage of people believe that accidents are caused by fate, destiny, or just bad luck. The term "accident," however, connoting a haphazard progression of events, should be replaced by the term *nonintentional injury*, the sixth leading cause of death in the United States for those 65 and older. While deaths from accidental falls declined by 29 percent from 1970 to 1988 (Table 7-2), "falls are the single leading cause of injury mortality in this group, accounting for 36 percent of the total deaths due to nonintentional injury" (Robinson and Conard 1986) (Figure 7-3).

TABLE 7–1. CONSEQUENCES OF FALLS

Medical
    Fractures, especially hip, wrist, vertebral, and rib
    Soft tissue injury, hematoma, laceration
    Subdural hematoma, contra coup injury, concussion
    Exacerbation of arthritis

Psychological
    Loss of confidence, depression, fear of falling

Social
    Social withdrawal, dependency
    Institutionalization

Functional
    Immobility, deconditioning, decreased joint mobility, decreased righting reflex
    Immobility may lead to hypothermia, thrombosis, dehydration, contractures, pressure
        sores, urine retention/incontinence, chest infection, osteoporosis

Source: Adapted from Hough, J. Christopher, 1991. Falls and Falling. In Richard J. Ham, and Philip D. Sloane (eds.), 1991. *Primary Care Geriatrics: A Case-Based Approach,* St. Louis: Mosby Year Book. Reproduced by permission.

Data also show that in a typical year, about one third of those over 65 have fallen at least once. This rate increases dramatically among the institutionalized elderly with reports of up to 20 percent of those hospitalized and 45 percent of those living in long-term care facilities experiencing falls sometime during their residency (Kay and Tideiksaar 1990).

While most falls do not result in injury, falls by elderly persons living at home are more likely to require treatment. They also lead to complications, such as painful soft-tissue injuries and hip fractures, and hot-water burns resulting from falling into the bathtub. Immobility resulting from

TABLE 7–2. DEATHS AND DEATH RATES FROM ACCIDENTAL FALLS: 1970–1988

Type of Fall	Deaths (Number)			Rate per 100,000 Population		
	1970	1980	1988	1970	1980	1988
Accidental falls	16,926	13,294	12,096	8.3	5.9	4.9
Fall from one level to another	4,798	3,743	3,317	2.4	1.7	1.3
Fall on the same level	828	415	433	0.4	0.2	0.2
Fracture, cause unspecified, and other unspecified falls	11,300	9,136	8,346	5.6	4.0	3.4

Source: Modified from Table No. 124. Deaths and Death Rates from Accidents, by Type: 1970–1988. U.S. Bureau of the Census, *Statistical Abstract of the United States: 1991* (111th edition). Washington, DC, 1991.

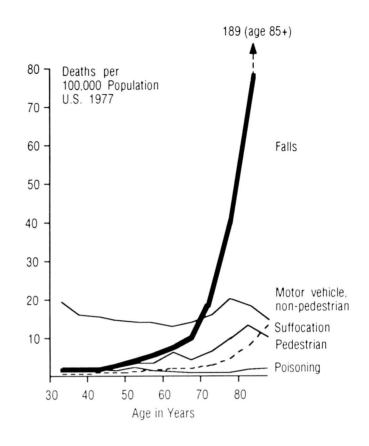

Figure 7–3. Relationship between accidental death and age.

Source: Adapted from Figure 15-1, Relationship between accidental death and age. In *Primary Care Geriatrics: A Case-Based Approach,* Richard J. Ham, and Philip D. Sloane (eds.). St. Louis: Mosby Year Book. 1991. Reproduced by permission.

falls can also contribute to hypothermia, dehydration, joint contractures, and pressure sores (Kay and Tideiksaar 1990).

Hip fractures top the list of all common, fall-related injuries that lead to hospitalization. Approximately 200,000 hip fractures occur in the United States each year—with 84 percent occurring in persons over age 65. Of these, about 25 percent result in death within 6 months of injury. Surviving a hip fracture leaves one vulnerable to one or more functional limitations. About 60 percent are left with decreased mobility and 25 percent become more functionally dependent (Kay and Tideiksaar 1990).

Falls by the elderly show a frequency rate of 14 to 19 falls per 100 people per year. They occur most frequently to older women who are in poor health and live alone—usually to those having more than one illness and who show a pattern of repeated falling.

Such recurrent falling is now becoming associated with a decline in general health with increased falling regarded as a signal of frailty—the greatest frequency occurring as death approaches. This is not to suggest that a solid relationship exists between falls and "identifiable medical factors." The medical community, according to Robinson and Conard (1986) believes that linking falls to a particular medical diagnosis, is "inappropriate." They now look to a broader assessment of the cause.

Professionals concerned with aging should become sensitive to the nature of falls and the environmental conditions that contribute to these occurrences. Thoughtful action based on these conditions can contribute to safer environments through the design of products and spaces that offer appropriate support. It is important for all professionals to recognize that falls can also be fatal (see Figure 7–3).

The most frequent activities resulting in falls are those associated with chairs, beds, and toilets. Robinson and Conard (1986) recommend that "the optimal design would be a height that allows the feet to be placed on the floor near the center of gravity with hips flexion 90° or less and a stable support object (bureau, safety rail) in reach." Unfortunately, many homes and institutional settings provide "beds that are too high, chairs too low, (and) unsecured support objects (beds, wheelchairs, other furniture on rollers)." Older people commonly push their chairs and furniture against the walls for stability. Similarly, when out-of-doors, they prefer sitting near such stable objects as trees, walls, benches, and other stable points of reference (DeLong 1968; Parker 1985).

Memory and Confusion

▶ DEMENTIA

The aging process causes our bodily organs to slow down upon reaching maturity. One of these organs is the brain—the core of our intellect and the control center for all bodily functions. As we age, millions of nerve cells gradually decrease and ten thousand processes linking other cells become less effective. The brain's function, however, is not necessarily lost; many linkages are available to take over damaged neural routes. But the brain's nerve cells do not regenerate. The brain, therefore, cannot replace its cells and continue functioning as can the skin, liver, and kidney. Consequently, diseases of the brain lead to permanent damage. Physical, cognitive, and sensory changes, left in the wake of this damage, affect the lives and life styles of many older adults, their spouses and children, and their care-givers (Fiber and Neurath 1985).

All illnesses in which the neuronal tissue and its supporting structures are destroyed are called *degenerative neurological diseases.* Of these, the most common are *Alzheimer's disease, parkinsonism, Huntington's disease,* and *muscular dystrophy.* The degenerative processes associated with these diseases are attributed to a number of causes; the most popular of these point to environmental toxins, immunological and viral processes, and factors causing premature aging. The most vital of our human processes—thinking, creating, conversing, feeling, and moving—are affected by these cerebral function disorders (Beare and Myers 1990).

▶ ALZHEIMER'S DISEASE

Today, many within the medical community believe that Alzheimer's disease is the most critical and challenging disease facing the elderly. It causes 50 to 60 percent of all dementia, a term described by Beare and Myers (1990) as a "diffuse progressive loss of mental function because of an organic disturbance." Fiber and Neurath (1985) add that "the term literally means, 'having lost the mind' and refers to progressive intellectual decline and memory loss."

Alzheimer's disease is the most common of the so-called degenerative neurological diseases. An estimated 1 million persons are affected by the disease (Beare and Myers 1989). It affects memory and other thought processes such as reasoning and identification. It also affects movement by producing falls, stiffness, rigidity, and difficulties in walking.

While the etiologic basis for the disease is unknown, extensive research has proposed numerous causes including genetics, abnormal protein, infectious agents, toxins, and inadequate blood flow (Bullock and Rosendahl 1988). It is generally accepted, however, that neurons (brain cells) in the region of the brain responsible for cognition, memory, and other thought processes, degenerate (Bullock and Rosendahl 1988).

Contrary to popular belief, Alzheimer's disease is not part of the normal aging process. This untreatable intellectual deterioration can occur at any age, but usually occurs among those aged 50 to 65. While also appearing in the seventies and eighties, it rarely occurs in those under 40. Within the over 65 group, 5 to 15 percent may have the disease. Its relentless duration ranges from 1 1/2 to 15 years with a 5- to 7-year average. Death usually occurs from such secondary causes as pneumonia and dehydration (Beare and Myers 1990).

The symptoms and progressive nature of Alzheimer's disease may differ from person to person (Bullock and Rosendahl 1988). Generally, however, the disease produces similar patterns of behavior. At first, persons with Alzheimer's disease begin to forget and lose things. They also tend to become careless in their dress and conduct. As the disease progresses, they become confused and experience increased difficulty with such daily living tasks as cooking, housekeeping, home maintenance, shopping, and transportation. As speech and written communication problems develop, they tend to withdraw from complex social groups (Beare and Myers 1990).

An advanced stage, called *ambulatory dementia,* brings complete disorientation. At this point they become increasingly self-absorbed and fail to recognize family members and friends. They begin to wander, becoming confused, agitated, belligerent, or combative. These mannerisms intensify as the day progresses. (This is known as *sundowning.*) Their impaired ability to reason, recognize others, and take safety precautions makes them increasingly dependent on care-givers. In the end, ambulation ceases with little purposeful activity. Moments of lucidity punctuate their inconsistent recognition of family members, body parts, and mirror images. They lose weight, forgetting how to eat, swallow, and chew. Death quietly ends their vegetative, bedbound life (Beare and Myers 1990).

Summary of Part 2

Are our body's cells genetically programmed to age? Do toxins cause human aging by damaging our cells gradually over time? Although "no single theory," we are told, answers the riddle of aging, functional declines in older people generally stem from three sources: disease, inactivity, and senescence (the aging process).

The good news here is that most people can expect to live longer than did past generations. Little correlation exists between chronological age and physical capability. Each of us ages at his or her own pace. This means that, while older people have more functional limitations, many impairments often attributed to "elderly" conditions are commonly experienced by younger people, many of whom are in worse physical condition than their older parents.

Poor eyesight is not an inevitable result of age. Only 3 percent of all Americans age 65 and over are totally blind, with 13 percent having some vision impairment. Most maintain good eyesight well into their seventies and eighties. All of us, however, will experience some decline in our ability to focus on nearby objects and see objects clearly in dim light. This occurs sooner for some than for others.

Hearing loss can impact one's life more profoundly than can loss of sight. Although not a normal condition of aging, hearing loss is most prevalent among older persons. But young people also lose their hearing sensitivity. Prolonged exposure to loud noise, such as rock concerts and portable cassette players, can result in gradual, but accelerating, permanent hearing loss. Such exposure causes many young people to exhibit hearing loss patterns of people two and three times their age.

The ability to move about is critical to one's independence. Dysmobility begins to affect people as young as age 40 when some form of joint deterioration limits the dexterity and bodily movements of 90 percent of U.S. adults. "Arthritis" is a generic term used to describe a number of degenerative and inflammatory joint changes. Although not considered part of the aging process, it interferes with the daily activities of 4 percent of all young adults, 50 percent of those in middle age, and about 80 percent of those in their seventies.

Almost 1 million persons in the United States have Parkinson's disease, which affects both sexes and all races, and appears most frequently in those between ages 50 and 79. About 70 percent of those with Parkinson's disease display tremor affecting the upper extremities. As the disease progresses, walking becomes increasingly difficult, body posture becomes more stooped, and the gait is reduced to a shuffle.

Falls occur when environmental demands exceed our postural competence (variable surface heights and textures significantly influence the chance of falling for all people). Chronic disease-related disorders affecting the central processing system, such as dementia, parkinsonism, and stroke, interfere with postural competence and increase one's chance of falling. Hip fractures lead the list of all common fall-related injuries leading to hospitalization. About 200,000 falls occur each year with 16 percent occurring in persons younger than age 65.

Alzheimer's disease is the most critical and challenging disease facing older people. Commonly called dementia, this degenerative neurological disease affects memory and other thought processes such as reasoning and identification. It also affects movement, producing falls, stiffness, rigidity, and difficulties in walking. While not part of the normal aging process, it usually occurs among those aged 50 to 65.

As we live on longer than our predecessors, more of us will acquire one or more functional limitations that will interfere with our activities of daily living. Such limitations need not, however, rob us of our dignity, independence, or our self-respect. Part 3 pursues these issues further, examining our freedom of choice and our ability to cultivate independence. It concludes by exploring the options and stating the promise of transgenerational design.

EXTENDING INDEPENDENCE

"There are many truths of which the full meaning cannot be realized until personal experience has been brought home."
—JOHN STUART MILL
(1800–1873)

Freedom to Choose

▶ THE IMPORTANCE OF CHOICE

One of the most precious—and fragile—human freedoms we enjoy is freedom of choice. Indeed, our independence depends on choice; only when we are free to choose can we be truly independent. That said, it also follows that the quality of life we experience as we perform activities of daily living (ADL) relates directly to the number and types of choices available.

When the environmental context offers the freedom to choose from a variety of options, we maintain our independence and the quality of our life is positive. On the other hand, when faced with unyielding environmental conditions that limit choices, frustrating encounters with hostile physical environments reduce our pleasure, independence, and quality of life.

It is easy for us to believe, however, that our freedom to make such simple choices as location of residence, the meals we eat, the furniture we use, or the recreation we seek, will remain unchallenged. It will not. At some point in our lives, if we live long enough, our ability to choose will be restrained by one or more functional limitations.

Functional Limitations

More than 37 million persons have functional limitations, although not severe in most cases. Storck and Thompson-Hoffman (1991) define functional limitations as "the inability to carry out sensory and physical activities." Murphy (1991) reminds us, however, that "functional limitations are not normal aspects of aging, but rather the result of one or more pathological processes." Rare is the person who reaches age 80 who is without one or more chronic disabling conditions (Sloane 1992). Yet, despite the pretension that most limitations affect older persons, most persons with disabilities are under age 65, with 14 million under age 55. Table 9-1 reveals the relationship between age and functional limitation.

TABLE 9–1. PERSONS 15 YEARS AND OVER WITH A FUNCTIONAL LIMITATION (IN THOUSANDS)

	TOTAL		SEVERE	
	Number	Percentage	Number	Percentage
Total by Age	37,304	20.6	13,537	7.5
15–24	2,054	5.2	346	0.9
25–34	3,049	7.5	596	1.5
35–44	4,074	13.4	890	2.9
45–54	5,110	23.0	1,431	6.4
55–64	7,552	34.2	2,734	12.4
65 years and over	15,465	58.5	7,539	28.5
65–69	4,052	45.4	1,682	18.8
70–74	4,078	55.3	1,691	22.9
75 years and over	7,335	72.5	4,166	41.2

Source: Used by permission of Springer Publishing Company, Inc., New York 10012, from Storck, Inez Fitzgerald, and Susan Thompson-Hoffman, 1991. Demographic characteristics of the disabled population. In *Disability in the United States: A Portrait from National Data*, Susan Thompson-Hoffman, and Inez Fitzgerald Storck (eds.). Copyright © 1991 by Springer Publishing Company.

Of those age 65 and older, about 60 percent have a sensory or physical condition, about half of which cause severe functional limitations. A similar picture emerges for those 75 years and older who are not institutionalized. Only 40 percent of this group experience severe limitations while one quarter report no functional limitations at all. A great many older people continue to retain their vision, hearing, and mobility (Storck and Hoffman 1991). Still, severe functional limitations, generally brought on by chronic conditions, will likely diminish the level of activity. Notwithstanding the obvious connection between disability and age, Storck and Hoffman (1991) remind us that, "while disability is highly prevalent among older persons, to overemphasize disability as a phenomenon associated with aging would be to ignore the unique characteristics and needs of younger disabled people."

▶ IMPAIRMENTS, DISABILITIES, AND HANDICAPS

People, according to Chapanis (1992), differ in every conceivable way. Certainly our anthropometric dimensions vary—"in height, sitting height, arm reach, and in the hundreds of different ways in which bodies can be measured" as well as sensory abilities, motor abilities, mental abilities, personalities, and attitudes. Chapanis (1992) states that the challenge (for industrial designers) is to "design for organisms no one of which is exactly like any other." His observation is especially true when applied to those with functional limitations, and good design—like good communication—begins with an understanding of common terms.

TABLE 9–2. PERSONS WITH ACTIVITY LIMITATION, BY SELECTED CHRONIC CONDITIONS

Condition	Total	Age			Sex	
		Under 45 Years	45–64 Years	65 Years and Over	Male	Female
Persons with limitations (millions)	32.7	11.6	10.4	10.7	15.3	17.4
Percent limited by						
Heart condition	17.4	4.7	21.5	27.1	18.2	16.7
Arthritis and rheumatism	18.9	5.4	22.8	29.7	12.4	24.6
Hypertension	10.5	2.9	15.2	14.2	7.9	12.8
Impairment of back/spine	9.2	12.5	10.4	4.4	8.9	9.4
Impairment of lower extremities and hips	8.9	10.7	8.2	7.8	9.4	8.5
Percent of all persons with						
No activity limitations	86.0	92.8	76.6	60.4	86.4	85.6
Activity limitation	14.0	7.2	23.4	39.6	13.6	14.4
in major activity	9.5	4.9	17.5	24.1	9.7	9.4

Source: U.S. National Center for Health Statistics, *Vital and Health Statistics*, Series 10, and unpublished data. In *U.S. Bureau of the Census, Statistical Abstract of the United States: 1991* (111th edition). Washington, DC, 1991.

Coming to Terms

A lack of consistent definitions for the measurement of disabilities exists in the United States. According to Brown (1991), many surveys "rely on concepts of disability developed by the National Center for Health Statistics (NCHS) for its National Health Interview Survey (HIS)." They examine the relationship between one's impaired ability and the expectation and assessment of one's performance, distinguishing between terms relating to (environmental) conditions and those relating to disability. Other systems of measurements or definitions are used by the Security Disability Insurance Program (SSDI), the Social Security Administration, the Census Bureau's Current Population Survey (CPS), and the U.S. Department of Education.

For the purpose of this book, I will use the *International Classification of Impairments, Disabilities, and Handicaps* (ICIDH) proposed by the World Health Organization (1993). This "conceptual framework," was developed, in part, to "provide detailed definitions to clarify terminology and promote comparability" (Brown 1991).

"Three distinct and independent classifications, each relating to a different plane of experience consequent upon disease" are offered by the World Health Organization: *impairment, disability,* and *handicap* (World Health Organization 1993). In reality, however, the situation is more complex. The consequence of disease, injury, or congenital malformations extend this set of ICIDH definitions into a linear progression of relationships (Weisgerber 1991).

> ▶ *Disease, injury,* or *congenital malformation* (the intrinsic pathology or disorder), leads to

> ▶ *Impairment* (loss or abnormality of psychological, physiological, or anatomical structure or function), which leads to

> ▶ *Disability* (restriction or lack [resulting from an impairment] of ability to perform an activity in the manner or within the range considered normal for a human being), which leads to a

> ▶ *Handicap* (a disadvantage for a given individual, resulting from an impairment or a disability, that limits or prevents the fulfillment of a role that is normal [depending on age, sex, and social and cultural factors] for that individual.)

These concepts are visualized in Figure 9-1.

A summary of the World Health Organization's International Classification of Impairments, Disabilities, and Handicaps is presented in Table 9-3.

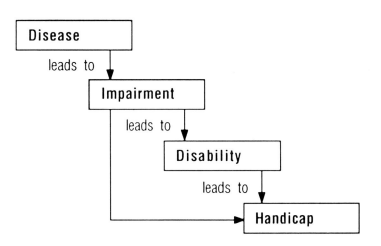

Figure 9–1 Progression of definition relationships.
Source: World Health Organization. 1993. *International Classification of Impairments, Disabilities, and Handicaps.* Geneva: World Health Organization. Reproduced by permission.

TABLE 9–3. SUMMARY OF THE WORLD HEALTH ORGANIZATION'S INTERNATIONAL CLASSIFICATION OF IMPAIRMENTS, DISABILITIES AND HANDICAPS

Impairment	Disability	Handicap
Definition in the context of health experience		
Any loss or abnormality of psychological, physiological, or anatomical structure or function	Any restriction or lack (resulting from an impairment) of ability to perform an activity in the manner or within the range considered normal for a human being	A disadvantage for a given individual, resulting from an impairment or disability, that limits or prevents the fulfillment of a role that is normal (depending on age, sex, and social and cultural factors) for that individual
List of two-digit categories or dimensions		
1. Intellectual	1. Behavior	Survival Roles—Scaled
2. Other psychological	2. Communication	1. Orientation
3. Language	3. Personal care	2. Physical independence
4. Aural	4. Locomotor	3. Mobility
5. Ocular	5. Body disposition	4. Occupation
6. Visceral	6. Dexterity	5. Social integration
7. Skeletal	7. Situational	6. Economic self-sufficiency
8. Disfiguring	8. Particular skill	Other—not scaled
9. Generalized, sensory and other	9. Other activity restrictions	7. Other
Characteristics		
Losses or abnormalities that may be temporary or permanent, and that include the existence or occurrence of an anomaly, defect, or loss in a limb, organ tissue, or other structure of the body, including the systems of mental function . . . represents exteriorization of a pathological state, and in principle reflects disturbances at the level of the organ (Note: "Impairment" is more inclusive than "disorder" in that it covers losses, e.g., loss of a leg is an impairment, but not a disorder.)	Excesses or deficiencies of customarily expected activity performance and behavior, may be temporary or permanent, irreversible or reversible, progressive or regressive . . . may arise as a direct consequence of impairment or as a response by the individual, particularly psychologically, to a physical, sensory, or other impairment . . . represents objectification or an impairment, and as such reflects disturbances at the level of person . . . concerned with abilities, in the form of composite activities and behaviors, that are generally accepted as essential components of everyday life	The value attached to individual situation or experience when it departs from the norm . . . a discordance between the individual performance or status and the individual's or member group's expectations . . . represents socialization of impairment or disability, and as such reflects consequences for the individual—cultural, environmental, economic, and social—that stem from the presence of impairment or disability . . . arises from failure to conform to the expectations or norms of individual's universe . . . occurs when there is interference with ability to sustain what might be designated "survival roles"

Source: Used by permission of Springer Publishing Company, Inc., New York 10012, from Brown, Scott Campbell, 1991. Conceptualizing and defining disability. In *Disability in the United States: A Portrait from National Data,* Susan Thompson-Hoffman, and Inez Fitzgerald Storck (eds.). Copyright © 1991 by Springer Publishing Company.

Expanded Views

Disease   People of all ages develop diseases and conditions. Lovering (1985) departs from conventional definitions and makes a unique distinction between these terms. He says, "a *disease* is characterized by a physical situation in which the body's immunization system would normally be activated." Catching a cold or developing pneumonia or measles are examples. A *condition*, he adds, "can be the result of a disease, but often is the result of an accident, a genetic backfire, a malfunctioning body chemistry, and naturally worn-out parts or organs."

Disability   Four factors determine the presence of a disability (DeLoach, Wilkins, and Walker 1983). Each is a potential barrier limiting a person's freedom and independence:

1. An "objective nature" associated with a medical condition

2. An "ongoing condition that is the result of an injury, illness, or congenital cause"

3. A disability "can usually be verified, described, or diagnosed by a physician or other appropriate professional" and

4. A disability "limits or impairs physical or mental functioning."

Disabilities tend to limit our choices in direct proportion to their severity. For example, a broken arm limits our choice of playing golf or listening to music; a hip replacement limits our choice of bathing or showering; and we cannot choose to drive a car if we are legally blind. Each of us develops what Weisgerber (1991) calls, "coping strategies" to maintain a "reasonable level of independence and quality of life." Thus, factors offering environmental support, such as products that accommodate the disability and help us in the ADL, contribute to self-reliance, and help maintain our independence.

People with disabilities say their difficulties are not caused so much by their disability as by society's attitudes about disabilities. Weisgerber (1991) reports that those with disabilities have "a unique perspective on life," which may be altered by social situations and interactions, which, in turn, develops functional skills. Self-sufficiency and independence, he adds, depend more on "opportunities to develop friendships and competence" than on the severity of the disability. Such individual qualities as "self-esteem, persistence, patience, and socially acceptable risk-taking behavior," also contribute.

Handicap   The word *handicap* is an obsolete term defined in the past as "the cumulative result of the obstacles which disability interposes between the individual and his maximum functional level" (Hamilton 1950). Clarifying the distinction between disability and handicap, DeLoach, Wilkins, and Walker (1983) cite G.N. Wright (1980) who further distinguishes between the two categories. A handicap, he says, is

> a disadvantage, interference, or barrier to performance, opportunity, or fulfillment in any desired role in life (e.g., vocational, social, educational, familial), imposed upon the individual by limitation in function or by other problems associated with disability and/or personal characteristics in the context of the individual's environment or role.

Thus, the concept of handicap is a relative term, much broader than disability. Moreover, identical impairments will affect different people in different ways, which in turn will vary with the situation.

While people with handicaps *may* be disabled, they are not *necessarily* disabled. For example, some functional impairments such as a broken leg or an arthritic hip can prevent the disabled person from freely standing and walking. Such an *imposed* limitation *can* become a handicap for someone who requires mobility (DeLoach, Wilkins, and Walker 1983). It may not, however, necessarily *be* a handicap for someone with little need for mobility.

Other factors can also inflict a handicap: age, education, employment, sex, race, or even the geographic location of one's residence. But regardless of the degree to which one develops a handicap, the functional limitation that caused the handicap remains identical for all who are similarly afflicted. In other words, the degree to which these functional limitations interfere with a person's freedom to choose roles and activities in commerce, society, and family is the degree to which that person experiences a handicap (DeLoach, Wilkins, and Walker 1983).

Other factors that handicap a person—advanced age, for example—acquire added significance when that factor is linked to a disability. "Such combinations," say DeLoach, Wilkins, and Walker (1983), "seem to be multiplicative rather than additive in terms of the problems they present to the individual." Unfortunately, as Blake (1983) points out, elderly people become disabled with greater frequency than the general population. This means that as one grows older, these disabilities and their resulting handicaps become an ever-growing concern.

Social stigma is also a handicap. The same prejudice and stereotyping that confront those who are disabled also face those who are old with or without disabilities. DeLoach, Wilkins, and Walker (1983) argue that "these negative reactions and attitudes from society can greatly hinder the older person's effective performance in various life roles," becoming, in fact, the "real handicaps."

Elderly   Over the years the question, "When do we become elderly?" has received no clear answer. Most demographic studies define the elderly in terms of some arbitrary chronological age, usually 65. This, of course, presents a distorted view of aging.

A useable definition of elderly is "that point in life when the functional limitations that tend to be associated with advanced age present a significant handicap to the individual in relation to his or her desired role in life." (DeLoach, Wilkins, and Walker 1983). Clearly, this definition can cover a wide range of ages and circumstances.

Fortunately, there is wide agreement among gerontologists that chronological age is not an accurate guide for assessing the likelihood of experiencing problems normally associated with becoming old. Such problems, say DeLoach, Wilkins, and Walker (1983), do not occur with regularity to all people at some predetermined chronological age. Each person ages at his or her own pace. This means that at any given age, one person may have an "old" heart and "young" eyes and another may have a "young" heart and "old" eyes. Even within the same individual, different bodily organs age at different rates. Thus our joints may "age" while our liver remains "young" (Pirkl and Babic 1988).

Functional problems—not chronological age—determine who is old. Nevertheless, problems normally associated with old age can also be found in younger populations. DeLoach, Wilkins, and Walker (1983) cite studies by Blake (1981) that show developmentally disabled postpolio patients and other groups, such as Native Americans, have "average life expectancies significantly lower than the total population." They experience the arrival of old age "as early as the mid-forties."

Semantics

These descriptive terms can also be misapplied through careless usage. The World Health Organization suggests that "the acid-test for a preferred nomenclature is whether it promotes practical benefits" (World Health Organization 1993). Two recommendations are given:

1. Avoid the same word to identify an impairment, a disability, and a handicap. Euphemisms tend only to blur the distinctions. While such descriptive adjectives as "mental" and "physical" are unsuitable for use in relation to handicaps, they may be correctly applied to impairments.

2. Use different parts of speech as descriptors: adjectives for the qualities of impairments, (e.g., adjectives for impairments and participles (-ing) for disabilities).

The World Health Organization illustrates their recommendations with the examples shown in Table 9-4.

TABLE 9–4. WORLD HEALTH ORGANIZATION'S RECOMMENDED NOMENCLATURE

Impairment	Disability	Handicap
Language	Speaking	
Hearing	Listening	Orientation
Vision	Seeing	
Skeletal	Dressing, feeding	Physical independence
	Walking	Mobility
Psychological	Behaving	Social integration

Source: World Health Organization. 1993. *International Classification of Impairments, Disabilities, and Handicaps.* Geneva: World Health Organization. Reproduced by permission.

▶ A THIRST FOR INDEPENDENCE

The ability to live independently serves as the key indicator of quality of life (Weisgerber 1991). "For many persons with disabilities," he argues, "living on their own is a viable goal, much preferred to living in the protective care of their family or in an institutional setting, where their needs are 'taken care of'."

Functional Dependencies

In the view of Weisgerber (1991), elderly persons with disabilities need personal assistance in noninstitutional living. He cites Chappel and Havens (1985) who suggest the term "interdependence" as the intermittent care required between formal and informal care models. Such care is mandated by government policies, which direct that communities maintain the independence of older persons by emphasizing home-care assistance (i.e., providing a personal assistant to help with daily tasks) rather than promoting supportive technology or other design accommodations to help those with functional impairments remain functionally independent (Pynoos, Cohen, Davis, et al. 1987).

Obviously, this position, emphasizing personal assistance and ignoring the potential of supportive (transgenerational) technology, encourages the continuation of discriminatory artifact environments and prevents millions of people with impairments and disabilities—of all ages—from reaching their full potential of independent living. Moreover, public and private policies to promote supportive technology would reverse the present condition and begin to fill the vacuum with transgenerational products.

A very clear relationship exists between independent living and a barrier-free environment. First, according to DeLoach, Wilkins, and Walker

(1983), those with severe disabilities cannot be functionally independent "without the absence of manmade barriers in architecture and various modes of public and private transportation." But not all in need of a barrier-free environment have severe disabilities. Most barriers to full independence depend on extending the present barrier-free environments—both public and private—from the macro- (architectural) to the micro- (product) level.

Service providers can and should also provide needed support, eliminate frustration, and extend the period of independent living for those whose impairments and disabilities do not require wheelchairs or the use of braille. DeLoach, Wilkins, and Walker (1983) identify four objectives for independent living "to enable severely disabled people of all ages to function to their maximum potential." These are

1. To help people with disabilities live as independently as possible

2. To maintain their highest level of functional independence for as long as possible

3. To live as fully integrated in the community as possible

4. To live each day in the same manner as persons without disabilities of the same age and background as far as possible.

Given the opportunity, older people prefer living independently in residences—but in residences *they themselves select* (Pynoos, Cohen, Davis, et al. 1987). With advancing years, however, their opportunity to make choices is made increasingly difficult by the onset of chronic illness and a variety of functional impairments, as well as financial concerns. Citing Brotman (1981), Pynoos, Cohen, Davis, et al. (1987) report that 50 percent of all people 65 years and older face limitations in ADL, and predict this figure will increase as the number of those 75 and over increases. Clearly, our choices decline as we grow older.

Still, categories of impairment alone do not determine our potential for living independently. An elderly person with a broken leg, for example, may have strong arms and hands, and excellent stamina. Another person with a broken leg may be young and obese, with very little stamina (Steinfeld 1987).

Maintaining independence is a strong desire of 90 percent of those living alone—their greatest fear is "too much dependence." Yet living alone can also bring negative side effects. Depression is common among those living alone. One third report depression problems with 60 percent of those over 75 experiencing severe loneliness. Despite their loneliness, their desire to live alone remains strong (Butler and Hyer 1990).

▶ THE NEED FOR ASSISTANCE

Over the years a variety of studies have probed the need for assistance in basic life activities by those living outside of institutions. Also examined was the extent to which the need for such assistance varies by age. The data indicates that the percentage of those needing assistance with daily activities range from 10.8% within the 65–74 age group to 20.5% of those 80 years and older. At the same time, it is important to point out that those between the ages of 15 and 64 account for 46.2% of all persons needing assistance, even though this group comprises only 2% of the total (see Table 9.5). Clearly, assistance is an issue of concern for younger as well as older people. Still, of all age groups, the elderly are most in need of help. And women outnumber men in the need for assistance, within all age categories. This is not surprising given the greater need for assistance among women and the declining rate of older men's survival (LaPlante, 1991).

According to the 1977 National Nursing Home Survey (Van Nostrand et al. 1979), 91 percent of nursing home residents require ADL assistance. Again, the women also tend to be older. Compared with those living independently within the community, the proportion for women is substantially higher than for men for each activity. Moreover, if residents of long-term care institutions were to live in the community, virtually all would require some level of support in performing ADL or other basic physical activities (LaPlante 1991). In this regard alone, transgenerational design can go a long way toward preserving, not only the individual's independence, but also the community's support resources that could be utilized more effectively by those with severe disabilities.

This is not only an age issue. The basis for age distinctions in long-term care is being questioned by researchers who, according to LaPlante (1991), are "identifying similarities between non-elderly and elderly persons with long-term service needs." He notes that data analysis "shows that the population with long-term service needs is more evenly distributed across the life span than is generally acknowledged." But within 10 years, he warns, "if rates of assistance needs are not reduced in successive age cohorts, the population with assistance needs will grow and become increasingly older." The sensitive application of transgenerational design principles is one strategy that can effect this reduction. Regnier (1987) reinforces this idea. To foster independence, he argues that new product forms should

▶ Encourage self-expression

▶ Provide free choice

▶ Maximize independence

▶ Allow self-governance

▶ Stimulate creativity

▶ Optimize environmental control

The aging of our population also masks another growing concern. LaPlante (1991b) observes that "the epidemic of AIDS, which has affected primarily young adults, will shift the age distribution of the population needing assistance in basic life activities toward nonelderly ages, potentially offsetting the effects of population aging over the short term." This promises to have profound implications for the already inflated set of health care costs expected to explode as the elderly population increases.

TABLE 9–5. PERSONS NEEDING ASSISTANCE WITH ACTIVITIES, BY TYPE OF ACTIVITY, AGE AND SEX: 1986

Age and Sex	Total (in 1,000's)	NEEDING ASSISTANCE WITH						No Assistance Needed
		One or More Activities*	TYPE OF ACTIVITY					
			Personal Care	Getting Around Outside	Preparing Meals	Doing House-work		
Total	186,022	8,206	3,211	5,213	4,830	5,927		177,816
Age: under 65 years old	158,359	3,794	1,383	2,077	2,315	2,821		154,564
65–69 years old	9,615	890	285	546	484	635		8,724
70–74 years old	7,319	806	336	525	472	566		6,586
75–79 years old	5,434	1,026	408	678	554	710		4,408
80–84 years old	3,126	738	311	595	365	473		2,388
85 years old and older	2,097	952	487	791	639	722		1,145
Male, total	88,958	2,551	1,258	1,606	1,413	1,418		86,407
Under 65 years old	77,547	1,300	642	753	739	759		76,247
65–69 years old	4,316	301	143	205	166	159		4,015
70–74 years old	3,208	281	115	167	157	132		2,927
75 years old and older	3,886	669	359	482	350	369		3,217
Female, total	97,064	5,655	1,953	3,607	3,417	4,508		91,409
Under 65 years old	80,812	2,497	741	1,324	1,576	2,062		78,317
65–69 years old	5,298	589	142	341	318	476		4,709
70–74 years old	4,183	525	220	358	315	435		3,659
75 years old and older	6,771	2,046	849	1,583	1,208	1,536		4,725

*Excludes duplication.
Source: U.S. Bureau of the Census, Current Population Reports, Series P-70, No. 19. Adapted from Table No. 197, p. 121, U.S. Bureau of the Census, Statistical Abstract of the United States: 1991 (111th edition). Washington, DC, 1991.

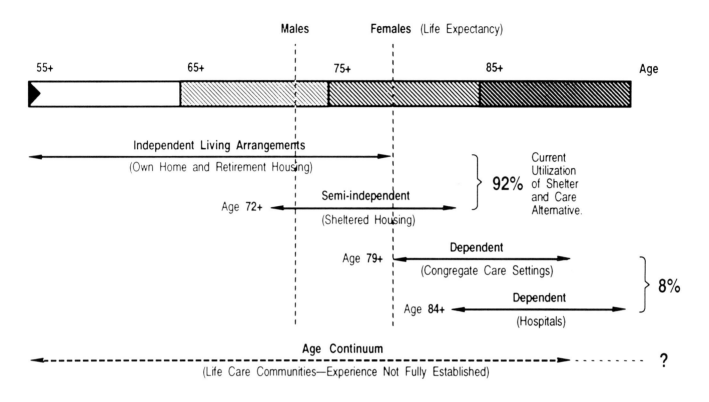

Figure 9—2 Relationship
between age, shelter, and services.

Source: Reprinted with the permission of
Lexington Books, an imprint of Macmillan,
Inc., from *Life Care: A Long Term Solution?*
by Robert D. Challis and Paul John
Grayson. Copyright © 1990 by Lexington
Books.

Keys to Compatibility

▶ ENVIRONMENTAL SUPPORT

A New Relationship

We cannot discuss the relationship of environmental support and independence without looking deeply into the impact made on this relationship by the range of functional limitations that deny us independence. It would be foolhardy to suggest that such a relationship is clear and simple. It is not.

The degree of independence (I) is a function (*f*) of environmental support (ES) and functional limitation (I = *f*(ES, FL). I have attempted to show a model of this relationship in Figure 10-1.

The vertical axis represents the spectrum of functional limitations ranging from mild (e.g., the need for corrective lenses) to severe (e.g., paralysis of the lower extremities). The horizontal axis represents the degree to which a particular product (microenvironment) supports independent living.

The model demonstrates that we maintain independence through a wide variety of combinations (options). This is shown by the central diagonal line tracing the level of *adaptive equilibrium.* Any point on this line balances the negative effects of the functional limitation with an appropriate environmental level of support—the more severe the functional limitation, the greater the environmental support needed to maintain a particular level of independence. For example, the limitation, presbyopia (inability of the eye to focus on nearby objects) demands far less environmental restructuring than does paraplegia (paralysis of the lower extremities).

The diagram is divided into four areas: On the left (area A) is the *zone of dependence.* Products located within this area are unsupportive, even hostile. Such products mitigate against independence and discriminate against those with functional limitations. On the right (area D) is the *zone of independence.* Products falling within this area support a wide range of functional limitations and permit independent living.

Two additional areas are located on either side of the line of *adaptive equilibrium:* products falling within the *zone of semidependency* (area B) demand that we modify our behavior to enhance *independence.* The zone of *semi-independence* (area C) requires modification of the environment to restore our independence.

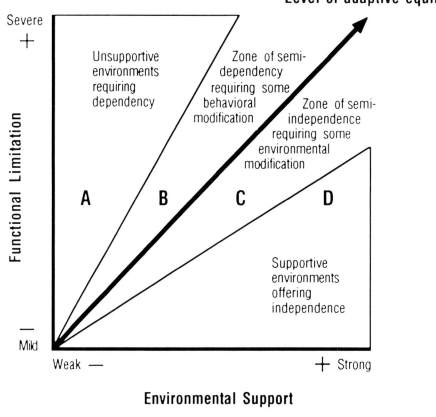

Figure 10–1 Environmental support and independence.

Source: Adapted by permission from Lawton, M. Powell, and Lucille Mahemow. 1973. Ecology and the aging process. In *The Psychology of Adult Development and Aging,* Carl Eisdorfer, and M. Powell Lawton (eds.). Copyright © 1973 by the American Psychological Association. Adapted by permission.

▶ THE CONTINUUM OF COMPETENCE

While most people 65 and older face their environment with competence, the number and severity of health-related functional limitations increases with age. As we have seen, when health decreases, more environmental support is needed to compensate for the associated functional losses.

Lawton and Nahemow's familiar ecological model of environmental press (Figure 10-2) shows the dynamic relationship that exists between the degree of environmental demand required to perform a given task and the competence level of the person performing it. "The basic premise of this model," according to Pollack and Newcomer (1986), "is that individual behavior and satisfaction are contingent upon the dynamic balance between the demand character of the environment (press) and the individual's ability to deal with that demand (competence)." Lawton (1986) explains his model's significance this way: "Any point on the schema represents the outcome of a person/environmental transaction . . . adaptive behavior and/or positive affect may result from a wide variety of combinations of individual competence and environmental press."

Any point falling in the shaded areas represents positive outcome—the level of environmental demand balances a person's ability to respond. By way of illustration, Ms. A. is 85 years old and, although she is legally blind, some peripheral vision allows her to perceive nearby objects. She also has rheumatoid arthritis in both hands which causes severe pain and limits her ability to grasp and manipulate most objects. Over the years she has modified her living spaces and acquired particular products that enable her to accomplish activities of daily living (ADL) and remain independent. She has modified her product environment (acquired transgenerational products) to reduce her level of dependency and frustration (environmental press), raised her competence level (functional ability) through the use of supportive products, and produced independence (positive adaptive behavior).

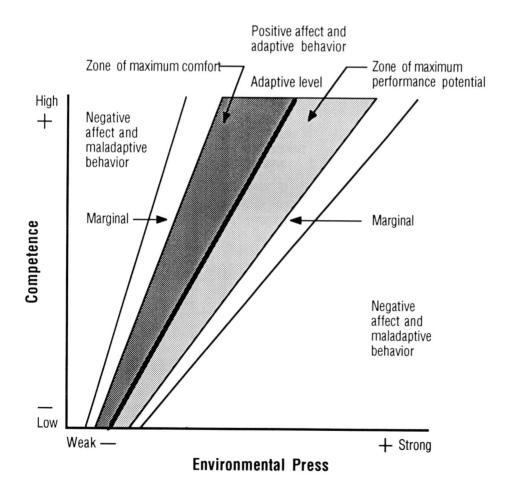

Figure 10–2 Ecological model.

Source: Lawton, M. Powell, and Lucille Mahemow. 1973. Ecology and the aging process. In *The Psychology of Adult Development and Aging,* Carl Eisdorfer, and M. Powell Lawton (eds.). Copyright © 1973 by the American Psychological Association. Adapted by permission.

Environment and Behavior

Conventional wisdom suggests that our activities are controlled by our environment. But picturing a less-than-competent person in a passive or reactive role mitigates against the fact that most people—including older people—choose and create their own product environments and will continue to do so for as long as they remain independent (Lawton 1989).

As health declines, more environmental support is needed. Lawton's model (Figure 10-2) shows the dynamic relationship between a person's competence and, in Lawton's words, "the kind of environment needed to optimize the outcome." Obviously, more supportive products are needed as health-related competence declines, especially with age. Levels of environmental press, explains Lawton (1989), "that would be in the optimal range for a fully competent person would be stressful for those of lesser levels of competence."

But moving to a retirement community or an extended care facility, whether congregate housing or a nursing home, does not guarantee that its product environment will provide the support function implied by sophisticated medical facilities or nursing care. While almost all housing for the elderly provides barrier-free designs offering such features as grab bars, flush thresholds, and waist-high electric outlets, their associated product environments usually fall far short of adequate transgenerational accommodation. Yet, many products provided by such facilities, such as beds, telephones, chairs, clothes washers and dryers, and door and bathroom hardware, fail to accommodate the residents' needs and level of competence. This usually occurs for one of three reasons: (1) either those who design, produce, specify, or purchase such products are unaware of transgenerational design; (2) such designs do not yet exist; or (3) the decisions were made for expediency. The latter choice carries no defense.

Environmental Coping

Age affects the incidence of disability and mitigates against our continued independence. While most people age 65 and older face their environment with confidence, the number and severity of decrements to health increases with age. As we develop one or more physical impairments, we turn to our products and environments to maintain our independence and support our ADL.

As our functional abilities decrease, many products that once provided years of enjoyment, stimulation, and maintained our independence, gradually become less supportive. We are forced to cope with an unyielding product environment that becomes frustrating at best (e.g., handles and knobs that are difficult to use), and dangerously hostile at its worst (e.g., slick, reflective floors and confusing range, oven, and faucet controls).

Compounding our ability to cope are the additional stresses of physical, social, and environmental changes brought about by retirement, pregnancy, reduction in income, and the death of family members and friends. While such events can occur at many ages, the elderly are particularly vulnerable. According to Neary (1990a), over half of those 85 and over experience major limitations in their daily living activities, which are "secondary to age-related changes." Add the extra burden of illness—physical, social, and psychological—and their ability to cope diminishes quickly. The appropriate question to ask is, To what degree could a transgenerational product environment reduce frustrations, injuries, and need to cope?

▶ QUALITY OF LIFE

The quality of life equates to the sum of our physical, social, and economic well-being. It is also influenced by the degree to which we experience difficulty as we perform ADL (Wiesgerber 1991).

Despite continual changes in the levels of our competence and environmental stress (press), the quality of our lives and our psychological well-being are determined by three additional environmental functions: *maintenance, stimulation,* and *support.* People of all ages require each of these functions, and some environments serve some functions better than others (Lawton 1989). For example, the routine act of sweeping a floor by someone who has no disability may be considered a maintenance function. This same activity may be a stimulating experience to someone recovering from a stroke. If the floor environment, however, is rough and uneven, it may not accommodate (support) a stroke victim's limited ability to stand, walk, or manipulate a broom. McRae (1989) suggests that such interactions between a person and the environment may be visualized as "personal characteristics and environmental characteristics coming together" (Figure 10-3).

The extent to which this "coming together" takes place becomes our individualized domain of environmental control. It is also the domain over which designers can demonstrate their professional ability and responsibility for accommodating these three environmental factors required by a transgenerational population.

Maintenance is the normal state of our relationship with the environment for most of us most of the time. It is the state when the demands of our environment and our ability (competence) to react appropriately (cope) to these demands are in equilibrium.

We know well the context of our daily living activities: our routine behaviors (e.g., toileting, dressing, eating, and walking) have become habitual through daily repetition. We have learned to adapt to the various

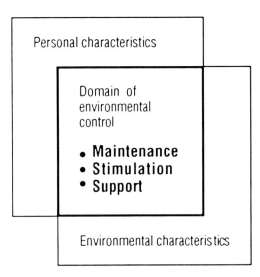

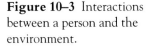

Figure 10–3 Interactions between a person and the environment.

environmental demands that press upon our lives. An important quality of environmental "maintenance" is, according to Lawton (1989), "being in the background." But we normally are not conscious of our background environment because it "fits" us and we "fit" it. Only when anomalies suddenly invade our consciousness do we react to our need to adjust.

Lawton's model points out that products (microenvironments) are sources of maintenance for most people, most of the time. But both products and people, however, change with time: their components break, run down, wear out, and become dysfunctional.

Stimulation can be thought of as a surprise departure from the maintenance function; a deviation from routine behaviors. It is characterized, according to Lawton (1989), as "situations where environmental demand is notably stronger than the range normally experienced by people of a given level of competence." Such situations provide a context calling for an emotional, cognitive, or behavioral response. They provide experiences involving novelty, learning, and problem-solving, and offer an affirmation of our competency level (e.g., learning a new task or skill).

Products move from maintenance to stimulation by upgrade through the purchase of a new model with new visual appeal and new features. Products are also used in new ways such as taking advantage of features previously unused or untried. New decorations, refinishing, or redecorating also introduce pleasure and enjoyment. Products that were once used routinely can also become stimulating as we experience declines in physical or sensory capabilities. Such products, used effortlessly in the past, can gradually become challenging to use, thereby offering a new form of satisfying activity (Lawton 1989). For example, riding a bicycle or skiing can offer stimulating experiences to older persons even though they may have mastered the challenge during their youthful years.

Environmental challenges can also be made too bland; they may not provide *enough* stimulation. Products that shelter us with excessive behavioral insulation can strip away the physical and mental stimulation necessary for a healthy mind and body. Such overprotection contains the danger of wringing out the last vestiges of independence and rendering impotent our motivation and residual skills for maintaining control of our life, our destiny, and our humanity.

Lawton (1989) reminds us that "stimulation is relevant to the least competent as well as to the most competent." Those who provide such service and support should, he insists, "be sensitive to the risks of overreacting to the impairments associated with aging or with illness by restricting press level too much."

Support—McRae (1989) argues that personal loss, such as physical disability (vision, hearing, movement, etc.) often reduces options. Environments thus become supportive or nonsupportive to the degree they accommodate the needs of those using the environment. A product that once met our needs adequately might fail to deliver its promised service if our competence falls outside Lawton's area of "positive effect and adaptive behavior" (Figure 10-2).

How we choose to design and furnish our living environment is, to a greater or lesser degree, a matter of personal choice. The better we learn to choose, however, the better the environmental support we provide. The better the environmental support, the greater maintenance achieved, and the higher our adaptive level will be.

In the end, however, "quality of life" refers to social and economic well-being in addition to our physical well-being. Weisgerber (1991) reminds us that "as we think of the quality of life for persons with disabilities, it is especially important to think in terms of how the quality of their lives is affected by the environment around them." This is particularly true when dealing with the elderly population. Their disabilities and impairments may not be readily apparent to younger persons without functional limitations who may, without realizing it, exclude opportunities. Quality of life is also affected by one's difficulty in accomplishing the many ADLs.

Weisgerber concludes that "there is little enjoyment to be gained from continuous encounters with physical barriers that stand in the way of the most fundamental life activities." Transgenerational design is an important tool for removing these barriers and obtaining environmental compatibility. The challenge is to preserve a person's sense of values and enhance the quality of life for both the young and old.

Cultivating Independence

▶ A SPECTRUM OF SUPPORT

Viewing the range of living environments occupied by older adults, Newcomer and Weeden (1986) suggest a "continuum" of housing types ranging from independent households, to semidependent households, to dependent households. He characterizes these by physical features and attributes of its occupants (Figure 11-1).

First, *conventional independent households* are those in which residents are capable of performing their own housekeeping chores: cooking, cleaning, laundry, and personal care. Single-family houses, apartments, retirement communities, and mobile homes are examples of such households (Newcomer and Weeden 1986). Most residents of conventional households would benefit from *transgenerational* products.

Second, *semidependent households* provide assistance to those requiring help in accomplishing one or more activities of daily living (ADL), e.g., cooking, cleaning, or personal care (Newcomer and Weeden 1986). Those needing and receiving assistance from family members or friends, and living in single-family homes or apartments, fall into this category. Also included are residents of boarding houses, retirement hotels, and continuing care houses. Such facilities may provide, or offer as optional, meals, cleaning, and personal care services. Most home-based care programs such as meals-on-wheels, adult day care, visiting nurses, and home chore services target this group. This is also the group that can benefit most from the availability of transgenerational products.

Finally, *dependent households* support those needing special assistance with personal care, e.g., grooming, bathing, eating, use of medication, and activities requiring ambulation. They normally reside in intermediate-care and skilled-care nursing facilities, although some would move to semidependent households if supportive environments were available. This form of dependency, and its onset, would be reduced by the early availability and use of transgenerational products.

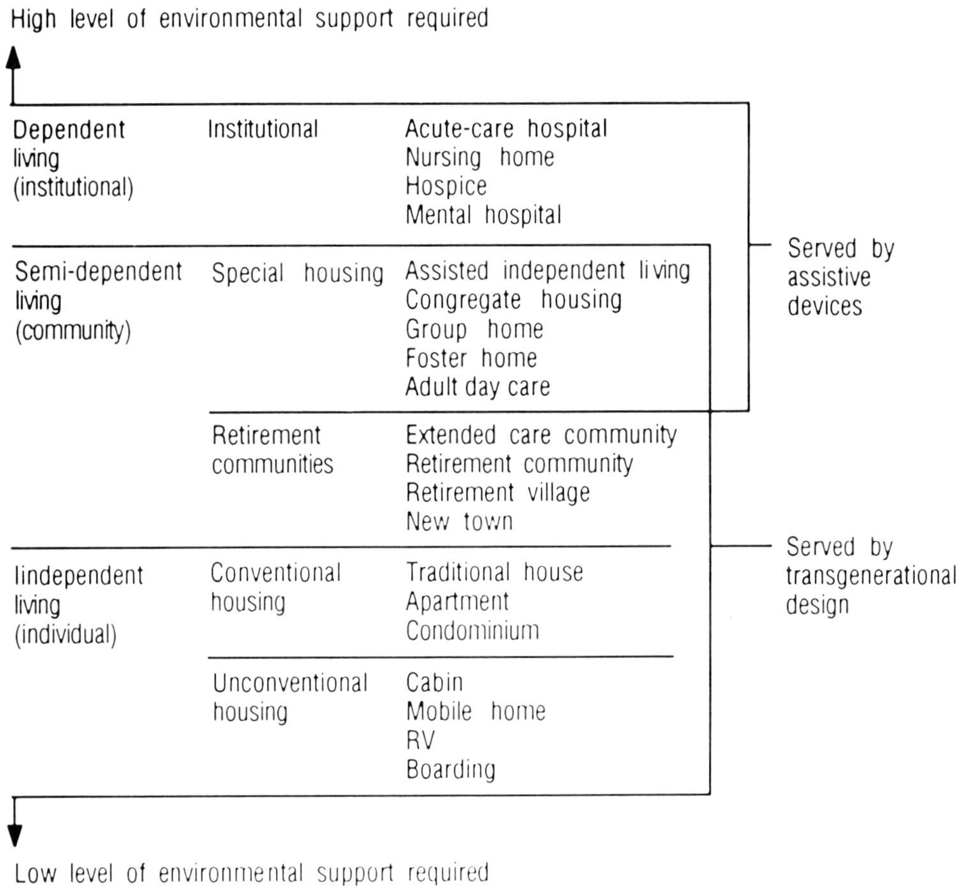

High level of environmental support required

Dependent living (institutional)	Institutional	Acute-care hospital Nursing home Hospice Mental hospital	Served by assistive devices
Semi-dependent living (community)	Special housing	Assisted independent living Congregate housing Group home Foster home Adult day care	
	Retirement communities	Extended care community Retirement community Retirement village New town	Served by transgenerational design
lindependent living (individual)	Conventional housing	Traditional house Apartment Condominium	
	Unconventional housing	Cabin Mobile home RV Boarding	

Low level of environmental support required

Figure 11–1 Continuum of environmental support.

Conventional Independent Living

Health problems are a challenge to people of all ages. The older we get, the more likely health problems will affect ADL. It is generally accepted that as we become elderly, we can expect to have at least one chronic health condition. Yet, while such conditions tend to restrict activities, they are not as limiting as one might expect. The overwhelming majority of older Americans are able to live and function independently—only 4 to 5 percent are institutionalized at any one time. While half of these may require some nursing assistance, the other half require only housekeeping assistance. Their need for such assistance, however, is directly related to age (Figures 11-2, 11-3, and 11-4).

This means that 95 to 96 percent of the older population are not institutionalized. Like the rest of us, they live in the same kind of spaces, use the same kind of products, and express the same desire to live independently as do younger people (Pirkl and Babic 1988).

This does not mean that older people are without limitations. In those households headed by an elderly person, a consistent pattern of

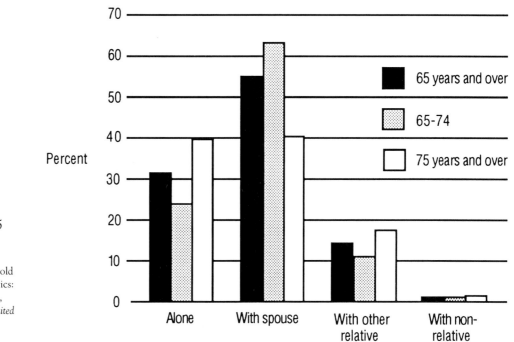

Figure 11–2 Living arrangements of persons 65 and over.

Source: Table No. 63. Living arrangements of persons 15 years old and over, by selected characteristics: 1989. U.S. Bureau of the Census, 1991. *Statistical Abstract of the United States: 1991* (111th edition). Washington, DC.

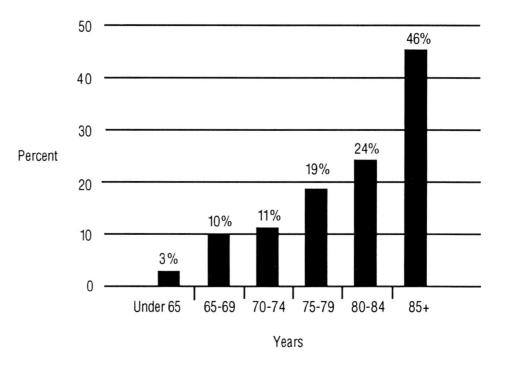

Figure 11–3 Persons needing assistance in activities of daily living (ADL).

Source: U.S. Bureau of the Census, *Current Population Reports,* series No. P-23, No. 173, and P-70, No. 19; and *Statistical Abstract of the United States: 1991* (111th edition), Table 197. Washington, DC, 1991.

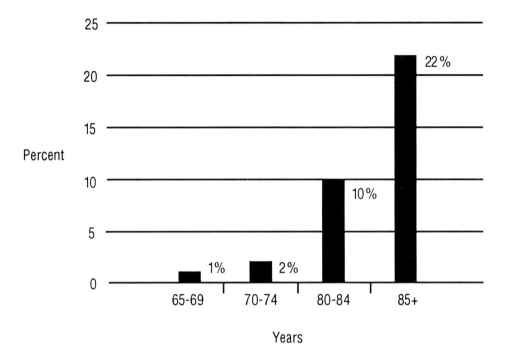

Figure 11–4 Living in homes for the aged.
Source: U.S. Senate Special Committee on Aging, 1980. Adapted from Pirkl, James J. and Anna Babic, 1988. *Guidelines and Strategies for Designing Transgenerational Products: A Resource Manual for Industrial Design Professionals.* Acton, MA: Copley Publishing Group.

limited activity emerges, highlighted by the need for supportive services. These limitations occur periodically and usually receive some assistance, mainly from outside the home, although a persistent need for such assistance is rare. Those with serious and persistent problems either change their environment, get outside help, or move to a more accommodating and supportive environment (Struyk and Katsura 1968).

Assisted Independent Living

Most older persons require some form of supportive service, which Turner (1986) defines as providing "limited assistance to persons having one or more functional limitations but who are otherwise able to live independently." Programs such as meals-on-wheels and homemaker assistance are common examples of such supportive services.

Access to such social service networks and homecare services can be critical to recuperation after a hospital stay. Without it many older persons risk permanent institutionalization and loss of independence (Butler and Hyer 1990). Most assistance, however, comes from family members and friends, with only 2.3 percent of those needing such services failing to receive it (Soldo 1983). Those who live alone, however, face the greatest risk. According to Butler and Hyer (1990) "almost 1/4 of those living alone report they have no one they could count on to help them for a few weeks, and 13 percent indicate they have no one to help them for even a few days."

To enhance the elderly's ability to maintain independence and remain in the community near friends and relatives, Struyk and Katsura (1968) suggest that those needing support:

▶ Shift from living alone to being a multiperson household with available "helpers"

▶ Obtain social support from family and friends living outside the household

▶ Receive assistance with daily living activities from others outside the home, e.g., family, friends, or hire

The availability of supportive transgenerational products can reduce the need for outside assistance and help the elderly maintain independence. Such accommodating technology can promote independent living and remove many of the frustrations experienced by the elderly as they undertake ADL.

Essential Home Services

DeLoach, Wilkins, and Walker (1983) identify three additional categories of essential home services required by those with severe physical limitations.

▶ Supplementary housekeeping services (e.g., cleaning, meal preparation, and yard maintenance)

▶ Supplementary medical and nursing care

▶ Assistance in daily self-care (e.g., bathing, dressing, and toileting)

"Without these services," they warn, "many severely disabled people cannot live within the community with safety and convenience." The need for each of these services, however, will be minimized by the availability of transgenerational products that permit those with functional limitations to accomplish many necessary tasks, either by themselves or with a minimum of help from care-givers.

Retirement Communities

A relatively recent American phenomena, retirement communities are living environments where many who retire choose to relocate their residences, seeking the benefits of a retirement life style based on social and leisure activities. Developed about 50 years ago to house several hundred persons, the first retirement villages were located in the Sunbelts of Florida and California. By contrast, today's retirement communities may contain thousands of houses with populations as large as 45,000 (Streib, LaGreca, and Folts 1986).

Neary (1990a) describes retirement communities as "aggregations of housing units with at least a minimal level of service planned for elderly people who are most often retired and healthy." She lists four broad categories:

1. *New towns* are self-contained communities offering residents a choice of housing options, facilities, and services. A range of recreational, commercial, shopping, dining, financial, and health care facilities are normally provided.

2. *Retirement villages* are usually located close to larger retirement communities. They also offer the same options, facilities, and services found in new towns, but to a lesser extent.

3. *Retirement subdivisions* are small, low-cost subdivisions for independent, elderly adults. Services not offered by the subdivision are usually accessed in nearby cities.

4. *Continuing care communities* are small retirement communities that provide continuing health care in a medically supportive environment. Life-care contracts usually provide personal care and nursing services for residents who become functionally dependent.

Retirement communities can be viewed as "ongoing laboratories" for selected aging and elderly populations and their associated dynamics (Streib, LaGreca, and Folts 1986). They offer developers and manufacturers ideal opportunities to design, develop, and test new transgenerational design concepts for maintaining independent living. I believe that the popularity of such *transgenerational communities*, integrating products, spaces, and architecture into comprehensive environments for living, would validate their existence and confirm their marketability.

Institutionalized Living

Very few old people live in institutional environments. On a given day only about 4 percent of all elderly persons are in nursing homes (Steinfeld 1987), and less than 1 percent of all elderly-headed households have a bedridden household member (Struyk 1987). This number will increase to 7.3 percent in 2010 (Zedlewski, Barnes, Burt, et al. 1990), and they "will most likely be very old, unmarried persons with significant numbers of ADL limitations." This relatively small but growing number has attracted much research that investigates housing and institutional settings specifically designed and built for old elderly adults (Pynoos, Cohen, Davis, et al. 1987). Indeed, such investigations seem to focus on environments for the frail elderly and/or those with severe functional limitations, requiring the use of a wheelchair.

Of this specialized research, the pioneering work of Howell, Koncelik, Raschko, and Steinfeld deserves special recognition. I must remind the reader, however, that barrier-free architecture, and specialized products and devices for those with severe limitations—of any age—lie outside the scope of this book's content.

▶ THE ENVIRONMENTAL LANDSCAPE

The completed act of communication has been described as someone saying something to someone with some effect. The essence of this model is contained in the fact that clear communication demands clear understanding. Thus it is important to understand certain key concepts that stake out the territorial boundaries of the environmental landscape.

As pointed out in Chapter 10, independence requires our competence level to be balanced by a corresponding level of environmental support. Stated another way, any environment must support our level of competency if we are to maintain our independence. Thus, if an impairment or disability decreases our level of competence, we must:

▶ Provide a new environment offering a higher level of support

▶ Raise our level of competence to meet the higher environmental demands, or

▶ Modify the existing environment to raise the support level and achieve equilibrium.

This suggests the importance of maintaining control (choice) over the environment. It also suggests that various environments confront us with greater or lesser degrees of control. But environmental control is not an either/or choice. Howell (1978) identifies four "environmental zones" ranging from those offering the user less to more control.

1. Public environments: shopping malls, theaters, transportation terminals, restrooms, drinking fountains, etc.

2. Semipublic environments: nursing homes, hospitals, supermarkets, restaurants, airline seating, waiting rooms, etc.

3. Semiprivate environments: congregate housing, offices, elevators, telephones, etc.

4. Private environments: private residences, bedrooms, automobiles, refrigerators, razors, etc.

Three zones are based on *shared* use: "public," "semipublic," and "semiprivate." One zone, "private," is based on *individual* use.

Control

Public (shared) environments provide us with little or no design control; they also offer us little or no opportunity to support our particular level of impairment or disability by modifying the surroundings. We cannot, for example, control light levels, select floor surfaces, or choose how the environment is furnished. We must either adapt to existing conditions or refrain from using such environments.

Semiprivate, semipublic, and public environments provide decreasing opportunity for freedom of choice and offer us the least control. Such shared environments shift the responsibility for providing transgenerational design support to others, whose decisions may or may not adequately accommodate our particular needs. We are not in control. Our independence depends on the degree to which the environment is supportive—and this depends on the sensitivity of those who design, specify, offer, or purchase the elements that comprise the environment.

In contrast, we normally control, to a relative degree, the design of our private (individual) environments—our living spaces, our car, or the furnishings of our house or apartment—acquired through our selective purchases. Thus, within financial and other constraints, private environments allow us to customize our surroundings according to the dictates of our individual aesthetic and social values, impairment, or disability. As our level of competence declines (or improves), we are free to modify and adjust these environments as we wish, replacing hostile elements with transgenerational design alternatives. Individual, private control permits us the maximum opportunity to modify the environment: change or adjust lighting, replace floor coverings, or install products more sympathetic to our ability to accomplish ADL. Private environments also provide us the greatest freedom of choice and offer us the most control because *we* supply the degree of transgenerational design support we require. Thus we retain maximum control over our environment—and our independence.

McRae (1989), who is sensitive to this issue, argues that designers and researchers (and care-providing professionals) have a major responsibility to ensure that the elements of our physical environments enhance the client's "sense of control" and their potential for remaining independent. Recognizing the need for designing, specifying, and selecting transgenerational design products can help serve this purpose.

Scope

The term "environment" implies a spatial context containing certain elements within and about which we interact. The environment of a shopping mall, for example, contains such items as shops, signs, walkways, elevators, escalators, directories, and telephone booths. The environment of the telephone booth contains such elements as a telephone, a seat, the sound barrier, a shelf, a phone book, and possibly a door. The environment of the telephone contains such elements as a receiver, a cord, a case, a dial or push-buttons, and alphanumeric information. Obviously, the spatial contexts of various environmental settings differ in size. Thus the scope of each setting may be classified as follows:

▶ Macroenvironments: shopping malls, arenas, urban landscapes, commercial spaces, residential spaces, etc.

▶ Minienvironments: telephone booths, kitchens, bathrooms, offices, transportation spaces, etc.

▶ Microenvironments: telephones, sinks, fire alarms, toilets, chairs, television sets, etc.

The distinctions that separate the scope of these various environmental settings are, according to Koncelik (1982), "vague in terms of social and psychological definitions." Notwithstanding, he notes that, "most researchers and designers would agree that the macro-environment is really an architectural and community level of design and structuring of the physical environment." On the other hand, microenvironments "are characterized by personal scale—the immediate surroundings of an individual," which, says Koncelik, "is that part of the physical environment that is within reach of a person. The more infirm that a person is, the tighter his or her personal micro-environment becomes."

Figure 11-5 is a model of the environmental landscape showing the interrelationship between the *scope* of environmental settings (ranging from macroenvironments to microenvironments), our *control* over them (private products to public products), and their use: *individual use* (products used by individuals), *shared use* (those shared by several individuals), and *public use* (those shared by many individuals).

I have located a number of familiar products and environments within the diagram. Three examples that illustrate this interrelationship are: an air terminal (a *macroenvironment* and a public product for public use), an office (a *minienvironment* and a semiprivate product for individual or shared use), and a razor (a *microenvironment* and a private product for individual use).

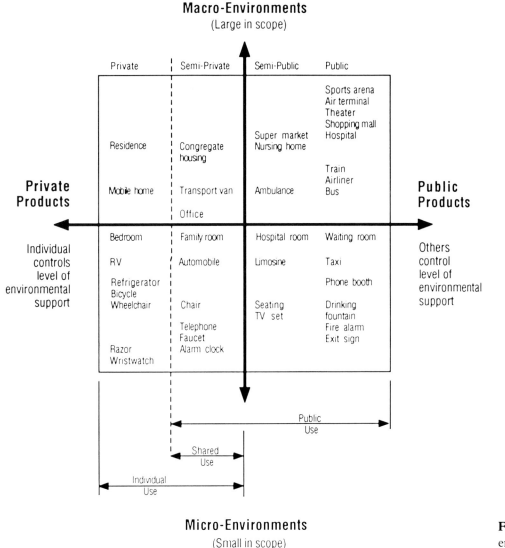

Macro-Environments
(Large in scope)

Private	Semi-Private	Semi-Public	Public
			Sports arena Air terminal Theater Shopping mall
Residence	Congregate housing	Super market Nursing home	Hospital
Mobile home	Transport van	Ambulance	Train Airliner Bus
	Office		
Bedroom	Family room	Hospital room	Waiting room
RV	Automobile	Limosine	Taxi
Refrigerator Bicycle			Phone booth
Wheelchair	Chair	Seating TV set	Drinking fountain
	Telephone Faucet		Fire alarm Exit sign
Razor Wristwatch	Alarm clock		

Private Products — Individual controls level of environmental support

Public Products — Others control level of environmental support

Public Use

Shared Use

Individual Use

Micro-Environments
(Small in scope)

Figure 11–5 The environmental landscape.

Responsibility

Private Environments   In order for us to gain or maintain our competence and remain independent, the products and environments we encounter must balance our need for support—either the environment must adapt to us or we must adapt to the environment. In the case of private environments, each of us controls the level of support we receive. We do this through choice and selection of such elements as our auto, residence, furniture, artifacts, appliances, and utensils. Sensitive choices can make private environments safe, comfortable, convenient, and supporting; insensitive choices can make private environments dangerous, frustrating, hostile, and demeaning—no matter what our age or condition. Regardless of the outcome, however, establishing the balance required for our continued independence remains our responsibility.

Public Environments   Unlike private environments, there is, of course, no easy way for us as individuals to ensure that any public environment will accommodate our functional limitations and support our independence. We must rely on those who plan, finance, design, specify, produce, and promote the countless environmental spaces and artifacts with which we interact daily. Indeed, the quality of any public environment depends on the collective decisions—often made on the basis of myths and erroneous preconceptions—by those with little or no understanding about the pressing needs of those who depend on the outcome.

Not all products maintain our independence. Many are ill-designed and, by their nature, result in an immediate decline in competence and an increased level of environmental press (Lawton 1989). Such products prevent those with functional limitations from participating fully in the public environment.

Over a decade ago Beattie (1978) forewarned us that

> Such designs and planning have for the most part failed to take into account the physiological, psychological, and sociological processes and changes associated with human aging. They are not designed to support the functions and capacities of individuals as they age. There is a need to design supportive environments for the life span (and) . . . to prepare and train architects, city planners, and those who build and design our transportation systems with a knowledge of aging and a conceptual capacity to provide for intergenerational and life-span orientations to our communities of the present and the future.

Clearly we all share the responsibility for reversing these conditions in all future products or environments we conceive, produce, manage, or promote. Transgenerational design is a viable means for achieving this goal.

The Transgenerational Design Promise

▶ DESIGN AND THE ADA[12]

What Is the ADA?

Here in the United States, aging is becoming a spirited societal issue, at least among professional groups. Encouraging this interest is Public Law 101-336, the *Americans with Disabilities Act* (ADA) of 1990, which became effective on January 26, 1992. Championed as the most important civil rights legislation in the last 25 years, this act "extends to individuals with disabilities comprehensive civil rights protections similar to those provided to persons on the basis of race, sex, national origin, and religion under the Civil Rights Act of 1964" (U.S. Department of Justice 1991).

The ADA is now a federal law that "prohibits discrimination on the basis of disability in places of public accommodation" and requires that all new places of public accommodation and commercial facilities be designed and constructed so as to be readily accessible to and usable by persons with disabilities. The ADA

▶ Mandates "the elimination of discrimination against individuals with disabilities"

▶ Provides "clear, strong, consistent, enforceable standards addressing discrimination against individuals with disabilities"

▶ Ensures that "the Federal Government plays a central role in enforcing the standards established in the Act on behalf of individuals with disabilities" and

▶ Invokes "the sweep of congressional authority, including the power to enforce the fourteenth amendment and to regulate commerce, in order to address the major areas of discrimination faced day-to-day by people with disabilities"

12. This section adopted from Pirkl, James J. 1992. The ADA: A timely matter of concern for us all. *DESIGNperspectives,* the Newsletter of the Industrial Designers Society of America, August, p. 1.

This act affects over 40 million Americans who may now join society's productive mainstream. The ADA removes the barriers that have denied them full access to the benefits, services, and opportunities enjoyed by their fellow citizens. It also increases the number of those with disabilities who now fit under this category. Title III of the ADA (U.S. Department of Justice 1991) guarantees public accommodation in such public environments as

▶ Inns, hotels, and motels

▶ Restaurants and bars

▶ Theaters, concert halls, and stadiums

▶ Auditoriums, convention centers, and recreation halls

▶ Stores, shopping centers, and malls

▶ Laundromats, banks, gas stations, and hospitals

▶ Transportation terminals and depots

▶ Museums, libraries, and galleries

▶ Parks, zoos, and amusement parks

▶ Nurseries, schools, colleges, and universities

▶ Daycare centers, senior citizen centers, and homeless shelters

▶ Gymnasiums, health spas, bowling alleys, and golf courses

Background

The Architectural and Transportation Compliance Board (ATCB) is an independent Federal agency established by Congress and created by the Rehabilitation Act of 1973 (Public Law) to "ensure that the requirements of the Architectural Barriers Act of 1968[13] are met and to propose alternative solutions to architectural, transportation, communication, and attitudinal barriers faced by individuals with disabilities" (Federal Register 1992).

Section 502 of the Rehabilitation Act of 1973 gave the Board responsibility for establishing accessibility standards and guidelines to help four Federal agencies[14] comply with the Architectural Barrier's Act of 1968. The Board was authorized to develop "Minimum Guidelines and Requirements for Accessible Design (MGRAD) (Federal Register 1992).

13. The Architectural Barriers Act of 1968 (Public Law 90-480) requires that buildings and facilities designed, constructed, altered, or leased by the federal government since August 12, 1968 be accessible to individuals with disabilities.
14. The General Services Administration, the Department of Defense, the Department of Housing and Urban Development, and the United States Postal Service.

As originally distributed by the Board, MGRAD contained detailed technical specifications which described how to make entrances, telephones, drinking fountains, toilet rooms, and other elements and spaces of a building or facility accessible to those with disabilities (U.S. Department of Justice 1991).

The Americans with Disabilities Act of 1990 (ADA) greatly expanded the Board's responsibilities to include "establishing accessibility standards for new construction and alterations in places of public accommodation and commercial for transportation facilities and vehicles." Section 304 of the ADA "provides for the guidelines to supplement the existing MGRAD and to establish additional requirements" which "ensure that buildings, facilities, and transportation vehicles are accessible in terms of architecture and design, transportation, and communication, to individuals with disabilities" (Federal Register 1992).

In carrying out its responsibilities, the Board, after lengthy debate, based its guidelines on research and studies conducted in the middle 1970s used to update the American National Standards Institute (ANSI) A117.1-1980 and 1988[15] standards on which the guidelines are based (Federal Register 1992). (See appendix for example of current ADA guidelines.)

A Timely Question

While one might ask what civil rights legislation has to do with transgenerational design, the answer, quite simply, is, "everything." It is naive to believe that the ADA's sole intended purpose lies in restructuring public architectural space, locating curb cuts, hanging signs, and installing lower drinking fountains. Its full impact will soon expand the nature and scope of all human activities, services, and operations contained within all public spaces.

Clearly, once those with disabilities gain their rightful access to our nation's commercial facilities, workplaces, cultural centers, and recreational areas, demand for "full and equal access" will rapidly shift from the architectural environment to the product environment. The lid on the Pandora's box of consumer products is now open. In response, a chorus of frustrated voices will soon demand a new category of consumer products sympathetic to the functional limitations of our elder population. If conversations with those challenged by today's product environment is any indication, the demand for transgenerational product innovation will be strong and unrelenting.

The powerful changes launched by the ADA, though targeted at the nation's millions with disabilities, will ultimately change the way all Americans perceive design, both good and bad. The act's provisions demonstrate

15. American National Standards Institute. 1980. *Specifications for Making Buildings and Facilities Accessible to, and Usable by, the Physically Handicapped.* New York: ANSI 117.1.

emphatically that "accessibility" or "usability" is sought neither by one disability group at the expense of another, nor by various disability groups at the expense of those with only minor or no impairments. Rather, its goal is to make accessible—to the greatest number of people the greatest number of public facilities—accommodations, goods, and services; and with the least number of exclusive or extraordinary provisions or features.

Finally, it has to do with opening a democratic, market-driven society to accommodate a wider range of human abilities and limitations than has ever before been considered. The ADA is challenging the design professions to extend traditional design principles to accommodate the full range of human abilities—and disabilities.

This new law reflects an awakening of the American conscience. It is particularly significant to those of us in the design community advocating a "transgenerational" environment; one in which legibility, accessibility, and adaptability of spaces and products, both public and private, provide an accommodating influence on the lives of all people, regardless of age or ability.

While many still refuse to acknowledge the realities and impact of our aging population, the fact still remains that the products used in ADL affect the independence of tens of millions of people who, in addition to those with disabilities derived from an accident or a disease, are growing older and developing functional limitations.

▶ ANATOMY OF ACCOMMODATION

Over a decade ago Byerts (1978) offered three attributes for achieving environmental quality that should be considered when developing or evaluating settings for use by elderly persons.

1. *Legibility* provides those environmental cues which enable us to perceive a sense of place, and which supply messages of orientation, direction, and differences.

2. *Accessibility* permits us to move freely and normally throughout an environmental setting.

3. *Adaptability* determines the range of adjustability offered by an environment.

I suggest a fourth attribute. Environments should also demonstrate *compatibility*. That is, artifacts and spaces should be yielding, tolerant, unassertive, and amenable to the functional limitations of people, offering such additional support as safety, comfort, convenience, ease of use, and ergonomic fit—qualities that humanize technology and form the core ingredients of transgenerational design.

Legibility

Product interaction requires us to "communicate" with products and, in turn, have products "communicate" with us. Human factors specialists term this interaction a *person/machine system.* Kantowitz and Sorkin (1983) call such a system "an arrangement of people and machines interacting within an environment in order to achieve a set of system goals."

In order to use a clothes washer, for example, we must first communicate our instructions. We begin by determining the set of washing conditions appropriate for the task (e.g., load size, water temperature, type of fabric, etc.). Next, we "tell" the washer our intentions by "instructing" the controls to perform the desired tasks (e.g., soak, wash, rinse, spin, etc.). Then, as the operation proceeds, the washer processes our instructions and "informs" us of its progress by "displaying" the status and progress information. Finally, when the cycle is complete, the washer turns itself off and "announces" that the instructions have been carried out.

This interactive communication between a product and its user takes place across the person/machine interface and depends on three factors:

1. *Perception* = perceiving information communicated by a product's form, components, controls, displays, instructions (visual, auditory, tactile)

2. *Interpretation* = understanding the information communicated, displayed, transmitted, or symbolized (clarity, readability, comprehension)

3. *Response* = reacting to the information received (human motor response, machine reaction)

Perception We rely on sensory clues to perceive the various forms of information displayed by products. Vision, for example, lets us perceive forms, shapes, and surfaces; positions and relationships; words and numbers; and graphic symbols and color codes. Our hearing alerts us to changes in a sound's pitch and intensity, and receives verbal and symbolic information from recordings and synthetic speech. Our sense of touch reacts to texture and surface modulations, as well as pressure and vibration cues associated with activating switches or push-buttons.

Each sensory cue can communicate a wide range of information—provided, of course, that our sensory receptors function normally. For example, Lovering (1985) notes that our sense of hearing provides an important element in personal safety; those who are deaf are unable to receive important audio clues and must rely on other signals, (e.g., facial expressions, body language, environmental conditions, etc.), to stay alive and prevent injury to themselves and others.

Interpretation   Our failure to understand environmental messages compromises our competence and safety, and prevents us from responding appropriately. Those of us with one or more sensory impairments or disabilities must rely on our remaining senses to complete the person/machine communication cycle. Consequently, product information that fails to deliver its message, regardless of our impairment or disability, discriminates against us and becomes a hostile element, militating against independence.

Redundant cuing is a strategy that enhances the independence of those with impairments and disabilities while, at the same time, benefiting users who are unaffected. Providing redundant cues that bridge the senses helps ensure that important product information is perceived and understood by all.

The future will see such redundant cuing extended to a variety of product applications. Its use requires that a product's control and information displays embrace more than one sense. For example, the identifying word "fire" on a fire alarm should consist of large contrasting letters (visual cue) raised from the background (tactile cue). In another example, the numbers and letters on a telephone's dial or push-buttons should feature large, high-contrast numbers and letters (visual cue), offer braille indicators along with raised or recessed letters (tactile cue), and induce a unique audio tone when pressed (audio cue). Such cross-sensory redundant cuing enables those with sensory impairments to *choose* their mode of communication and interact with products no less effectively than those who are unimpaired.

In the face of demands for greater environmental support, the ADA has recognized the importance of redundant cuing as a means for promoting greater independence. It requires redundant tactile, braille, and visual indicators on such environmental elements as elevator controls, fire alarms, room designations, and directional and warning signs. The use of such redundant indicators must become a common practice throughout the artifact environment.

Responding to the Information   Most products that we use in ADL require some form of response from us. This response can take many forms. The late Henry Dreyfuss[16] stated prophetically almost four decades ago that products are

> going to be ridden in, sat upon, looked at, talked into, activated, operated, or in some way used by people individually or en masse. If the point of contact between the product and the people becomes a point of friction, then the industrial designer has failed. If on the other hand, people are made safer, more comfortable, more eager to purchase, more efficient—or just plain happier—the industrial designer has succeeded (Dreyfuss 1955).

The problem is, of course, that many persons with physical and sensory limitations are prevented from responding to the dictates of a product's functional demands. For example, a person with impaired gripping and grasping capability has difficulty operating round doorknobs. A lever requires a more sympathetic action to operate. A person with limited eyesight has difficulty responding to a set of instructions or a warning label printed in very small type against a low-contrast background. Large, well-contrasted typography is easier to read. Design affects one's response either positively or negatively. Transgenerational design offers positive choices.

Accessibility

Koncelik (1987) tells us that "to know the environment is to reach it, touch it, manipulate it, and understand it." Indeed, each environment— public or private—should be accessible by all who would use it; good product design solutions accomplish this goal. The fact remains, however, that most consumer products and living accommodations found in today's private and public environments still deny accessibility and equality of use and support to millions of older people, most of whom do not have severe disabilities.

The ADA includes many guidelines and standards for ensuring accessibility, the result of the barrier-free design movement—a wide constituency of dedicated persons representing many organizations and professional specialties. While these guidelines and standards are becoming effective in removing the architectural barriers that bar those with disabilities from accessing public spaces and buildings, these standards do not apply to the majority of consumer products. It is only a matter of time before the demographic shift of age develops the degree of market pressure required to have similar standards developed for consumer products. Such standards will evolve, either voluntarily by industrial and professional organizations, or by legislation.

I believe that transgenerational design can fill the current void by answering the growing demands of older people. Today, under the banner of "universal design," barrier-free architectural and interior design accommodation provides accessibility that is protected by civil rights legislation to architectural and interior spaces for persons who are blind or deaf, or use wheelchairs. But in today's world—and certainly in tomorrow's—this is not enough. Thirty-two million Americans of all ages, who experience some form of functional limitation, are still denied a product environment that enhances their quality of life, continued independence, and ability to

16. Henry Dreyfuss was one of America's pioneer industrial designers. In 1947, following the administrations of Walter Dorwin Teague, and Raymond Loewy, he became the third president of the Society of Industrial Designers (SID). In 1965 he was elected the first president of the newly formed Industrial Designers Society of America (IDSA).

accomplish the ADL (see Table 9-2). The availability of transgenerational design products would go a long way toward eliminating this problem.

Adaptability

The transgenerational design idea is congruent with the rich diversity of people. It is a concept that promotes sympathetic products that adapt to the widest range of individual needs. For example, it should make no difference whether a fire extinguisher, a detergent package, a can opener, or a telephone is used by a teenager or an octogenarian. Each requires equal access. Unfortunately, however, the very group that needs the most environmental support is offered the least.

From a transgenerational design perspective, adaptive design does not mean adapting or modifying existing products or environments to accommodate a range of disabilities. Rather, it means that all products should be designed at the outset to accommodate the widest range of abilities of those who would use them. Thus, in a broad sense, there should be little or no need for further adaptation.

In 1987, the U.S. Energy Information Administration's Residential Energy Consumption Survey determined that of households using appliances: 92.7 percent had a color television, 74.9 percent a clothes washer, 67.3 percent a refrigerator, 65.8 percent a clothes dryer, 60.8 percent a microwave oven, 56.8 percent an electric range, and 56.6 percent an electric oven. These and many similar products are often purchased when we are middle-aged and without impairments or disabilities. These same products are likely to be used by us one, two, or even three decades later when we acquire one, or more functional limitations. Tasks, such as manipulating knobs and dials, grasping handles, opening doors, lifting heavy and awkward pots of food or bundles of clothes become difficult, if not impossible, for those with debilitating physical or sensory conditions.

Transgenerational products, designed to accommodate those with the least competency, may succeed in raising their competency level and extend their period of valued independence. Transgenerational products are also better products for the young and able-bodied, particularly when normal ability is restricted by a temporary illness or accident.

Compatibility

Transgenerational products demonstrate an allegiance to the consumer and a commitment to provide features that are compatible with the widest degree of individual abilities. They help promote and maintain independent functioning for all who would use them, not just the young, the able, or those who can afford customization. Such products agree with our life style, support independence, and bring about a more compassionate environment. They continue to do so over the product's lifetime—and ours. In addition, transgenerational products offer increased safety, better comfort, added conveniences, simplified use, ease of handling, and bodily fit—elements that form a harmonious bond between us and the environment.

Safety   Products should be free from danger, injury, or damage under reasonable conditions by all who may be expected to handle, use, or operate them. Such products should be designed to anticipate a wide variety of physical and sensory impairments, providing safe, supporting features before they may be needed.

Comfort   Products should be free from disturbing, painful, or distressing forms or features. Products that offer comfort to those with impairments will also provide better comfort for those who are able-bodied. In many cases, comfort for all can be achieved with simple adjustments of type size, contrast, color, proportion, or dimension.

Convenience   Products should be designed to provide convenient, handy, and appropriate use for all who would operate them. This means such things as convenient storing, repair, cleaning, packaging, and carrying. Planning, foresight, and sensitivity go a long way toward providing convenient use by all.

Ease of Use   Products should be designed for simple, easy, and uncomplicated use, regardless of our age or limitation. We should demand understandable instructions, simple operations, and logical controls that do not confound our intelligence, tire our muscles, or defy our dexterity.

Bodily Fit   Products should be designed to accommodate and fit the widest possible range of appropriate human dimensions. We should recognize that while bodily dimensions reach their full limits during our late teens and early twenties, they also diminish as we reach the older years. Eye glasses, hearing aids, crutches, canes, walkers, and seeing-eye dogs become extensions of one's body and should be considered along with the person who must use them, as a single anthropometric unit.

Generic Guidelines

Pirkl and Babic (1988) developed the following generic guidelines for designing—or selecting—transgenerational design products in a joint study conducted in 1987 by Syracuse University's All-University Gerontology Center, the Center for Instructional Development, and the Department of Design.[17] They are not offered as a definitive set of "how-to" directives, but rather are intended to prime the mind—sketching the form, but not the details, of transgenerational design requirements. "These apply equally to all users, and their adoption by the design community can lead to better products for all users, regardless of age" (Pirkl and Babic 1988).

1. Provide cross-sensory redundant cuing for all alarms, signals and controls (combine an audio signal with a visual indicator)

2. Offer redundant modes of operation utilizing the next larger set of motor movements (finger to hand; hand to arm; arm to foot)

3. Establish consistent display/motion relationships left to right and forward/up to increase, backward/down to decrease)

4. Provide definitive feedback cues (control positions (detents) should "snap" into position)

5. Reduce the complexity of all operations (minimize the number of tasks)

6. Place critical, and frequently used controls within easiest reach (cluster controls on basis of priority)

7. Prevent accidental actuation of critical controls (relocate, recess, or provide a guard)

8. Provide adjustable product/user interfaces (horizontal/incline, vertical/incline, raise/lower, push/pull)

9. Design for use by a variety of populations (male/female, young/old, weak/strong, large/small)

10. Design to facilitate physical and cognitive function (encourage user to practice and improve by making operations easy and enjoyable)

11. Design beyond the basic physical/functional need (enhance the user's independence, self-respect, and quality of life)

12. Compensate for a range of accommodation levels (provide for some exercise through user interaction/participation)

13. Strive to make task movements simple and understandable (clockwise for "on" or "increase," counterclockwise for "off" or "decrease")

17. This project was supported, in part, by grant number 90-AT-0182, from the Administration Office of Human Development Services, Department of Health and Human Services, Washington, DC 20201.

▶ A MATTER OF OPTIONS

There is a tendency to regard transgenerational design as an optional activity for designers; a desirable goal but not strictly necessary and given the difference in our ages and convictions, maybe not even possible. This attitude, of course, is understandable. But its foundation rests on a basic misunderstanding.

Transgenerational design is not about producing specialized "elderly" or "adaptive" products. On the other hand, this does not minimize the importance of such products for those with severe disabilities or those that require special environmental assistance.

Transgenerational design is about designing all products at the outset to accommodate the widest possible spectrum of those who would use them—regardless of age. Transgenerational design also involves critical thinking about human accommodation, arguing about who should be accommodated and how best to achieve it. Our professional lives rarely revolve around dramatic decisions about good and evil, but, instead, normally deal with making choices between competing alternatives. Transgenerational design is about making appropriate choices.

This brings us back to the question of options. Transgenerational design cannot be separated from broader moral and ethical considerations. Far from being optional, transgenerational design is a professional imperative. Professional issues lie behind each decision we make regardless of our specialty.

Now, if we understand transgenerational design in this way, accommodating the elderly or any other special population need not begin with a list of "dos" and "don'ts." These will develop, of course, and our professions would not be complete without them. But all the guidelines and strategies won't make much sense without grasping the full dimension of the environmental need for human accommodation. Thinking about transgenerational design has to begin by asking what it is that products and environments must contribute to extend human independence and improve the quality of life for all persons—young and old.

What makes transgenerational design a moral imperative is that it unites forms of human understanding, forms of beauty, and forms of function which are the essence of professional design practice. It would be foolish to suggest, however, that every product can accommodate persons of every age and all degrees of physical competency. But is it not reasonable to demand products and environments that serve the widest possible spectrum of potential users?

It seems that the design and care-giving professions echo common evolutionary values. Yet, while each specialty branches off in different directions, each also develops from the common roots of human service. Weisgerber (1991) taps these roots and urges us to "provide a caring and continuing system of intervention and support that

▶ Bridges the transitions across life stages

▶ Is responsive to individual differences and abilities

▶ Affords the individual an opportunity to develop a sense of worth and dignity through employment and community participation

▶ Encourages personal and social interaction, as well as close friendships, between nondisabled persons and persons with disabilities

A product environment that offers such support to the transgenerational population reflects the highest level of professional service. Clearly, society's relentless demographic shift demands—and deserves—no less.

Summary of Part 3

Independence demands choices. The availability of environmental options helps determine the quality of life; the degree to which we are able to maintain independence. Our choices, however, tend to be limited in direct proportion to the severity of the disability. Environmental conditions that are insensitive to our physical and sensory limitations restrict our choices, and frustrate our desire and ability to remain independent. But this loss of independence does not only affect old people. While age is the most general indicator of disability and loss of independence, most persons with disabilities are under age 65.

The term "disability," however, means different things to different people. Researchers have organized various definitions associated with functional limitations into a linear progression of relationships: *disease* (an intrinsic pathology or disorder) leads to *impairment* (a loss or abnormality in structure or function), which leads to *disability* (a restriction or lack of ability considered normal), which leads to *handicap* (a disadvantage for a given individual).

Obviously, for many disabled persons, including those who are elderly, independent living is a viable goal. Moreover, government policies mandate assistance for them in settings of noninstitutional living. But many of these policies tend to promote *dependence,* focusing on the use of personal home-care assistants rather than cultivating *independence* by encouraging the development, availability, and use of supportive products and environments. It is debatable whether current policies fully serve intended purposes.

Researchers have established a strong relationship between independence and environmental support. While most older people face the environment with competence, a strong correlation exists between age and the number and severity of health-related functional limitations. Evidence shows that when health decreases, more environmental support is needed to compensate for the associated functional loss.

As our functional abilities decline, many products and environments that once provided enjoyment and enhanced the quality of life, gradually become less supportive. We are forced to cope with products and environments that increasingly limit choices, reduce options, and weaken our ability to remain independent.

Still, a variety of living environments ranging from conventional housing (independent living), to retirement communities and special housing, (semidependent living), to institutions (dependent living) form a continuum of environmental support. Each type provides a different level of environmental support, and each maintains a different degree of independence.

Contrary to popular opinion, 95 to 96 percent of the older population do not depend on institutional support. Most are not blind, deaf, or in need of a wheelchair or other specialized adaptive devices. And despite their functional limitations, most live in the same kinds of spaces, use the same kinds of products, and express the same desire for independence as younger people. But remaining independent means retaining control over the micro- as well as the macroenvironment. Control means choice—the opportunity to modify the environment to accommodate one or more functional limitations.

Still, some environments and products offer more control (choice) than others. *Private* products and environments (e.g., our home, our car, our refrigerator, etc.) offer the greatest opportunity for support—we "choose" these elements for the degree of support they offer. On the other hand, *public* products and environments (stores, buses, drinking fountains, etc.) offer us little opportunity to modify the elements to suit our particular needs—they have already been "chosen for us" by others.

The spatial context of public and private products and environments differs in size: *macroenvironments* are large in scale, and exist at the community or architectural level (e.g., shopping malls, theaters, sports arenas, etc.). *Microenvironments* are small in scale, and exist at the personal level, normally within convenient reach (telephones, chairs, television sets, etc.). Obviously, the more severe our functional limitation, the closer and tighter our environmental support must be to maintain independence. Unfortunately, by failing to accommodate the functional limitations associated with normal human aging, many products and environments further limit the competence of disabled users, blocking attempts to remain independent. Transgenerational design seeks to minimize this prospect.

The *Americans with Disabilities Act* (ADA), which became effective on January 26, 1992, "prohibits discrimination on the basis of disability in places of public accommodation." It removes another layer of barriers affecting 40 million Americans who have been denied full access to all commercial facilities and places of public accommodation. Moreover, its full impact will undoubtedly expand the nature and scope of all human service activities within all public and private environments to eventually include a broad spectrum of products at the microenvironment level. Such products used in activities of daily living (ADL) can also affect the independence of tens of millions of people who are growing older and developing a variety of functional limitations. Their needs are no less significant.

In providing such products for use by older people, four attributes of environmental quality should be considered: *legibility* provides cues that enable us to perceive a sense of place, and supplies messages of orientation, direction, and differences; *accessibility* permits us to move freely and normally throughout an environmental setting; *adaptability* determines the range of adjustability offered by a product or environment; and *compatibility* demands that artifacts and spaces be yielding, tolerant, unassertive, and amenable to our functional limitations. In addition, all products and environments should provide safety, comfort, convenience, ease of use, and ergonomic ("user-friendly") fit—qualities that humanize technology and form the core ingredients of transgenerational design.

Transgenerational design is not about producing specialized "elderly" or "adaptive" products. It is about designing all products at the outset to accommodate the widest spectrum of those who would use them—regardless of age—and without penalty to any group. The idea behind transgenerational design asks the question, What must products and environments contribute to extend human independence and improve the quality of life for all persons—young and old? In the end, the answer must come by uniting forms of human understanding, forms of beauty, and forms of function—the essence of all professional service, whatever the discipline.

Epilogue

The problem of unresponsive design is not new; but it is reflective of today's deeper societal problems. Addressing these problems, however, by adhering strictly to the letter of governmental guidelines without addressing their spirit, becomes a compelling reason to pause and reexamine the ethical foundations upon which any claim to professional status rests. It calls for an enlarged conception of professional accountability.

A ground swell of concern for intelligent design accommodation is being heard from a small but growing collection of voices in a number of disciplines. Much has already been done, but much more remains to do. Responding to the challenge are the tacit alliances being formed by a growing number of designers, who are reaching out to psychologists, physicians, gerontologists, ergonomists, nurses, and other professionals in allied academic and business disciplines. I would hope that these collaborations signal the start of a new, interdisciplinary movement—away from the design-it, make-it, peddle-it syndrome of the past and toward a more compassionate and humane design direction and focus.

Transgenerational design is offered as a way to correct one societal area affected by design discrimination. It also addresses the deeper problem of priorities facing the future direction of all professions—and our nation.

I believe that transgenerational design holds the answer to the older generation's plea for equality. Without question, barrier-free design accommodation is recognized and acknowledged for achieving today's comprehensive civil-rights protection for people who are blind or deaf, use a wheelchair, or are otherwise disabled. But despite these achievements and accomplishments, the fact remains that over 28 million of our nation's aging population still experience discrimination by design.

A collective commitment to transgenerational design by all professional specialties may help solve a variety of critical, human accommodation problems faced by today's elderly consumers. Given the pressing needs to accommodate an aging population, unprecedented demands will be placed on today's age-related professionals. Our goal is to equip all with sensitive solutions. Needed information is available. Rationalizations, therefore, will no longer excuse designs that fall short.

What can you do?

▶ Recognize that the problem of design discrimination is world wide, affects tens of millions of people of all ages, and can be prevented or eliminated.

▶ Discard yesterday's preconceptions and false distinctions about who is young and who is old.

▶ Sensitize yourself to the changing needs of aging people. Understand that the aging process starts at birth and ends with death. It does not begin suddenly at age 65.

▶ Collect specialized information. Familiarize yourself with available guidelines and strategies for designing, developing, specifying, or acquiring transgenerational products and environments.

▶ Learn to differentiate good design from bad design. Remember that bad design can look attractive, but fail to deliver the human service it may also promise or imply.

▶ Consider the needs of older people as an integral part of the design, specification, and purchasing processes.

▶ Vote with your wallet. Seek out and purchase transgenerational products when given the choice.

▶ Write letters to all who can effect change: politicians, governmental agencies, professional organizations, manufacturers, and retailers—letters of praise as well as condemnation.

Many professional organizations are also available to help you—particularly the Industrial Designers Society of America (IDSA), the American Institute of Architects (AIA), the American Society of Interior Designers (ASID), the Gerontological Society (GSA), and the Human Factors and Ergonomics Society (HFES). Each can provide you with specialized professional information and advice.

Winning one battle, however, does not win a war. We ought not become complacent and rest on past accomplishments. Now is the time to strengthen our resolve and respond to technology's new challenge. We must carry the banner beyond the boundaries of "accessibility" and secure the rights of all in need of environmental support. Our collective effort can extend the independence of countless older Americans and postpone the day when they become institutionalized. It could also free us all to celebrate the wisdom, experience, and dignity reflected in the rich variety of talents represented by the elders of our society. After all, in a few years, *they* are *us*.

References

Abrams, William B., and Robert Berkow (eds.). 1990. *The Merck Manual of Geriatrics.* Rahway, NJ: Merck & Co.

Achenbaum, Andrew W., and Peggy Ann Kusnerz. 1978. *Images of Old Age in America: 1790 to the Present.* Ann Arbor, MI: Institute of Gerontology.

Allan, Carole B. 1981. Over 55: Growth market of the '80s. *Nation's Business,* April 1981, pp. 26–32.

American Foundation for the Blind. 1993. *Social Research Department Typescript.* New York: American Foundation for the Blind, Inc.

Architectural and Transportation Barriers Compliance Board. 1974. *To the Congress of the United States: First Report of the Architectural and Transportation Barriers Compliance Board.* Washington, DC: U.S. Department of Health, Education, and Welfare.

Beare, Patricia G., and Judith L. Myers (eds.). 1990. *Principles and Practice of Adult Health Nursing.* St. Louis: C.V. Mosby.

Beattie, Walter M. 1978. Transcultural aspects of aging. Paper presented at the VIIIth International Conference of Social Gerontology, December 13, 1978, Mohammedia, Morocco.

Besdine, Richard W. 1990. Introduction. In *The Merck Manual of Geriatrics,* William B. Abrams and Robert Berkow (eds.). Rahway, NJ: Merck Sharp & Dohne Research Laboratories, Division of Merck & Co., Inc., pp. 2–4.

Bikson, Tora K., and Jacqueline D. Goodchilds. 1978. *Production Decision Processes Among Older Adults.* Santa Monica, CA: The Rand Corp. ([Report]—Rand Corp. R-2361-NSF).

Blake, R. 1981. Disabled older Americans: A demographic analysis. *Journal of Rehabilitation* 47(4):19–27.

Brody, Jacob A., and Victoria W. Persky. 1990. Epidemiology and demographics. In *The Merck Manual of Geriatrics,* William B. Abrams and Robert Berkow (eds.). Rahway, NJ: Merck Sharp & Dohme Research Laboratories, Division of Merck & Co., Inc., pp. 1115–1127.

Brotman, Herman B. 1976. Who are the aged? In *The Elderly Consumer*, Fred E. Waddell (ed.). Columbia, MD: The Human Ecology Center, Antioch College, pp. 9–28.

Brotman, Herman B. 1981. Every ninth American. In *Development on Aging. Report #96-55*. Washington, DC: Government Printing Office.

Brown, Scott Campell. 1991. Conceptualizing and defining disability. In *Disability in the United States: A Portrait from National Data*, Susan Thompson-Hoffman and Inez Fitzgerald Storck (eds.). New York: Springer, pp. 1–4.

Bullock, Barbara L., and Pearl Philbrook Rosendahl. 1988. *Pathophysiology: Adaptions and Alterations in Function*, 2nd ed. Glenview, IL: Scott, Foresman.

Butler, Robert N., and Kathryn Hyer. 1990. Living alone. In *The Merck Manual of Geriatrics*, William B. Abrams and Robert Berkow (eds.). Rahway, NJ: Merck, Sharp & Dohme Research Laboratories, Division of Merck & Co., pp. 1162–1165.

Byerts, Thomas. 1979. Toward a better range of housing and environmental choices for the elderly. In *Back to Basics: Food and Shelter for the Elderly*. Proceedings of 27th Southern Conference on Gerontology, 1978. Patricia A. Wagner, and John M. McRae (eds.). Gainesville, FL: Center of Gerontological Studies, University of Florida.

Chapanis, Alphonse. 1992. To communicate the human factor message you have to know what the message is and how to communicate it: Part 2. *Human Factors Bulletin* 35(1):3–6. Santa Monica, CA: Human Factors Society.

Chappel, N., and B. Havens. 1985. Who helps the elderly person: A discussion of informal and formal care. In *Social Bonds in Later Life*, W. Peterson and J. Quadagno (eds.). Beverly Hills, CA: Sage Publications.

Chellis, Robert D., and Paul John Grayson (eds.). 1990. *Life Care: A Long-Term Solution?* Lexington, MA: Lexington Books.

Cluff, Pamela J. 1990. Designing for the elderly and the disabled: The Canadian experience. In *Life Care: A Long-Term Solution?* Robert D. Chellis, and Paul John Grayson (eds.). Lexington, MA: Lexington Books, p. 122.

Comfort, Alex. 1990. *Say Yes to Old Age: Developing a Positive Attitude Toward Aging*. New York: Crown Publishers.

Dahlman, Sven. 1989. Declaration of intent. In *ICSID Interdesign: Design for Elderly*, Sven Dahlman and Nils J. Tvengsberg (eds.). ICSID Interdesign Long Term Project 2. Helsinki: International Congress of Societies of Industrial Design (ICSID), pp. 16–17.

DeLoach, Charlene P., Ronnie D. Wilkins, and Guy W. Walker. 1983. *Independent Living: Philosophy, Process, and Service.* Baltimore: University Park Press.

DeLong, Alton J. 1968. The administrator and the environmental language of the older person. *Directions '68, AAHA Report No. 6.* New York: American Association of Homes for the Aging, pp. 22–26.

Dreyfuss, Henry. 1955. *Designing for People.* New York: Simon and Schuster.

Dychtwald, Ken. 1986. *Wellness and Health Promotion for the Elderly,* Ken Dychtwald (ed.). Rockville, MD: Aspen Publishers.

Dychtwald, Ken. 1988. *The Age Wave Featuring Dr. Ken Dychtwald,* Sponsored by American Express Travel Related Services Company. Video recording. Greensborough, NC: American Express Travel Related Services.

Ettinger, Walter H. 1990. Joint and soft tissue disorders. In *The Merck Manual of Geriatrics,* William B. Abrams and Robert Berkow (eds.). Rahway, NJ: Merck Sharp & Dohme Research Laboratories, Division of Merck & Co., Inc., pp. 676–702.

Federal Register. 1992. Architectural and Transportation Barriers Compliance Board, *Federal Register* 12 May 1992. Washington, DC: Department of Justice, 57(92):20360.

Fiber, Elaine, and Otto Neurath. 1985. Senility: Putting an end to the myth. In *Our Aging Parents: A Practical Guide to Eldercare.* Colette Browne and Roberta Onzuka-Anderson (eds.). Honolulu: University of Hawaii Press.

Glenn, Jerome C. 1989. Conscious technology: the coevolution of mind and machine. *The Futurist,* September-October, p. 140.

Gray, Muir, and Gordon Wilcock. 1981. *Our Elders.* Oxford: Oxford University Press.

Greene, Vernon L., Deborah Monahan, and Patricia D. Coleman. 1991. Demographs. In *Primary Care Geriatrics: A Case-Based Approach,* Richard J. Ham and Philip D. Sloane (eds.). St. Louis: Mosby Year Book, pp. 3–17.

Gulya, Julianna A. 1990. Ear disorders. In *The Merck Manual of Geriatrics,* William B. Abrams and Robert Berkow (eds.). Rahway, NJ: Merck Sharp & Dohme Research Laboratories, Division of Merck & Co., Inc., pp. 1083–1108.

Haan, Mary. 1991. The longitudinal dynamic: Linking many factors. In *Aging Today,* the bimonthly newsletter of the American Society on Aging, February/March 1991, 13(2):10.

Hale, Glorya (ed.). 1979. *The Source Book for the Disabled: An Illustrated Guide to Easier More Independent Living for Physically Disabled People, Their Families and Friends.* New York: Paddington Press, Ltd.

Ham, Richard J. 1986. *The Geriatric Medicine Annual.* Oradell, NJ: Medical Economics.

Ham, Richard J. 1991. Assessment. In *Primary Care Geriatrics: A Case-Based Approach,* Richard J. Ham and Philip D. Sloane (eds.). St. Louis: Mosby Year Book, pp. 64–94.

Hambrook, Ann. 1990. Marketing life care. In *Life Care: A Long-Term Solution?* Robert D. Chellis and Paul John Grayson (eds.). Lexington, MA: Lexington Books, pp. 35–48.

Hamilton, K. 1950. *Counseling the Handicapped in the Rehabilitation Process.* New York: Ronald Press.

Harris, C., et al. 1975. *The Myth and Realities of Aging in America.* Washington, DC: National Council on Aging.

Hiatt, Lorraine, G. 1987. Designing for the vision and hearing impairments of the elderly. In *Housing the Aged: Design Directives and Policy Considerations,* Victor Regnier and Jon Pynoos (eds.). New York: Elsevier, pp. 341–371.

Howell, Sandra C. 1978. *Shared Spaces in Housing for the Elderly: Design Evaluation Project, October 1976 (Revised).* Cambridge, MA: The Project, Massachusetts Institute of Technology, Department of Architecture.

Industrial Designers Society of America. 1992. The design principles of environmental stewardship. *Innovation: Journal of the Industrial Designers Society of America* 11(3):3.

Kantowitz, Barry H., and Robert D. Sorkin. 1983. *Human Factors: Understanding People-System Relationships.* New York: John Wiley & Sons.

Katchadourian, H. 1987. *Fifty: Midlife in Perspective.* New York: W.H. Freeman & Co.

Katz, S., T.D. Downs, H.R. Cash, and R.C. Grotz. 1970. Progress in development of the index of ADLs. *Gerontologist* 10:20–30.

Kay, Arthur D., and Rein Tideiksaar. 1990. Falls and gait disorders. In *The Merck Manual of Geriatrics,* William B. Abrams and Robert Berkow (eds.). Rahway, NJ: Merck Sharp & Dohme Research Laboratories, Division of Merck & Co., Inc., pp. 52–68.

Kirchner, C., and C. Lowman. 1978. Sources of variation in the estimated prevalence of visual loss. *Journal of Visual Impairment and Blindness,* 72(8):329–333.

Koncelik, Joseph A. 1982. *Aging and the Product Environment.* Strouds-burg, PA: Hutchinson Ross Publishing Co.

Koncelik, Joseph A. 1987. Product and furniture design for the chronically impaired elderly. In *Housing the Aged: Design Directives and Policy Considerations,* Victor Regnier and Jon Pynoos (eds.). New York: Elsevier, pp. 373–398.

Kupfer, Carl. 1990. Ophthalmologic disorders. In *The Merck Manual of Geriatrics,* William B. Abrams and Robert Berkow (eds.) Rahway, NJ: Merck Sharp & Dohme Research Laboratories, Division of Merck & Co., Inc., pp. 1055–1081.

LaPlante, Mitchell P. 1991a. Medical conditions associated with disability. In *Disability in the United States: A Portrait from National Data,* Susan Thompson-Hoffman and Inez Fitzgerald Storck (eds.). New York: Springer Publishing Company, pp. 34–72.

LaPlante, Mitchell P. 1991b. The need for assistance in basic life activities. In *Disability in the United States: A Portrait from National Data,* Susan Thompson-Hoffman and Inez Fitzgerald Storck (eds.). New York: Springer Publishing Company, pp. 73–106.

Laufer, M. Barbara. 1984. *Have You Heard? Hearing Loss and Aging.* Washington, DC: American Association of Retired Persons.

Lawton, M. Powell. 1986. *Environment and Aging,* 2nd ed. Albany, NY: Center for the Study of Aging.

Lawton, M. Powell. 1989. Three functions of the residential environment. In *Lifestyles and Housing of Older Adults: The Florida Experience,* Leon A. Pastalan and Marie E. Cowart (eds.). New York: Haworth Press, pp. 35–50.

Lawton, M. Powell, and L. Nahemow. 1973. Ecology and the aging process. In *Psychology of Adult Development and Aging,* C. Eisdorfer and M.P. Lawton (eds.). Washington, DC: American Psychological Association, pp. 619–674.

Levitt, Theodore. 1986. Cited in Lorenz, Christopher, in *The Design Dimension.* Oxford: Basil Blackwell, pp. 25.

Lovering, Robert. 1985. *Out of the Ordinary: A Digest on Disability.* Phoenix, AZ: ARCS, Inc.

McRae, John M. 1989. Spatial implications of design for the elderly. In *Lifestyles and Housing of Older Adults: The Florida Experience,* Leon A.

Pastalon and Marie E. Cowary (eds.). New York: Haworth Press, pp. 105–110.

Mellström, Dan. 1989. Physical aging and its consequences: New perspectives on old age. In *Design for Elderly: Design for Independent Living*, Sven Dahlman and Nils J. Tvengsberg (eds.). ICSID Interdesign Long Term Project 2. Helsinki: ICSID Secretariat.

Modern Maturity. 1992. What's new on cable? April–May 1992, p. 21.

Moos, Rudolf H., Sonne Lemke, and Thomas G. David. 1987. Priorities for design and management in residential settings for the elderly. In *Housing the Aged: Design Directives and Policy Considerations*, Victor Regnier and Jon Pynoos (eds.). New York: Elsevier, pp. 179–205.

Murphy, John B. 1991. Dysmobility and immobility. In *Primary Care Geriatrics: A Case-Based Approach*, Richard J. Ham and Philip D. Sloane (eds.). St. Louis: Mosby Year Book, pp. 313–335.

National Center for Health Statistics. 1988. *Current estimates from the National Health Interview Survey: United States. 1987.* Washington, DC: U.S. Department of Health and Human Services.

National Center for Vision and Aging. 1986. *A Better View of You: A Community Guide for Vision and Aging.* New York: The Lighthouse National Center for Vision and Aging.

National Institute on Aging. 1986. *Age Words: A Glossary on Health and Aging*, NH Publication No. 86-1849, January 1986. Bethesda, MD: National Institute on Aging, National Institutes of Health, Public Health Services, Department of Health and Human Services.

National Institute on Aging. 1987. *Help Yourself to Good Health.* Bethesda, MD: National Institute on Aging, National Institutes of Health, Public Health Services, Department of Health and Human Services.

Neary, Mary Anne. 1990a. Chronic illness in elderly people. In *Nursing in the Community*, Bonnie Bullough and Vern Bullough (eds.). St. Louis: C.V. Mosby, pp. 492–517.

Neary, Mary Anne. 1990b. Psychosocial issues in the older adult: Nursing implications. In *Nursing in the Community*, Bonnie Bullough and Vern Bullough (eds.). St. Louis: C.V. Mosby, pp. 470–491.

Nelson, K.A., and E. Dimitrova. 1993. Statistical brief No. 36, Severe Visual Impairment in the United States and in each state, 1990. Reprinted from *Journal of Visual Impairment and Blindness*, March 1993, 87(3):80–82, 84–85.

Neumann, Leonard, and Duncan Boldy. 1982. *Housing for the Elderly.* New York: St. Martin's Press.

Newcomer, Robert J., and Joel P. Weeden. 1986. Perspectives on housing needs and the continuum of care. In *Housing an Aging Society*, Robert J. Newcomer, M. Powell Lawton, and Thomas O. Byerts (eds.). New York: Van Nostrand Reinhold Company, pp. 3–9.

Osterburg, Arvid E. 1987. Evaluating design innovations in an extended care facility. In *Housing the Aged: Design Directives and Policy Considerations*, Victor Regnier and Jon Pynoos (eds.). New York: Elsevier, pp. 399–420.

Ostroff, Jeff. 1989. *Successful Marketing to the 50+ Consumer*. Englewood Cliffs, NJ: Prentice-Hall.

Parker, Sheridan W. 1988. Characteristics of the elderly population. In *A Bathroom for the Elderly: Aging Factors, Design Evaluation Criteria and a Design Proposal*, Robert F. Graeff and Len D. Singer (eds.). Blacksburg, VA: Center for Product and Environmental Design, College of Architecture and Urban Studies, Virginia Polytechnic Institute and State University, pp. 11–31.

Parsons, Mary Ann, and Gwen Felton. 1990. Young and middle adulthood: The working years. In *Nursing in the Community*, Bonnie Bullough and Vern Bullough (eds.). St. Louis: C.V. Mosby, pp. 404–437.

Pirkl, James J. 1991. Transgenerational design: A design strategy whose time has arrived. *Design Management Journal* 2(4):55–60.

Pirkl, James J. 1992. The ADA: A timely matter of concern for us all. *Design Perspectives: The Newsletter of the Industrial Designers Society of America*. August, p. 1.

Pirkl, James J., and Anna L. Babic. 1988. Guidelines and Strategies for Designing Transgenerational Products: An Instructor's Manual. Acton, MA: Copley Publishing Group.

Pirkl, James J., and Anna L. Babic. 1988. *Guidelines and Strategies for Designing Transgenerational Products: A Resource Manual for Industrial Design Professionals*. Acton, MA: Copley Publishing.

Pollack, Lance M., and Robert J. Newcomer. 1986. Neighborhoods and the aged. In *Housing an Aging Society: Issues, Alternatives, and Policy*, Robert J. Newcomer, M. Powell Lawton, and Thomas O. Byerts (eds.). New York: Van Nostrand Reinhold, pp. 119–126.

Pulos, Arthur J. 1988. *The American Design Adventure*. Cambridge, MA: MIT Press.

Pynoos, Jon, Evelyn Cohen, Linda J. Davis, and Sharmalee Bernhardt. 1987. Home modifications: Improvements that extend independence.

In *Housing the Aged: Design Directives and Policy Considerations*, Victor Regnier and Jon Pynoos (eds.). New York: Elsevier, pp. 277–303.

Raschko, Bettyann. 1987. Universal Design. *ASID REPORT*, American Society of Interior Designers 13(2):8–10.

Regnier, Victor. 1987. Design directives: Current knowledge and future needs. In *Housing the Aged: Design Directives and Policy Considerations*, Victor Regnier and Jon Pynoos (eds.). New York: Elsevier, pp. 3–24.

Regnier, Victor, and Jon Pynoos (eds.). 1987. *Housing the Aged: Design Directives and Policy Considerations*. New York: Elsevier.

Robinson, Bruce E., and Christine Conard. 1986. Falls and falling. In *The Geriatric Medicine Annual*, Richard J. Ham (ed.). Oradell, NJ: Medical Economics, pp. 198–212.

Shalit, Anita. 1987. Alerting business to the needs of older Americans: A look at federal initiatives. *Innovation: Journal of the Industrial Designers Society of America*, Summer 1987, pp. 12–14.

Sheehy, G. 1989. The happiness report. *Redbook*, July.

Sloane, Philip D. 1992. Normal aging. In *Primary Care Geriatrics: A Case-Based Approach*, 2nd ed., Richard J. Ham and Philip D. Sloane (eds.). St. Louis: Mosby Year Book, pp. 20–39.

Smedley, Lawrence T. 1976. The patterns of elderly retirement. In *The Elderly Consumer*, Fred E. Waddell (ed.). Columbia, MD: Human Ecology Center, Antioch College, pp. 155–173.

Soldo, B.J. 1983. *A National Perspective on the Home Care Population*. Washington, DC: Georgetown University, Center for Population Research, CPR 83-004.

Steinfeld, Edward. 1987. Adaptive housing for older disabled people. In *Housing the Aged: Design Directives and Policy Considerations*, Victor Regnier and Jon Pynoos (eds.). New York: Elsevier, pp. 307–339.

Storck, Inez F., and Susan Thompson-Hoffman. 1991. Demographic characteristics of the disabled population. In *Disability in the United States: A Portrait From National Data*, Inez Fitzgerald Storck and Susan Thompson-Hoffman (eds.). New York: Springer, pp. 15–33.

Streib, Gordon F., Anthony J. LaGreca, and William E. Folts. 1986. Retirement communities: People, planning, prospects. In *Housing and an Aging Society*, Robert J. Newcomer, M. Powell Lawton, and Thomas O. Byerts (eds.). New York: Van Nostrand Reinhold, pp. 94–103.

Struyk, Raymond J. 1987. Housing adaptations: Needs and practices. In

Housing the Aged: Design Directives and Policy Considerations, Victor Regnier and Jon Pynoos (eds.). New York: Elsevier, pp. 259–275.

Struyk, Raymond J., and Harold M. Katsura. 1968. *Aging at Home: How the Elderly Adjust Their Housing Without Moving.* New York: Hayward Press.

Svanborg, A. 1985. Biomedical and environmental influences on aging. In *Productive Aging: Enhancing Vitality in Later Life,* R. Butler and H. Gleason (eds.). New York: Springer Publishing Co., pp. 15–27.

Thackara, John. 1988. *Design After Modernism.* New York: Thames and Hudson.

Toufexis, Anastasia. 1991. Now hear this—if you can. *Time,* August 5, 1991, pp. 50–51.

Turner, Lloyd. 1986. Public policies and individual housing choices. In *Housing and an Aging Society,* Robert J. Newcomer, M. Powell Lawton, and Thomas O. Byerts (eds.). New York: Van Nostrand Reinhold, pp. 42–52.

U.S. Department of Health and Human Services. 1988. *Vital Statistics of the United States, 1988.* Volume I, Natality Table 1-20. Washington, DC: Department of Health and Human Services.

U.S. Department of Justice. 1991. Americans with Disabilities Act (ADA) Accessibility Guidelines for Buildings and Facilities: Final Guidelines. *Federal Register,* 56(144):35408–35455, July 26, 1991.

Van Nostrand, J.F., A. Zappolo, E. Hing, B. Bloom, B. Hirsch, and D.J.

Foley. 1979. The National Nursing Home Survey: 1977 Summary for the United States. *Vital and Health Statistics,* Series 13(43). Washington, DC: U.S. Public Health Service.

Wallin, David E. 1965. A marketing profile of the senior citizen group. In *Dimensions of Consumer Behavior,* James U. McNeal (ed.). New York: Appleton-Century-Crofts, Division of Meredith Publishing, pp. 218–227.

Weisgerber, Robert A. 1991. *Quality of Life for Persons with Disabilities: Skill Development and Transitions Across Life Stages.* Gaithersburg, MD: Aspen Publishers.

World Health Organization. 1993. *International Classification of Impairments, Disabilities, and Handicaps: A manual of classification relating to the consequences of disease* (Revised). Geneva: World Health Organization.

Wright, G.N. 1980. *Total Rehabilitation.* Boston: Little, Brown.

Yahr, Melvin D., and Stuart W.H. Pang. 1990. Movement disorders. In *The Merck Manual of Geriatrics,* William B. Abrams and Robert Berkow (eds). Rahway, NJ: Merck & Co., pp. 973–993.

Zedlewski, Sheila R., Roberta O. Barnes, Martha K. Burt, Timothy D. McBride, and Jack A. Meyer. 1990. *The Needs of the Elderly in the 21st Century,* Urban Institute Report 90-5. Washington, DC: Urban Institute Press.

Zukav, Gary. 1989. *The Dancing Wu Li Masters: An Overview of the New Physics.* New York: Bantam Books.

THE TRIUMPH
OF CONSCIENCE

*"I expect to pass through life
but once. If therefore, there
be any kindness I can show,
or any good thing I can do to
any fellow being, let me do it
now, and not defer or
neglect, as I shall not pass
this way again."*
—WILLIAM PENN
(1644–1718)

▶Product Name
Newport™ Rehabilitation Collar

▶Manufacturer/Supplier
California Medical Products, Inc. A Laerdal Company.

▶Design Firm/Designer(s)
In house/Joseph Kemme, Geoffrey Garth, Charlie Patterson

▶Description

Designed for us by cervical spine injury patients during rehabilitation, the collar promotes healing by providing effective immobilization while being comfortable to wear for an extended period. This innovative design features a dynamically cushioned chin piece and a unique *Extension Support Strap*™ that allows the back of the collar to precisely conform to each patient. The unit stores flat to save space in hospital inventory and is available in a range of sizes including two for children.

▶Touch

Comfort is enhanced by large front and back airflow openings and breathable foam pads that wick prespiration away from the skin to the outersurface of the pad where it evaporates. Pads are easily removed for washing or replacement, enabling the patient to keep the collar sanitary.

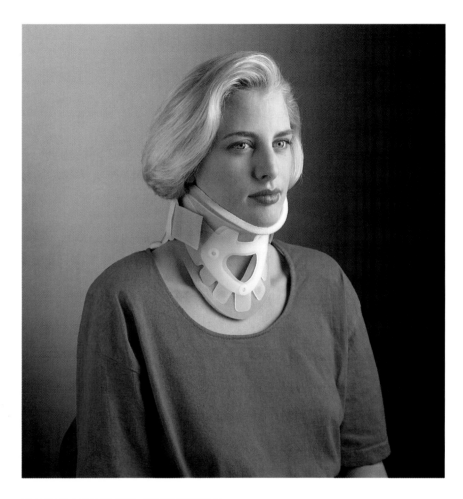

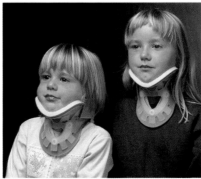

Photos by Charlie Patterson. Courtesy of California Medical Products.

▶Manual Handling

Self-adjusting chin piece and support tabs provide even, constant mandible support regardless of the activities being performed by the patient.

► **Product Name**
Aqua Pill Timer™

► **Manufacturer/Supplier**
Zelco Industries, Inc.

► **Design Firm/Designer(s)**
Not available

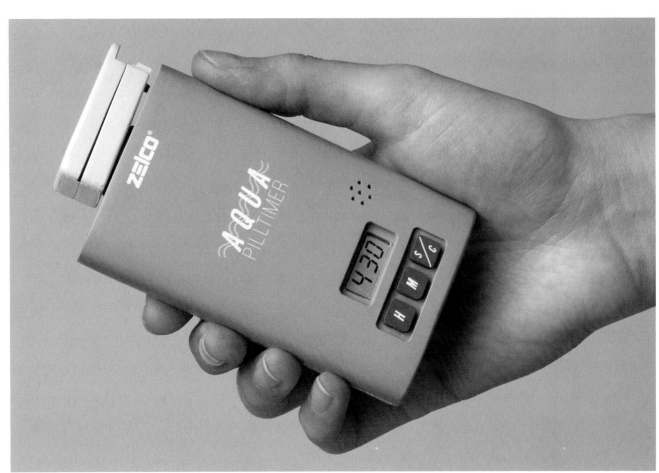

Photos courtesy of Zelco Industries, Inc.

► **Description**

The handy, compact Aqua Pill Timer is so easy to use you can take it wherever you go. Keep it in your pocket, purse, briefcase, or at home on your nightstand. This smart pillbox lets you simply program the electronic alarm and a beep will remind you when to take your medication. Since it carries its own water and straw, there is no need to search for a glass, faucet, or water fountain. The unit holds approximately 2 ounces of water.

► **Hearing**

A beep alarm alerts you when it's time to take your medication.

► **Manual Handling**

The compact design fits in a pocket or purse to go wherever you go. It features a slide-out drawer for storing pills.

► **Mobility**

The unit carries 2-ounces of water and a straw, thus eliminating the need to search for a glass, faucet, or fountain.

▶**Product Name**
Ultramark 4 Sonography
System

▶**Manufacturer/Supplier**
Advanced Technology
Laboratories

▶**Design Firm/Designer(s)**
Joseph Ungar, Leroy Laceue

▶**Description**
The Ultramark 4 sonography
system is used primarily for
ultrasound imaging in obstetric
and gynecology applications in
clinical and hospital
environments. The unit is
designed to accommodate both
male and female users ranging in
size from the 5th to the 95th
percentile. The system, including
the monitor, keyboard, and
transducers, may be operated in
either a sitting or standing
position. Providing comfort and
minimizing stress to patients of all
ages was also a design parameter.

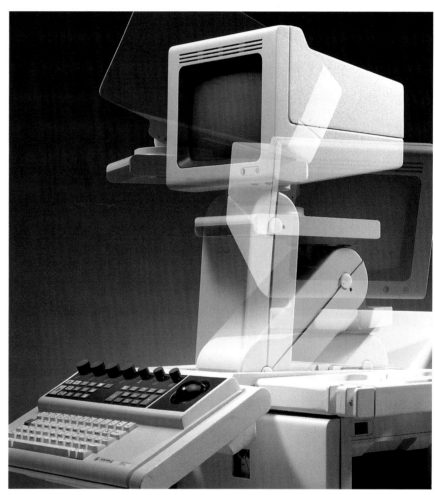

Photos courtesy of Advanced Technology Laboratories.

▶Vision

Adjustable monitor features forward/backward and up/down positioning. Both monitor and keyboard accommodate the operator's position, whether sitting or standing. The swiveling monitor allows viewing by the patient. All elements adjust for various age-related focus ranges.

▶Hearing

The unit's Doppler stereo speakers are located at maximum separation distance and feature adjustable volume control. The keyboard's "beep" feedback can also be adjusted to achieve a variety of sonography comfort levels.

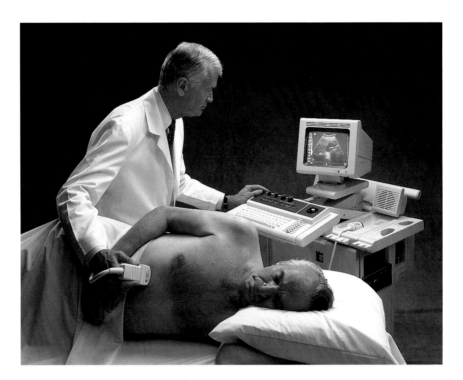

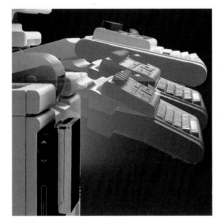

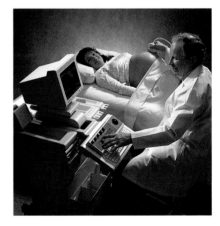

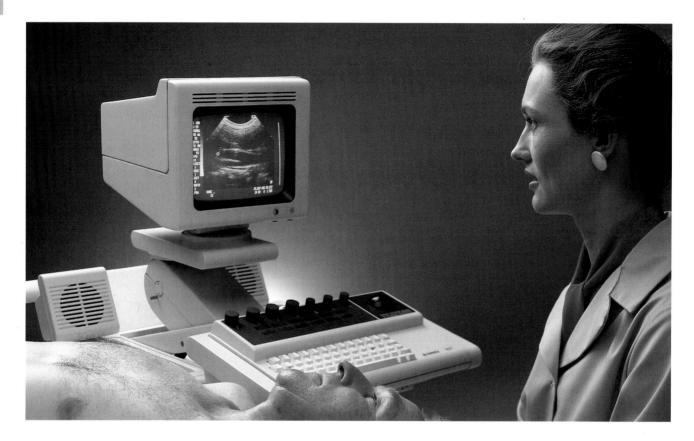

▶Touch
The knobs and keyboard are molded of soft rubber, providing the operator a comfortable "feel" and a sense of accuracy.

▶Manual Handling
Handles located at the rear of the unit and placed at midrange height provide an easy and comfortable means to move the lightweight cart. For difficult positioning of the cart, the keyboard can be removed. As an added convenience, all tilting and height adjustments can be released and made with one hand.

▶Mobility
The "weightless" movements of the monitor and keyboard allow the operator to easily change the monitor's tilt or the height of the monitor and keyboard. These effortless movements provide a stress-free work environment for operators of all ranges of ages and strengths.

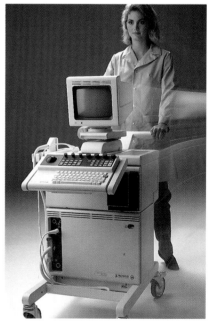

► **Product Name**
Orthovision Orthopedic Table

► **Manufacturer/Supplier**
AMSCO International, Inc.

► **Design Firm/Designer(s)**
In house/Ward Sanders, Dennis Coon, Stephen Leonard

► **Description**

The Orthovision orthopedic table provides a safe patient support and posturing platform. It offers the surgical team and their supportive equipment convenient access to the patient and the operative site. The table features an adjustable padded patient surface mounted on a mobile base and column. Adjustable abductor bars extend from the table's superstructure and can be positioned around the table for storage. The table's design focuses on accommodating elderly and disabled persons.

► **Touch**

The Akros table mattress pad helps prevent decubitus ulcers (bed sores) particularly common to elderly and disabled patients. The pad also provides comfort for long stationary procedures lasting several hours. Additional padding for the foot, arm, and perineum provide support and reduce nerve damage associated with orthopedic procedures.

► **Manual Handling**

Patented carbon fiber abductor bars minimize adjustments to intensify and clarify the image by allowing the intensifier (C-ARM) to project with little or no interference. This reduces uncomfortable and potentially dangerous adjustments to patients due to orthopedic table posturing.

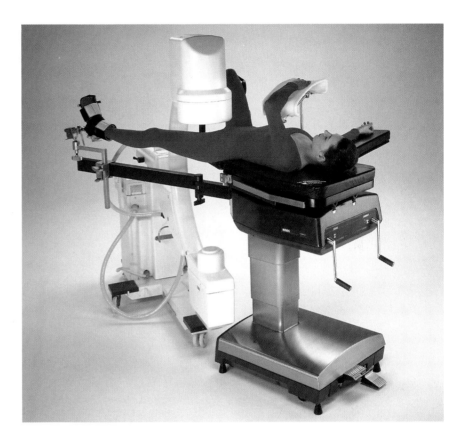

Strains to the joints of elderly and disabled patients are thus reduced.

► **Mobility**

Ease of moving the orthopedic table was a key design objective. The design of the four-swivel caster base makes moving the 550-pound table equally easy and effortless for the 2.5 percentile female as well as the 95th percentile male.

Photo by Tal Advertising. Courtesy of AMSCO International, Inc.

135

▶**Product Name**
Quantum 3080 RL Surgical
Table

▶**Manufacturer/Supplier**
AMSCO International, Inc.

▶**Design Firm/Designer(s)**
In house/Ward Sanders, Joe
Sestak

▶**Description**

The Quantum 3080 RL table
provides the patient safety and
comfort during all general surgical
postures. It offers anesthesiologists
logical, easy-to-use control systems
and provides the surgical team and
their equipment unimpaired access
to the patient and the operative
site. A four-section articulated
padded patient surface provides a
wide range of reverse or standard
surgical postures, positioned by a
tethered hand control.

▶**Touch**

The Quantum 3080 RL table
incorporates the Akros table
mattress pad to alleviate the
problem of decubitus ulcers (bed
sores) particularly common to
elderly and disabled patients. The
pad also provides comfort for the
patient during long, stationary
procedures lasting several hours.

▶**Manual Handling**

The table top surface is
transparent to x-ray and image
intensification. It improves
imaging access to particular bodily
organs by eliminating the past
need to reposition the patient.
Approximately 80 percent of the
body can now be imaged at one
time, greatly reducing
uncomfortable and potentially
dangerous patient movements.

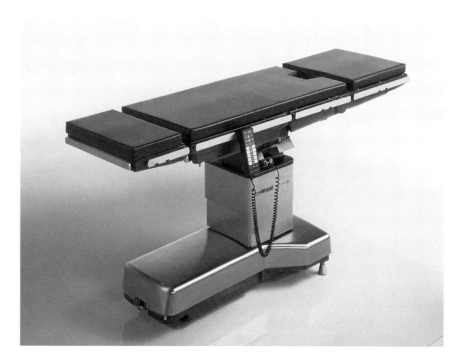

▶**Mobility**

The computer-controlled table
movement/posturing capability
offers smooth patient positioning,
and a return-to-level feature
ergonomically controls the
patient's movement, reducing
strain on bodily joints. A
four-swivel caster base makes
moving the 800-pound table easy
and effortless for the 2.5 percentile
female as well as the 95th
percentile male.

Photo by Tal Advertising. Courtesy of AMSCO
International, Inc.

▶Product Name
Eye Drops Applicator

▶Manufacturer/Supplier
Clement Clarke International

▶Design Firm/Designer(s)
IDEO Product Development:
Colin Burns

▶Description

The eye drops applicator is an adaptor device designed for use with most available eye drops bottles. It enhances the user's control of gripping and positioning the bottle while self-administering eye drops. The user places an eye drops bottle in the applicator, positions the applicator cup over the eye, and merely squeezes the applicator "wings" to release a dose of eye drops into the eye.

▶Manual Handling

The applicator is lightweight and its "wing" grips are easy to hold by the elderly and those with diminished finger dexterity. The cup fits comfortably over the eye and the amount of pressure required to activate a dose of eye drops is minimal.

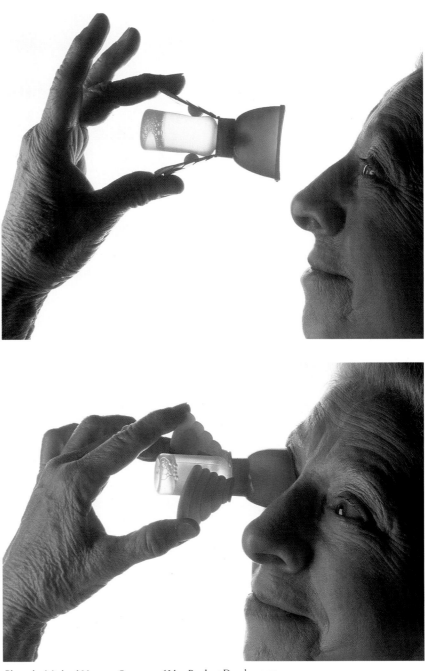

Photo by Michael Venera. Courtesy of Ideo Product Development.

▶**Product Name**
Horizon Infusion Pump

▶**Manufacturer/Supplier**
Mc Gaw, Inc.

▶**Design Firm/Designer(s)**
IDEO Product Development,
San Francisco, CA: Tim Parsey,
Peter Spreenbery, Jane Fulton,
Tony Fields, Walt Conti

▶**Description**
The infusion pump is simple to use
and highly accurate. In areas
where space is limited, the design
permits more pumps to be put on
intravenous (IV) poles. The pump
also allows easy manipulation of
complex performance data.
Additionally, an important design
goal was to achieve patient trust
through a comfortable,
nonthreatening appearance.

▶**Vision**
The clean design features an
organized display of clustered,
legible controls. Readability is
enhanced by the large,
high-contrast san-serif type.
Simple, unequivocal graphic
symbols, sized and positioned to
communicate priorities, order, and
relationships, provide
easy-to-understand redundant
cues.

▶**Touch**
Tactile controls offer easy
identification and feature a
distinctive raised shape for
distinguishing each set of message
units.

▶**Manual Handling**
The wide, easily gripped handle is
positioned for comfortable
transport and set-up.

Photo by Giampiero Bienvenutti. Courtesy of
IDEO Product Development.

▶Product Name
Left Ventricular Assist System
(LVAS)

▶Manufacturer/Supplier
Baxter Healthcare Corporation,
Novacor Division, Oakland,
CA

▶Design Firm/Designer(s)
IDEO Product Development,
San Francisco: Nauto
Fukosawa, Tim Parsey, Robin
Sarre, Jane Fulton

▶Description

The system supports diseased or
damaged hearts for patients
waiting for a donor heart for
transplant. The patients, who
would normally be tethered to a
large console in a hospital, are
able to live close-to-normal lives.
The system consists of an
implanted mechanical pump
which is controlled by an external
microprocessor-based unit, capable
of following the natural rhythms of
the heart. A controller unit, a
main battery, and a support
battery are worn in a harness by
the patient.

▶Vision

The strong, linear surface contours
reveal the product's form to those
with limited vision. Important
information is oriented to the
unit's position when worn by the
user. Isolated from the product's
textured surfaces readouts are
identified legibly by large, white
type contrasted effectively against
the dark background.

Photo by Charles Kemper. Courtesy of IDEO Product Development.

▶Manual Handling

The product's gently curving forms
give the unit a nonthreatening
appearance. The unit's slim design
hugs the wearer's body
comfortably; reduces the effort and
inconvenience of donning,
wearing, and removing the
harness; and offers the dignity that
comes with visual discretion.

▶Mobility

This product breaks the patient's
physical connection to the
hospital, freeing him or her from
its confines. The system, designed
for use during showering,
exercising, sitting, and sleeping,
maintains the patient's
independence and permits daily
living activities to continue in a
near-normal manner.

▶**Product Name**
Digital Finger Blood Pressure
Monitor

▶**Manufacturer/Supplier**
Omron Healthcare, Inc.,
Vernon Hills, IL

▶**Design Firm/Designer(s)**
Not available

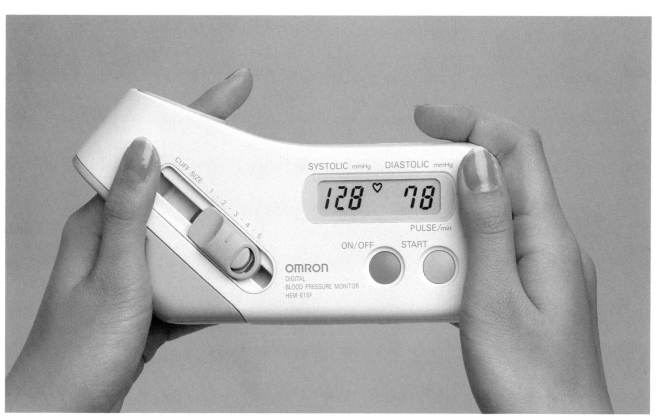

Photo courtesy of Omron Healthcare, Inc.

▶**Description**
The Omron HEM-815F is an
electric digital blood pressure
monitor that measures systolic,
diastolic, and pulse measurements
from the left index finger. The
user holds the unit in the palm of
the left hand and inserts the left
index finger into the finger cuff.
When the start button is pressed,
the cuff automatically inflates to
the correct pressure. Systolic,
diastolic, and pulse measurements
are displayed on an easy-to-read
liquid crystal display (LCD) panel.

▶**Manual Handling**
The natural positions of the index
finger and a grasping hand dictate
the product's clean form with
simple directness, making the unit
easy to hold and operate by those
with limited hand or finger
dexterity. The soft edges, which
are easy to handle, invite the hand
to hold and grasp the unit.
Portable and lightweight, the
monitor fits easily into a purse,
briefcase, or gym bag.

▶**Vision**
The simple controls are clearly
differentiated with contrasting
colors. The LCD panel displays
large, easy-to-see measurement
numbers.

▶**Touch**
The cuff-size is set by a convenient
thumb-operated slide and features
a tactile indicator bar that can be
read redundantly by touch as well
as sight. The large, push-button
controls are indented and
positioned for easy thumb location
and operation.

▶Product Name
Prescript™ TimeCap
Medication System

▶Manufacturer/Supplier
Wheaton Medical Technologies,
Division of Wheaton Industries,
Inc., Millville, NJ

▶Design Firm/Designer(s)
Moore Design Associates

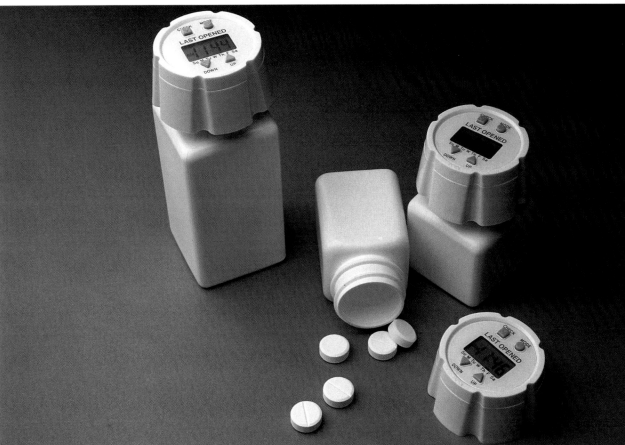

Photo courtesy of Moore Design Associates.

▶Description
PRESCRIPT™ was designed to remind people when they last took their medication. It recognizes that older people are most vulnerable to the life-threatening practice of "double-dosing" (accidently repeating a medication dosage because the first dosage was forgotten). Whether the user is a busy homemaker who forgets the occasional antibiotic, or an older person managing a daily multiple pill regimen, PRESCRIPT™ supports the cognitive and physical parameters of taking medications.

▶Vision
Large numerals on the timer display aid those with visual impairments. The symbolic arrow-shaped buttons offer a visual reinforcement for identifying the "down" and "up" buttons.

▶Touch
Each of the four input buttons has a different shape, offering redundant, tactile cues that helps the user identify each button's particular function. This is particularly helpful in low-light environments or for those with sight impairments.

▶Manual Handling
The large-diameter cap accommodates those who have difficulty gripping and grasping. Six bold recesses along the cap's side provide extra gripping edges and reduce the forces needed to twist the cap open or shut.

►**Product Name**
Easy Street Environment®

►**Manufacturer/Supplier**
La Grange Memorial Hospital,
La Grange, IL

►**Design Firm/Designer(s)**
Guynes Design Incorporated

►**Description**
Easy Street Environments® are unique, real-life home and urban environments located in hospitals and clinics throughout the United States and Canada. Therapists and families work together to help patients regain physical and mental capacities lost due to injury or illness. Patients learn to walk, eat, shop, and drive so that, after a stroke or an auto accident, the patient can go home rather than to a nursing home. Using the Easy Street Environments, ability is celebrated and enhanced, regardless of age.

►**Hearing**
Audiotapes of impatient mutterings about their slowness "holding up the line" are used at stimulated bank teller windows and grocery story checkout counters. Such experiences prepare patients for the real-life situations they will encounter when they return to their normal daily living activities.

►**Manual Handling**
Each *Easy Street* reflects its regional home-town surroundings. Patients practice and hone their coordination skills needed to manipulate such environmental elements as self-service gas pumps, lunch counters, kitchens with large and small appliances, coin-operated laundries, automated teller machines, restaurants, and self-service groceries.

►**Mobility**
Easy Street installations using driving simulators, real automobiles, and parts of buses to provide exercise opportunities for exercising the large-muscle groups needed to navigate such environmental obstacles as bus aisles, car trunks, car doors, and automobile interiors.

Photos courtesy of Guynes Design, Inc.

▶Product Name
Press N' Pour Beverage Pitcher

▶Manufacturer/Supplier
Tucker Housewares, Inc., a Mobil Company

▶Design Firm/Designer(s)
Goldsmith Yamasaki Specht Inc.: Marlan Polhemus

▶Description
The easy-to-open/easy-to-close lid of this unique 2-quart beverage pitcher was designed to be ergonomically correct for all ages, particularly accommodating those with limited motor impairments, children, and older persons. This simple, durable, impact-resistant product offers all users upscale functionality; the lid features a water-resistant seal for shaking or storing juices and other liquids. Satisfying to use, this innovative proprietary product saves storage space both within the refrigerator and on the door.

▶Manual Handling
The rocking lid was designed to open and close by simple thumb pressure, providing easy use by elderly persons, children, and those who suffer from arthritis or other motor impairments. It can also be rocked open or closed by those without thumb strength or dexterity by using the palm of the hand.

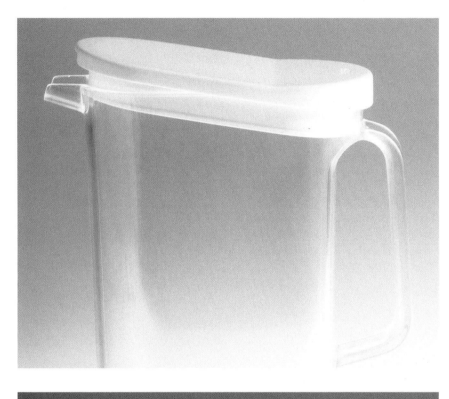

Photo by Claude Cummings. Courtesy of Goldsmith Yamasaki Specht, Inc.

▶Product Name
Good Grips

▶Manufacturer/Supplier
Oxo International

▶Design Firm/Designer(s)
Smart Design, Inc.: D. Stowell,
T. Viemeister, D. Formosa,
S. Russack, S. Allendorf,
M. Calahan, J. Laub, S. Wahl

▶Description
Good Grips kitchen tools offer special handles designed to be comfortable and easy for everyone to hold. The large-diameter, nonslip Santoprene™ rubber handles are easily gripped and provide better leverage. They feature patented softspot grips on either side, which develop extra friction and act as universal contact points. The handle design distributes gripping forces, thus minimizing the hand strength normally required for comfortable and secure manipulation of the tool.

▶Vision
Large, clear markings on the measuring cups and spoons offer high-contrast size identification for those with vision impairments. Additional color coding provides a redundant cue that helps identify particular sizes.

▶Touch
The handle's rubber-like material feels soft and inviting and won't slip, even in wet hands. The finned, flexible softspots guarantee a comfortable, cushioned grip for everyone, regardless of age or functional ability.

▶Manual Handling
The extraplump oval handle, resilient and rounded at the end, nestles in the palm comfortably and securely. The tapered, oversized hole guides the handle onto the hook without the user looking. Scissor design spreads out the stress and cushions the hand for easy, ambidextrous use.

Photos courtesy of Smart Design, Inc.

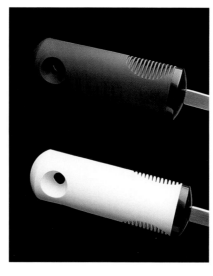

▶**Product Name**
Wonderlier Bowl

▶**Manufacturer/Supplier**
Tupperware

▶**Design Firm/Designer(s)**
In house/Morison Cousins,
Brian Aiken

Photo courtesy of Tupperware.

▶**Description**

Tupperware's classic Wonderlier Bowl was redesigned in response to the company's growing awareness of its customer's needs. Recognizing the increased demands on the average person as well as the growing incidence of arthritis, Tupperware created a seal and bowl combination which functions better than the original classic; the new design allows the seal to be easily cleaned, burped, and removed. Moreover, the bowl's simple form and vibrant colors appeal to all generations.

▶**Vision**

The lid-lifting tabs create a strong visual impact and communicate their function cleanly and directly. The strong color contrast between lid and bowl distinguishes each element for quick identification.

▶**Touch**

The lifting tabs feature an easy-to-grasp texture that enhances the user's grip and aids in breaking the seal and removing the lid.

▶**Manual Handling**

The new design corrects many problems. The original structural rim felt harsh to the touch and made cleaning difficult. The new rim provides more structure, offers the hand a softer touch, and cleans more easily. The bowl's new form presents an elegant appearance while increasing its capacity and achieving greater stability.

▶Product Name
Adjust-A-Measure (adjustable measuring spoons and scoop)

▶Manufacturer/Supplier
E. Stanley Robins, Robins Industries, Inc., Kitchen Art Division

▶Design Firm/Designer(s)
Lee Payne Associates, Inc.: Lee Payne, Darrell Watt, Frans Weterrings, Wendell Wilson

▶Description
The spoons can measure to 1 teaspoon and to 1 tablespoon, and the scoop can measure to a half-cup. Simple geometric forms produce an adjustable volume, which is sized by moving a sliding cover to the appropriate position. Graphic indicators label the various volumes, and incremental detents located on the side of the spoon and the top of the scoop create positive stops. The tapered edges of the sliding cover permit each unit to be easily inserted into jars and cans.

▶Vision
The diagonal, black position line and bold type provide a strong contrast with the cover's white background and enhance readability of the measurements.

▶Hearing
The incremental detents snap audibly as each measure division is reached, providing a redundant cue for those with poor eyesight.

▶Touch
The indicator detents that identify each measure division provide the user with redundant tactile feedback cues.

▶Manual Handling
The large gripping surfaces of each device provide easy handling for those with manual impairments.

Photo by Peter Hogg. Courtesy of Lee Payne Associates, Inc.

▶**Product Name**
Softouch Scissors

▶**Manufacturer/Supplier**
Fiskars, Inc.

▶**Design Firm/Designer(s)**
Fiskars Research and
Development Group: Doug
Birkholz, industrial designer;
Craig Melter, engineer

▶**Description**

The Fiskars Softouch is a scissors
that assists individuals who have
low hand strength, are afflicted
with arthritis, or use scissors daily.
The scissors are used by grasping
the handles and pulling back the
orange switch, releasing the upper
and lower handles. This
ambidextrous, lightweight design
features spring-loaded handles
with a cushion grip, a locking
switch to disengage the handles,
and stainless steel blades.

▶**Touch**

An injection molded thermoplastic
rubber grip gives the scissors a soft
feel, nonslip grip, and increased
comfort while cutting.

▶**Manual Handling**

The Softouch utilizes a
compression or "squeeze" motion
to operate the scissors. This
motion takes the work normally
done by the thumb and transfers it
across the surface of the palm,
distributing the load along four
fingers rather than one. Opening
the scissors is spring-assisted,
reducing the hand's workload. It
accommodates both right and left
hand users.

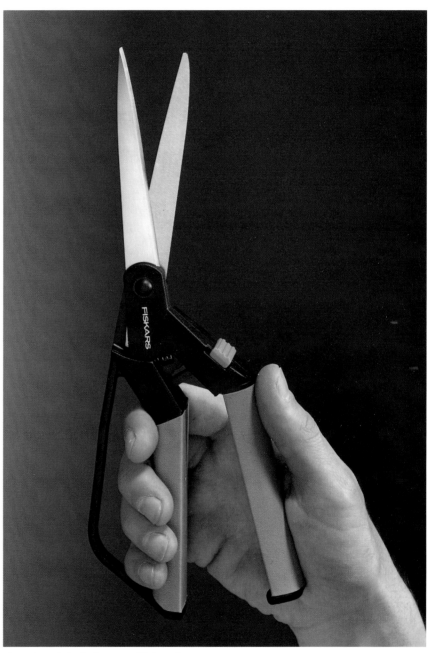

Photos by Dale Hall. Courtesy of Fiskars, Inc.

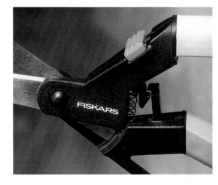

▶**Product Name**
Hillcrest Motorcaddie

▶**Manufacturer/Supplier**
Kangaroo Motorcaddies

▶**Design Firm/Designer(s)**
Machen Montague, Inc.:
Edmund H. Machen, James
Machen, Edgar B. Montague

▶**Description**

The Hillcrest Motorcaddie promotes healthy walking without the burden of pulling or carrying a golf bag. Popular with senior golfers, the unit is designed to be light weight for easy steering and handling, simple to operate, and maintenance-free. Even men and women in their eighties can continue to play golf and get healthy exercise walking, but without having to lug their golf bags. The powerful motor enables the Hillcrest to help pull elderly golfers up long grades or steep hills.

▶**Touch**

An ergonomic speed control features a thumb wheel built into the handle which allows safe control by those with arthritis or other functional hand impairments. Speed and steering can be controlled by just one hand, right or left.

▶**Manual Handling**

The unit transports easily. Two simple latches permit disassembly or assembly of the unit without knobs, wing-nuts, or levers. A built-in handle helps to lift the chassis easily.

▶**Mobility**

Using the Hillcrest avoids the twisting strain to the torso and shoulder normally associated with pulling a golfcart. It also eliminates the strain to shoulder and back muscles which occurs while carrying a golf bag.

Photo by Christopher Bartol. Courtesy of Kangaroo Motorcaddies.

▶ **Information and Communication**

Photo by John Betts. Courtesy of Henry Dreyfuss Associates.

▶ **Description**

The Polaroid Spectra Camera is an instant camera designed for use by amateur photographers spanning a wide age range. Its LCD panel and five buttons reduce the number of switches required to use the controls and allow the user to program the camera simply. Should the need arise, the user can return to the standard setup by pressing only one button.

▶ **Vision**

A large eye-cup can easily accommodate users with glasses or those whose reduced vision requires holding the viewer closer to the face. The camera also features clear, readable icons and large numerals, offering camera status information to users with a wide range of seeing capabilities.

▶ **Manual Handling**

A binocular-style rubber grip on both the top and bottom of the camera adds to the user's comfort and provides a secure grip. A hand strap offers additional security to those whose grip might weaken while photo shooting.

► **Product Name**
Pro Release bowling wrist
positioner

► **Manufacturer/Supplier**
Moro Design

► **Design Firm/Designer(s)**
Moro Design: Joseph Moro

► **Description**
Maintaining the correct wrist
position is one of the most
important aspects of the sport of
bowling. The Pro Release is an
adjustable wrist positioner. It
holds a bowler's wrist firmly in
position while he or she delivers
and releases a bowling ball. It
allows a bowler to preset the
desired wrist position (angle) and
holds the wrist firmly in that
position throughout delivery and
release of the bowling ball. This
product benefits bowlers of any
age.

► **Manual Handling**
Holding a 16-pound bowling ball
throughout delivery causes a great
amount of strain on one's wrist. If
the wrist is not firm at the point of
release, the bowler cannot impart
the necessary finger lift to roll the
ball. The result is a weaker driving
ball and less striking power.

► **Mobility**
The Pro Release serves the older
bowler who has lost wrist strength.
It supports the wrist firmly and
comfortably while finger, arm, and
leg strength impart the necessary
finger lift to deliver a strongly
rolling ball.

Photos courtesy of Moro Design.

151

▶**Product Name**
Men's Outdoor Cross Training
Shoe

▶**Manufacturer/Supplier**
NIKE, Inc.

▶**Design Firm/Designer(s)**
In house design/Tinker
Natfield, Steve McDonald

Photo courtesy of NIKE, Inc.

▶**Description**

The air escape outdoor
cross-training athletic shoe is a
durable, breathable product adept
at allowing the wearer to perform a
variety of activities including
walking, trekking, cycle touring,
relaxing, and mowing the lawn. It
includes a sturdy rubber outsole,
comfortable uppers of leather and
sturdy mesh, and a cushioning
midsole of polyurethane.

▶**Mobility**

The polyurethane midsole wraps
up into the upper, especially in the
heel area, to cradle and assist in
stabilizing the foot on uneven
terrain.

▶**Product Name**	▶**Manufacturer/Supplier**	▶**Design Firm/Designer(s)**
Women's Walking Shoe	NIKE, Inc.	In house design/Pam Greene

Photo courtesy of NIKE, Inc.

▶Description

The women's air essential athletic walking shoe is an all-leather shoe with a lightweight Phylon™ midsole, which cushions the foot against the shock of impact through the heel. The low-profile, rubber outsole contributes to postural stability by offering the wearer traction and durability. The shoe is available in several widths and requires little break-in time.

▶Mobility

The soft leather contouring of the midsole cradles the foot and minimizes foot discomfort caused if stiffer material rubbed against the foot. It also helps stabilize the foot throughout the sequence of walking motions.

153

▶**Product Name**
Timex Easy Reader® Watches

▶**Manufacturer/Supplier**
Timex Corporation

▶**Design Firm/Designer(s)**
In house/J. Houlihan, J. Riley, J. Gazzola

Photos by Jon Van Gorder. Courtesy of Timex.

▶**Description**

Timex Easy Reader® Watches are designed for easy reading while maintaining their function as fashion accessories attractive to people of all ages.

▶**Vision**

People with less than 20/20 vision find the Easy Reader® collection very desirable. They can "read the time without their glasses." Large, black, clearly defined numerals and hands contrast with the clean white dials, enhancing legibility—particularly in low-light environments.

▶Product Name
Clear Solutions Calculator™

▶Manufacturer/Supplier
Zelco Industries, Inc.

▶Design Firm/Designer(s)
Not available

▶Description

This is the see-through calculator with the light touch. Clear Solutions features a light touch keyboard and large "no mistake" numbers, making it easy to use by those with manual or visual impairments. The calculator is powered by either daylight or artificial light, and there are no batteries to replace. A fold-out stand provides the right angle for desk operation.

▶Vision

The large, clean numbers are isolated from the background, reducing clutter and helping those with poor vision. The transparent plastic case allows the user to increase or reduce the contrast between the numbers and the background by placing the unit on an appropriately dark or light surface.

▶Touch

The flat surface with large numbers have eliminated the usual small, hard-to-push buttons. Heat from the fingers activates this calculator, making it ideal for people with arthritis or other hand dysfunctions.

Photo courtesy of Zelco Industries, Inc.

▶**Product Name**
AT&T Big Button Phone

▶**Manufacturer/Supplier**
AT&T

▶**Design Firm/Designer(s)**
Henry Dreyfuss Associates: Jack McGarvey, Partner; Al Tilley, Human Factors Specialist

▶**Description**
The AT&T Big Button Telephone is an ergonomically sensitive product that can accommodate a large population of users, including older adults. This design, and its various versions, has been mass marketed through AT&T for over 20 years.

▶**Vision**
The large, bold graphic numerals enable those with reduced vision to place calls easily. An added benefit comes from the numerical layout, which is identical in each set and easily memorized by blind callers who can also access the phone without the need for a braille template.

▶**Touch**
Those with tremor or other manual limitations require little accuracy or effort to locate or activate the large, touch-sensitive buttons.

Photo courtesy of Henry Dreyfuss Associates.

►**Product Name**
AT&T VideoPhone 2500

►**Manufacturer/Supplier**
AT&T

►**Design Firm/Designer(s)**
Henry Dreyfuss Associates: Jack McGarvey, partner, Michael Zambelli, associate, Johnathan Marks, designer

►**Description**

The AT&T VideoPhone 2500 is the world's first full-color motion videophone that works in any home in the United States. The phone sends and receives video calls over existing lines for the same price as regular voice calls and plugs into standard telephone outlets. The console features a regular touch tone telephone with an adjustable tilt and swivel camera to accommodate the image of callers of various sizes. Full-color caller images can be transmitted at 2–10 frames per second.

Photo by Johathan Marks. Courtesy of Henry Dreyfuss Associates.

►**Vision**

The miniature color camera provides a focus range from 1 to 9 feet with equal clarity on a LCD screen. The movement speed allows those with declines in vision to easily perceive caller images. A hinged module allows adjustment of the camera to improve viewing by those requiring closer access to the screen.

►**Hearing**

The video component allows hearing impaired users who depend on visual communication for lip reading and/or sign language to communicate. This method is better than current typewriter-like devices which are slow and can't transmit the important nuances of expression.

►**Touch**

The phone features easy-to-use contoured buttons for efficient dialing and a frequently called numbers automatic dial with a memory for up to 12 numbers.

►**Manual Handling**

A built-in speaker phone serves those not able to hold the receiver manually.

►**Mobility**

For the housebound, the videophone provides a welcome means of social interaction with the outside world. Particularly for older people, it provides an opportunity to "see" family members. It is also an invaluable tool for doctors, allowing them to maintain between-visit contact with patients, thereby personalizing the doctor-patient relationship.

▶**Product Name**
AT&T Public Phone 2000

▶**Manufacturer/Supplier**
AT&T

▶**Design Firm/Designer(s)**
Henry Dreyfuss Associates: Jack McGarvey, Partner; Al Tilley, Human Factors Specialist

▶**Description**
The wall-mounted AT&T Public Telephone 2000 is available nationally in airports, hotels, and various public domains. Accessed by major credit cards, it offers travelers a unique set of user-friendly, innovative services. The apparatus includes a color monitor that gives clear-to-understand, sequential automatic instructions in four languages, a teletype keyboard allowing access to remote databases, and a data port allowing connection of laptop computers/facsimile machines.

▶**Vision**
The 9-inch color monitor displays text and graphics in sizes that accommodate those with declining vision.

▶**Hearing**
The phone includes a telecommunications device for the deaf (TDD) accessibility, which allows the hearing impaired to communicate free of charge via keyboard with another person at a TDD. The phone is compatible with hearing aids, providing feedback-free service. Control buttons allow users to adjust volume by 20 decibels, 5 decibels at a time.

Photo courtesy of AT&T Archives.

▶**Manual Handling**
The screen and function buttons accommodate a large and varied user population in the same manner as automatic teller machines. Thus, buttons are labeled with an up and down arrow, enter/yes, and control/no enabling users to control feature selection.

▶**Mobility**
Certain modified versions of the telephone accommodate wheelchair users. Their lowered height, however, still permits use by the general population.

▶Product Name
A.R.T. Bar Code Scanner

▶Manufacturer/Supplier
Advanced Retail Technologies, Inc.

▶Design Firm/Designer(s)
Henry Dreyfuss Associates: James Ryan, partner; Chris Johnson, associate; Tor Bonnier, designer

▶Description
The bar code scanner is used to translate coded information and place merchandise orders by modem over regular telephone lines. Typically used by consumers to order items from catalogs, it offers entry into a two-way transaction-based information network designed for order processing and inventory management. A built-in printer furnishes instant written order confirmations, allowing consumers to always know the status of their order(s).

▶Vision
The bar code scanner eliminates the need for reading small-print catalogs and transferring complex merchandise details onto forms. The built-in printer gives instant product status data, eliminating the need for repetitive phone calls to customer service representatives.

▶Hearing
The scanner is ideally suited for those who are deaf or have a hearing impairment. Orders can be placed using the modem and confirmed in writing by the built-in printer. The entire process can be accomplished without any auditory interaction.

Photo by Mikio Sekito. Courtesy of Henry Dreyfuss Associates.

▶Manual Handling
The scanner is lightweight with a dimpled feature that facilitates gripping. Designed for either right- or left-handed use, the unit can be easily used by a broad spectrum of adults, including the aging population.

▶Mobility
This device offers individuals with mobility limitations the opportunity to continue making consumer purchases without leaving their home.

▶**Product Name**
Easylistening

▶**Manufacturer/Supplier**
Anderson Design Associates

▶**Design Firm/Designer(s)**
Anderson Design Associates:
Scott A. Johnstone

▶**Description**
The Easylistening radio/tape player was designed to provide an attractive, user-friendly method of keeping people informed and entertained. It addresses ergonomic issues frequently ignored by current radio styles, such as dexterity problems, vision impairments, and ease of operation. The Easylistening player removes the frustration felt by those whose functional abilities prevent them from easily using most radios or tape players.

▶**Vision**
The upright design enhances the visibility of the control displays, regardless of whether the user is standing or sitting. Users access the controls and displays logically, guided by their front-forward locations. Their contrasting colors, sizes, and shapes are easily perceived by those with limited vision.

▶**Touch**
Button shapes are designed to communicate symbolically; i.e., an arrow pointing forward is fast forward; a round red disk is stop, etc. General controls are differentiated by orientation: the on/off/volume lever moves up and down, while the tuner lever slides side to side. The different spatial levels of the controls provide an added tactile reference.

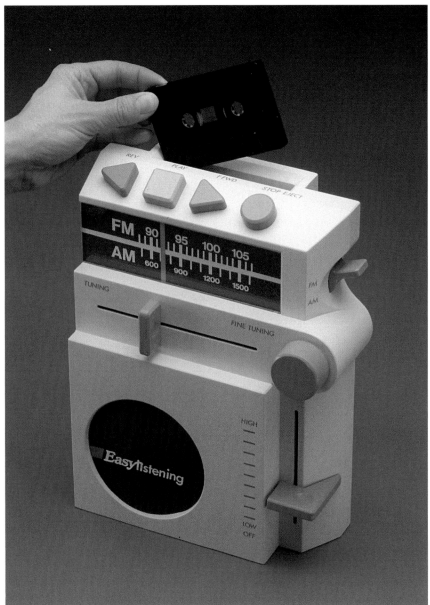

Photo by Dominic Caporale (for Autograph). Courtesy of Anderson Design Associates.

▶**Manual Handling**
The fine-tuning knob eliminates the repetitive twisting movements normally required to locate precise stations. The unit's easy-access tape player loads cassettes from the top, toaster style.

▶ **Product Name**
PosiTector 5000/6000

▶ **Manufacturer/Supplier**
DeFelsko Corporation

▶ **Design Firm/Designer(s)**
Cleminshaw Design Group:
Douglas Cleminshaw. In house:
Frank Koch, Leon Vanderwalk,
Rashid Aidun.

▶ Description

The PosiTector electronic gauge measures coating thickness. It features only two finger-sized buttons, replacing the complex array normally found on such devices. Sliding the dark cover exposes the probe and turns the instrument on. Placing the probe on a surface displays the measurement, storing it in memory for unloading later to a computer. Two buttons calibrate the reading, convert measurements, return the factory settings, and permit technicians to perform many calibration, test, and service functions.

▶ Vision

The unit's clean, functional appearance symbolizes the assurance of precision measurement, and ease of learning and use. The contrasting color used for the probe cover and buttons provide redundant visual cues, identifying the parts that actuate and control the instrument.

▶ Hearing

Audio cues from a high-pitched "beeper" alarm alert the user to inaccurate measurements.

▶ Touch

The adjustment buttons are marked with large, tactile + and − symbols. Tactile, raised-dot patterns on the probe cover and battery access slide identify the movable parts and assist one's grip. The probe-cover locks lightly into notched detents, establishing the cover's travel limits; and a V-notch in the probe-cover permits tactile centering on curved surfaces.

Photo by Rober Kent. Courtesy of Cleminshaw Design Group.

▶ Manual Handling

The PosiTector is comfortable to hold and easy to grip by a variety of hand sizes. The demands of a thumb-and-four-finger grip determined the unit's 25-mm central thickness and 22-mm at the edge. The case's swelling contour at the display area prevents the instrument from slipping through the fingers if the grip loosens slightly.

▶ Mobility

The unit is sized to fit into a shirt pocket, and a wrist strap provides physical and psychological security from damage by dropping. A leather pouch with a belt clip permits the user to easily carry or store the unit.

▶**Product Name**
LODEX™

▶**Manufacturer/Supplier**
Kevcor Limited

▶**Design Firm/Designer(s)**
In house design/Kevin Jameson,
Bill Goralski, Mark Beard

Photo by Bill Goralski. Courtesy of Kevcor Limited.

▶**Description**
Derived from the words "low" and "dexterity," LODEX provides a gateway opportunity to answer the fire safety needs of elderly and disabled people. Universally accessible, this first-of-its-kind manual fire alarm device may be configured for a variety of activating options, and can replace ordinary manual stations already installed without moving or repositioning the alarm system wires or hardware.

▶**Manual Handling**
The sculptured activator handles permit the alarm to be sounded with low-impact. Their unique design minimizes pinching, squeezing, and pulling. A choice of radial or pull down actions may be configured as single or double action to prevent false alarms, while enabling those with limited hand movement to activate the alarm.

▶**Vision**
The large, high-contrast lettering, visable from up to 75 feet away, helps draw attention to the unit and assists those with low vision during a time of great stress.

▶**Touch**
The ergonomically designed, molded plastic activator handles feature a nonslide surface. This redundant cue identifies them and prevents hands, wrists, or elbows from slipping upon activating. Their form symbolically communicates the action necessary for operating in the dark or by those with impaired vision.

► **Product Name**
Home Information System

► **Manufacturer/Supplier**
Zanussi/Zeltron

► **Design Firm/Designer(s)**
META.FORM design:
A Delser; M.A. and
R. Pezzetta

► **Description**
Developed with a user-centered approach, the interactive, user-friendly Home Information System connects the user to an information data base through a telephone line. This electronic device allows consumers to gain access to such services as home shopping, home banking, and message sending without having to leave the home.

► **Mobility**
Persons who are disabled or housebound are the target population for this domestic communications terminal, allowing them to gain access to certain activities of daily living without having to leave their home.

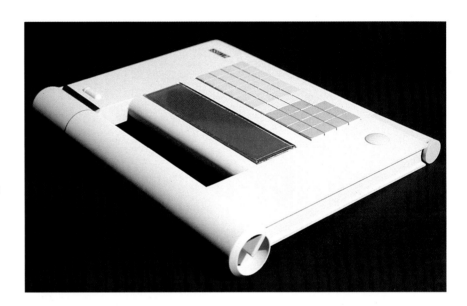

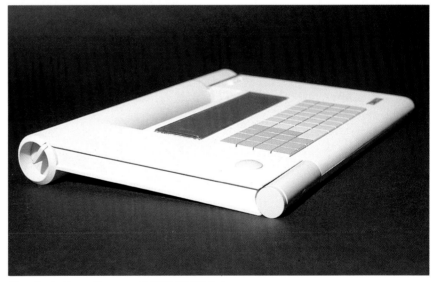

Photo by A. Vosca. Courtesy of META.FORM design.

▶**Product Name**
Driver Improvement Simulator

▶**Manufacturer/Supplier**
Doron Precision Systems, Inc.

▶**Design Firm/Designer(s)**
In house/Not available

▶**Description**
A realistic substitute for on-street driving, the Doron driver simulators bridge the theory and practice of driving. With Doron's L-300 System, trainees of all ages can practice hazardous driving situations safely and with a greater degree of realism, and develop the ability to recognize, analyze, and correctly respond to traffic situations. Those who are physically impaired or who have cognitive and perceptual deficits are likely candidates for the simulator.

▶**Vision**
A driver analyzer provides an accurate measurement for evaluating a driver's perceptual skills, reaction time, and threat recognition abilities. The visual evaluation aspects of the system are especially helpful to clients with visual scanning, visual attention, or visual field impairments.

▶**Touch**
Switches offer realistic feel, simulating actual operations.

▶**Manual Handling**
Tilt steering eases client transfer and improves their comfort during training and assessment. Assist grips provide ease of client transfer. A headlight dimmer and switch on column helps assess a drive's ability to use a column-mounted dimming device for headlights.

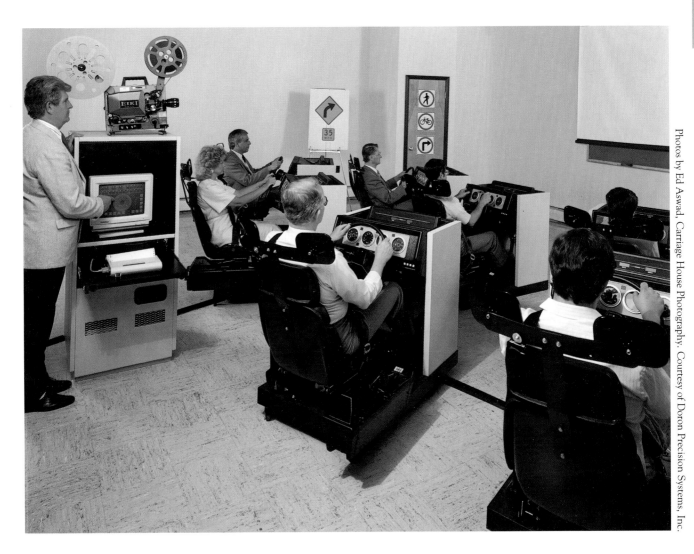

Photos by Ed Aswad, Carriage House Photography. Courtesy of Doron Precision Systems, Inc.

►Mobility

The system can help train those with decreased or lost mobility to become drivers. It identifies deficiencies which rule out the individual as a candidate for driving; evaluates whether an individual needs adaptive equipment and, if so, what type; and determines what therapy or training would help the individual improve his or her driving ability.

►**Manufacturer/Supplier**
Prince Corporation

►**Design Firm/Designer(s)**
Advanced Design Studio: Dave
Muyres, Scott Bainbridge

►Description

The average age of most full-size
and luxury vehicle owners is about
60 years. The Prince Corporation
uses this vehicle interior simulator
as a research tool to better
understand the wants and needs of
this group. Built to aid the
decision-making process, the
simulator is used by Prince
Corporation designers to mock-up
interior product proposals. It plays
a significant role in viewing and
testing design concepts in their
final three-position, thus ensuring
product receptivity across all ages.

►Vision

Such interior products as visors,
consoles, mirrors, and arm rests
are evaluated in the simulator to
see if they intrude into a driver's
cone of vision, and to minimize
the time a driver's eyes are
diverted from the road. The goal
is to simplify operations by
improving the legibility of graphic
displays and/or minimizing the
driver's need to see them.

►Touch

Designers investigate the
effectiveness of tactile feedback
(redundant cueing) to enhance
such nonvisual operations as
opening and closing windows,
operating the ventilation controls,
and adjusting the seat position.

►Manual Handling

Such mechanical devices as
buttons, knobs, handles, and
levers are evaluated for their
comfort, convenience, ease of use,
and simplicity of operation.

Photos by Jim Bielski. Courtesy of Prince Corporation.

►Mobility

The simulator's full-size offers an
opportunity to test the entrance
and egress requirements of a wide
range of drivers. To better
understand the particular needs
and limitations of older drivers,
designers frequently videotape
people between the ages of 55 and
80 years interacting with such
products as grab handles, center
arm rests, and sun visors.

▶Product Name
Lytestream (fluorescent lighting fixture)

▶Manufacturer/Supplier
Lightolier

▶Design Firm/Designer(s)
In house/Corporate design team

▶Description
Lytestream is a wall-mounted bathroom lighting fixture. Two 32-watt fluorescent lamps distribute light onto the face for grooming and throughout the room for a bright, glare-free ambiance. The fluorescent source features excellent color quality, is very energy efficient, and offers easy maintenance.

▶Vision
Lytestream delivers about twice as much light as conventional bath lighting. Its well-shielded indirect light source offers a comfortable glare-free environment that benefits those vision impairments.

▶Manual Handling
The lamps used in Lytestream have a rated life of 20,000 hours, producing a bright, diffused light with low energy cost. Their 4–5 year life expectancy minimizes changing manipulations by increasing the time between lamp changes. Their lack of heat build up protects those lacking thermal sensitivity from being burned while replacing lamps.

Photo courtesy of Lightolier.

▶**Product Name**
SARAH Reclining Chairs

▶**Manufacturer/Supplier**
Herman Miller, Inc.

▶**Design Firm/Designer(s)**
William Stumpf & Associates:
William Stumpf

▶**Description**

SARAH reclining chairs were designed to promote comfort, health, and relaxation. They also encourage work and activity, thereby supporting the vitality of older people. They permit "active rest"—the comfortable pursuit of activities while semireclined—by positioning the body ergonomically for useful long-term activity. They encourage participation in group activities and allow for solitary work or rest. These chairs can also be used with all or parts of the Sarah Accessory Group.

▶**Touch**

SARAH seating reduces unhealthful pressures on the intervertebral discs of the spine caused by long-term sitting.

▶**Manual Handling**

Manual controls allow the chairs to lock into a number of finite positions from upright to almost horizontal. The control also unlocks the chair and allows the user to readjust the chair's position. An adjustable shoulder pivot also locks into a finite number of positions designed to let the user support the upper body and head as desired.

▶Mobility

The designs maintain the ankle joint as the true center of rotation of the body as it reclines in spaces with the feet on the floor. Moreover, pressure under the leg normally experienced using a conventional rocking chair is eliminated. Unlike conventional rockers that rotate the arms with the torso, this chair rotates between fixed armrests.

▶**Product Name**
SARAH Accessory Furniture

▶**Manufacturer/Supplier**
Herman Miller, Inc.

▶**Design Firm/Designer(s)**
William Stumpf & Associates:
William Stumpf

Photos courtesy of Herman Miller, Inc.

▶**Description**
Designed for function, comfort, and convenience, the SARAH chair accessories are lightweight, rearrangeable furniture units designed to group around a recliner or lounge chair and support a person's activities—work or leisure. Used individually or in combination, these accessory pieces enable the user to create a personalized activities center, accommodating a wide variety of tasks including reading, writing, conversing, watching television, sewing, eating, and napping.

▶**Manual Handling**
The bookcase serves the limited range older people can reach as they sit in a chair. It provides storage for objects used in and around the chair: books, newspapers, knitting, bookkeeping materials, pens and pencils, magazines, clocks, radios, etc., keeping these objects close at hand and easily accessible.

170

▶Mobility

The convertible table provides a
stable surface on which to read,
write, or work while seated. It
functions as a side table or a work
surface pivoting across a person's
lap. This position reveals storage
compartments on the top of the
pedestal. Easily movable, both the
table and bookcase are lightweight
without compromising stability.

►**Product Name**
Relay™ Furniture

►**Manufacturer/Supplier**
Herman Miller, Inc.

►**Design Firm/Designer(s)**
Hollington Associates: Geoff
Hollington

Photo courtesy of Hollington Associates.

►**Description**

Relay™ is a comprehensive range of freestanding office furniture for building workstations in open plan offices and for private office environments. It has many unique features, particularly the fact that adjacent pieces do not connect mechanically, but simply dock together. Relay's flexibility addresses the needs of the entire working population, including the special needs of those disabled or elderly users.

►**Touch**

Relay furniture uses a diverse mix of materials and textures on details and surfaces to help users differentiate the various functions by touch.

►**Vision**

The tilting display surface at the rear of the high performance table desk enables users to assemble reference materials on a visual plane close to the user and at a comfortable angle, which reduces or eliminates disturbing glare from reflective surfaces.

►**Hearing**

Mobile folding screens offer temporary privacy—both visual and acoustical—reducing visual clutter and background noise. Offered in three heights, they can mark boundaries, diffuse glare from windows or on computer screens, or shut out distractions.

▶Manual Handling

Drawer pulls are substantial, full-width, ergonomic **D**-pulls, easily operated with one hand. All units are on large, smooth glides or castors for easy movement. Desk surfaces rise from 28 to 44 inches to accommodate a wide range of needs. The adjustment is a one-hand operation—simple, easy, and fast—requiring a minimum of effort.

▶Mobility

All units can move easily at a moment's notice. Relay furniture allows the user to configure—or reconfigure—the work environment quickly and easily to suit the idiosyncrasy of his or her individual requirements by pulling all required functions into easy reach.

▶**Product Name**
Honeywell T87F Round
"Easy-to-See" and
"Easy-to-Use" Thermostat

▶**Manufacturer/Supplier**
Honeywell

▶**Design Firm/Designer(s)**
In house/James A. Odom

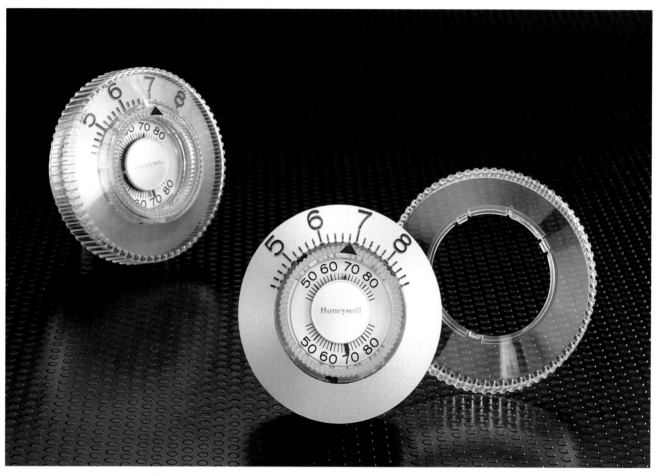

Photo courtesy of Honeywell.

▶**Description**

The Honeywell T87F Round
"Easy-to-See" Thermostat was
conceived in response to customer
requests for better visibility of the
set and room temperature scales.
The "Easy-to-Use" version was an
internal, human factors effort to
address the difficulties of
manipulating the control knob by
those with disabilities affecting the
hand and grip. The goal was to
produce a design based on an
existing product that minimized
costs and looked "normal" rather
than "adaptive."

▶**Vision**

The larger numerals on the
primary scaleplate; the
high-contrast oversize numerals on
the outer ring cover; and large
arrow pointer have eased the task
of setting and reading the
temperatures for the visually
impaired.

▶**Touch**

The oversize numerals on the
outer ring cover, along with the
associated indices, are
three-dimensional. This permits
the user to locate or set positions

by touch. Detents paired with
each index position provide tactile
feedback for users who may be
blind and who must rely on
counting the degree increments.

▶**Manual Handling**

The design features an extended,
coarse-knurled knob for secure grip
and precise setting control.

▶**Mobility**

The thermostat is wall-mounted,
normally at 60 inches above the
floor, but can be positioned lower
for wheelchair users.

▶Product Name
Helper

▶Manufacturer/Supplier
Anderson Design Associates

▶Design Firm/Designer(s)
Anderson Design Associates:
Robert L. Marvin, Jr., David
W. Kaiser

▶Description
The Helper combines the features of both a cane and a reacher. It provides an effective and easy-to-use reaching device, while serving as a stable means of support for anyone in need of mobility and extended-range assistance. The Helper combines a useful reaching device with a reliable support for walking, leaning, and rising out of chairs.

▶Vision
The form and placement of the simple trigger and lock controls ensures an easily operating reach function, while providing security and safety when used as a cane.

▶Touch
The comfortable, soft-skinned, foam handle is molded to fit the hand and designed to be ergonomically correct for either right- or left-handed use. The trigger grip is angled 15 degrees for easy use, and a full-hand-span trigger provides increased leverage.

▶Manual Handling
The Helper's light weight and padded handle helps those with limited hand strength to grip the handle effectively while walking or grasping objects outside their reach.

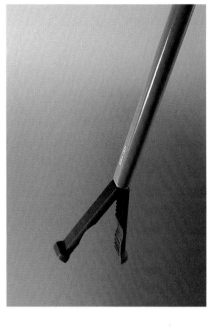

▶Mobility
The Helper restores the independent pursuit of daily living activities such as grasping objects outside the arm-span, lifting and supporting heavy objects without fully extending the arm, or eliminating stooping for items dropped on the floor. In case of overbalance or stumbling, the Helper becomes a cane simply by releasing the gripper jaws.

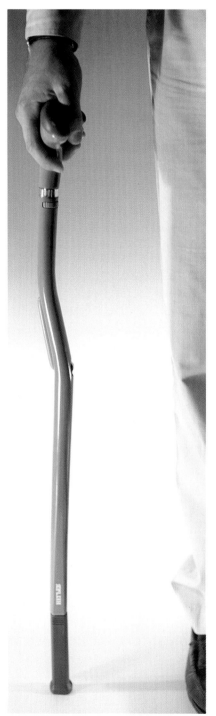

Photos by Richard J. Carbone. Courtesy of Anderson Design Group.

▶Product Name
A Living Environment to
Extend Elderly Independence

▶Manufacturer/Supplier
Research funded by Kohler Co.
and University of
Wisconsin–Stout

▶Design Firm/Designer(s)
University of Wisconsin–Stout
Design Research Center/
University of Wisconsin–
Stout students and faculty

▶Description
Six activity areas were identified
and investigated: cooking and
eating, private interest areas,
toileting and grooming, sleeping,
socializing, and water therapy. A
full-size demonstration model was
constructed and tested for varied
population segments. Although
intended to create an environment
that will encourage self-sufficiency
and independence for elderly
residents, evaluation results show
equal acceptability and enthusiasm
by younger age groups, including
primary school children.

▶Vision
Work surfaces are elevated and
incorporate high-level task
lighting. Controls are configured
to simulate functions and legends
are enlarged for ease of reading.
Low-level lighting illuminates the
floor for nighttime excursions.

▶Hearing
Carpeting, installed throughout
the environment, plus the
extensive use of various
sound-absorbing materials,
dampens the ambient noise level
and produces a quiet, soothing
environment.

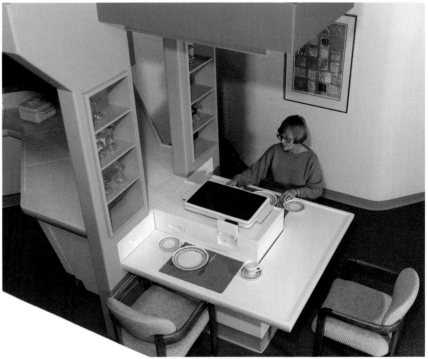

Photo courtesy of Martin Springer, University of Wisconsin–Stout.

▶Touch

Textured surfaces optimize the user's grasping and gripping capabilities. Smooth surfaces, used appropriately where soiling conditions normally occur, permit easy cleaning and maintenance. Surface burners were not incorporated into this concept, eliminating a variety of possible thermal hazards.

▶Manual Handling

The design minimizes the need for carrying objects. It locates storage areas for food and equipment adjacent to where such items are normally used. Users avoid lifting such heavy objects as cooking and serving vessels by sliding them across the counter's flush surfaces.

▶Mobility

Low-nap carpets and minimum thresholds are installed to help prevent tripping. Grab rails are integrated into wall surfaces and counter edges to offer stability when needed. Storage areas are located at fixed heights and eliminate climbing, stooping, and kneeling.

▶**Product Name**
Sew It

▶**Manufacturer/Supplier**
Anderson Design Associates

▶**Design Firm/Designer(s)**
Anderson Design Associates:
Robert L. Marvin, Jr.

▶**Description**

The *Sew It* makes hand sewing easier, especially for those with impaired or diminished eyesight, hand strength, or motor skills. This compact sewing kit combines a variety of features that make thread unrolling, cutting, needle-threading, and knot-tying easier and more enjoyable for those of any age or ability.

▶**Vision**

The cover lifts off for use as a free-standing, lighted magnifying glass for close work. The thread bobbins are organized and color-coded, making thread selecting easy. A high-contrast, bright-colored block provides a guide for a needle-threading device.

▶**Touch**

The magnifier's soft foam cover offers the user a sure grip. All other surfaces are smooth with gentle curves for easy, comfortable handling. Small pieces of Velcro capture the thread ends, which are easily seen and grasped.

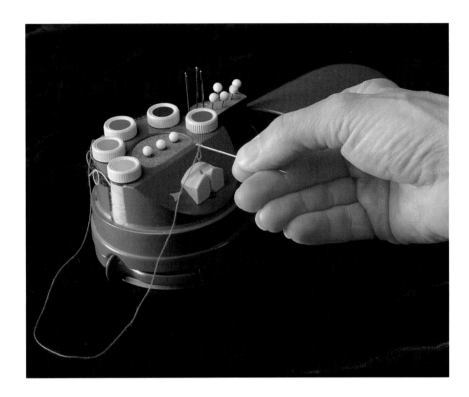

▶**Manual Handling**

The one-handed needle-threader simplifies a sometimes impossible task. It works by sliding a needle over a wire loop inside a bright yellow block, pushing the thread through the indicated path, and pulling out the threaded needle. A knot-tying guide works in a similar manner. Spring-loaded scissors with a larger gripping area are also included.

Photos by Dominic Caporale (for Autograph).
Courtesy of Anderson Design Associates.

178

▶**Product Name**	▶**Manufacturer/Supplier**	▶**Design Firm/Designer(s)**
Precedence™ Bath Whirlpool	Kohler Company	In house/Todd Dannesberg

▶Description

The Precedence™ Bath is a 24 inch deep bath/whirlpool with an easy-access water-tight door and multiple interior seating options. People with varying abilities of all ages can enjoy safe, independent bathing at home. Operation of the seating options and automatic sealing door is easy, even for those with limited strength and dexterity. And, unlike many products designed for those with different abilities, the style, design, and color options of the unit complement contempory home decor.

▶Vision

Color contrasting grab bar and door release button provide easy visual recognition of these critical functions for those with visual impairments.

▶Hearing

Several pumps capable of inflating the seal were examined. The designers rejected those that are ultraquiet, selecting instead one that emits a low-frequency rumble, which tells the user that the seal is inflated.

Photos courtesy of Kohler Company.

▶Touch

The bath floor is covered with a slip-resistant Ceramite coating, offering the user sure footing. The fold-down seat provides a textured surface which also helps prevent the bather from slipping. The bath's walls are smooth and generously curved, and prevent injuries to the bather by eliminating sharp edges.

▶Manual Handling

An automatic water level sensor and door sealing system minimizes the need for manual operation of these functions. A large push-button door-latch release eliminates the need for hand strength to open the door. For bathing, the user simply swings the door closed and the door latches automatically.

▶Mobility

The low height threshold allows for easy access to the bath. The integral grab bar aids the bather when choosing either the integral seat or the fold-down seat. The integral seat, fold-down seat, and deep soak position offer a wide range of options designed to meet a variety of ages, sizes, and physical abilities.

▶**Product Name**
Bedside Commode

▶**Manufacturer/Supplier**
Guardian Medical Sunrise, Inc.

▶**Design Firm/Designer(s)**
David Hodge Design: David
Hodge, Neil Goldberg, Dennis
Dressel/Guardian Medical
Sunrise, Inc: Eric Rose

▶Description

This molded composite bedside
commode has a pleasant
furniture-like form that blends
into the bedroom environment.
Designed with dignified forms and
clean lines, it introduces a new
aesthetic paradigm that respects
the user's humanity and dignity.
Challenging the assumption that
all medical equipment must look
institutional, the design benefits
equally young persons recovering
from surgery as well as the frail
elderly with ambulatory
difficulties.

▶Touch

The seat is ergonomically
contoured and angled, making it
comfortable for protracted periods.
For an infirm person distracted by
pain, discomfort, and loss of
independence, maintaining
dignity becomes essential to their
psychological and physical
well-being.

▶Manual Handling

The commode fits easily over a
standard or extended toilet bowl,
allowing the unit to be used as a
raised toilet seat. Ease of cleaning
and less strain while getting a
patient in and out of the
commode, provide additional
benefits to the caregiver.

▶Mobility

Armrests are raised in the front
and brought forward to provide a
firm "grip" within reach while
sitting and standing. Their
position helps elderly users pull
themselves off the commode
independently, thus minimizing
the need for assistance and
preserving their dignity.

Photos courtesy of David Hodge.

▶**Product Name**
The Dispenser™

▶**Manufacturer/Supplier**
Better Living Products, Inc.

▶**Design Firm/Designer(s)**
Not available

▶**Description**

The Dispenser™ provides a convenient method of organizing bathroom clutter and dispensing liquid personal care products safely, easily, and economically. The unit eliminates the hassle of cumbersome, environmentally unsafe plastic bottles, dropped bottle caps, elusive lids, and messy spills. Large 16-ounce chambers are easy to refill and allow the user to purchase larger, more economical sizes. Its clean, contemporary appearance complements any bathroom decor.

▶**Vision**

Round viewing windows continually indicate the level of solutions, informing the user when a refill is necessary.

▶**Touch**

The large push-buttons are easily located and operated by touch, benefiting those with visual impairments.

▶**Manual Handling**

One or two strokes on the smooth-working push-buttons release a premeasured amount of soap, shampoo, or lotion into the palm of the hand. The cover lifts up and stays up, allowing easy one-hand access for filling and cleaning.

Photo courtesy of Better Living Products, Inc.

▶**Mobility**

The Dispenser™ eliminates the bottle clutter and the necessity of stooping to reach dropped soap, shampoos bottles, etc. The unit is easily installed at a comfortable height and in a convenient location, accommodating a wide variety of user needs.

▶Product Name
Cushioned Insert for Bathtub

▶Manufacturer/Supplier
Diversified Fiberglass
Fabricators, Cherryville, NC

▶Design Firm/Designer(s)
Pascal Malassigne, James A.
Bostrom

▶Description

The full-sized Cushioned Insert for Bathtubs is designed to help maintain a stable seated position during bathing. The insert is safe, comfortable, and easy-to-use by persons who can walk, or transfer from a wheelchair, with or without assistance. Both the shape and design of the backrest provide a stable and secure sitting position for the user, allowing safe and easy bathing. The unit is also removable to allow conventional use of the bathtub.

▶Touch

The insert's nonslippery, cushioned surface provides comfortable seating and helps reduce the possibility of bruising the skin.

▶Mobility

With the proper placement of grab bars, the insert offers those with limited mobility, safe and easy access to a shallow bathing platform. When installed at wheelchair height, the unit fully supports and surrounds the body with a nonslip, padded surface.

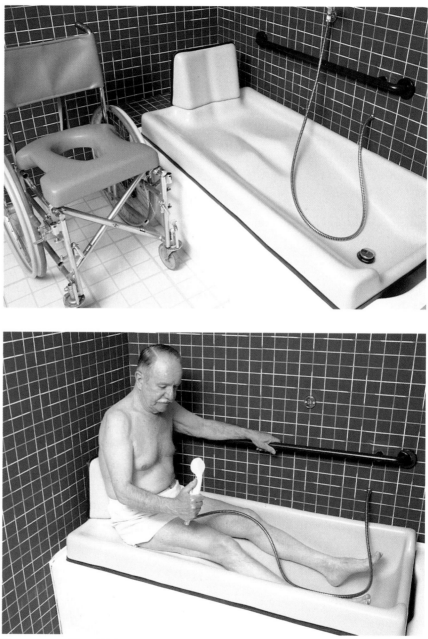

Photo courtesy of Pascal Malassigne.

▶**Product Name**
Wall-Mounted Seat for Showers

▶**Manufacturer/Supplier**
Diversified Fiberglass
Fabricators, Cherryville, NC

▶**Design Firm/Designer(s)**
Pascal Malassigne, James A.
Bostrom

▶**Description**

The Wall-Mounted Seat for
Showers is designed to facilitate
wheelchair transfer and help
maintain a stable seated position
while showering. Used with proper
placement of grab bars, the design
satisfies most critical concerns of
access for disabled or older people
including safety, sitting position,
and usage. The unit installs at
wheelchair height on either right-
or left-handed shower stalls, and
requires fastening to a reinforced
wall for safe usage.

▶**Touch**

The seat is cushioned with a
closed cell foam that provides a
nonslippery soft surface.

▶**Mobility**

The seat is designed to fully
support the user's body and
provides easy access for ambulatory
users as well as those in
wheelchairs. It is reached either
from a standing position or by
making a side transfer from a
wheelchair, with or without
assistance.

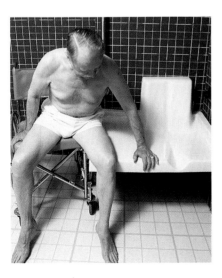

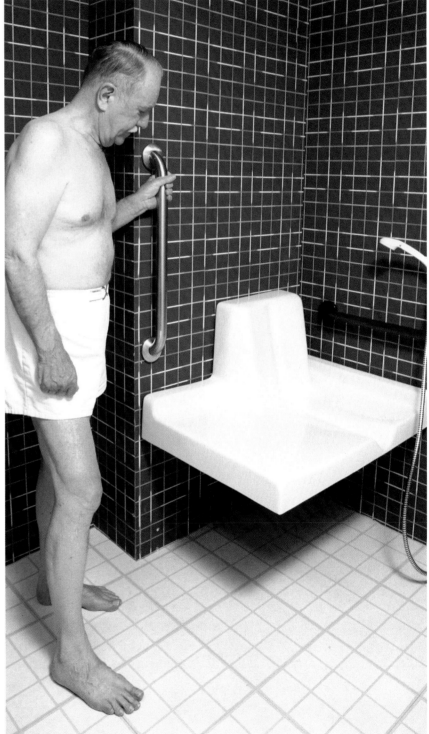

Photo courtesy of Pascal Malassigne.

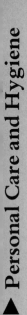
►**Product Name**
Metaform Personal Hygiene System

►**Manufacturer/Supplier**
Herman Miller Corporation

►**Design Firm/Designer(s)**
Design Continuum Inc.: Gianfranco Zaccai, principal designer; T. Dearborn, L. Pedraza, N. Dye, A. Ziegler, R. Miller, A. Rousmaniere, D. Porat

►**Description**

The Metaform system consists of a series of "activity nodes" (Upper Body Care—Sink; Elimination—Toilet; and Total Body Cleansing—Shower/Tub), which can be installed as an integrated system or independently to replace existing fixtures. Each node is a dynamic module designed to adjust rapidly to the needs of individual users within a household, offering features that accommodate and appeal to users of all ages and abilities. Patents on the system and its key features are pending.

Photos by Link Cornell. Courtesy of Design Continuum, Inc.

184

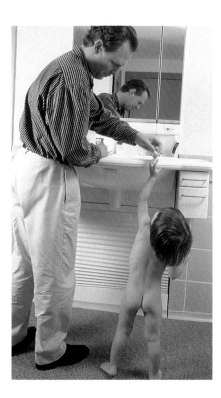

▶ Vision

The "water column" provides torchiere-type quartz halogen lighting to the room and shower. The sink node provides halo lighting from above and below the mirror. Lighting is also integrated into the toilet node. Shower and tub controls are solid state temperature control devices with large light emitting diode (LED) displays and color-coded directional arrows.

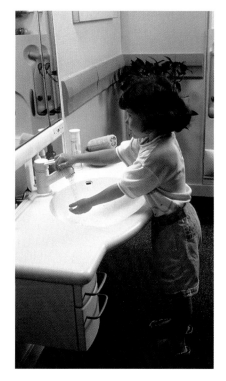

▶**Manual Handling**

The sink and toilet nodes adjust easily to accommodate the height of a standing or sitting user, allowing access by a small child, a tall adult, or a wheelchair user. The rail system and its accessories allow users to tailor the bathroom to fit individual needs and preferences. Accessories are kept off the floor to minimize stooping and facilitate cleaning.

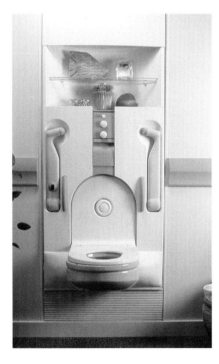

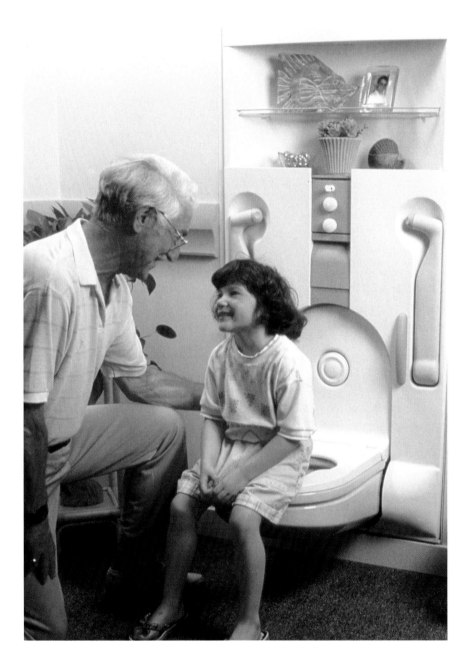

▶Touch

Controls are large elastomeric keys offering redundant tactile cues. The tub and sink modules feature soft resilient surfaces for comfort and safety. Controls for flushing the toilet and operating the bidet are activated by the elbow. A support bar system, featuring proprietary geometry with an outer layer of resilient foam, offers users a secure grip.

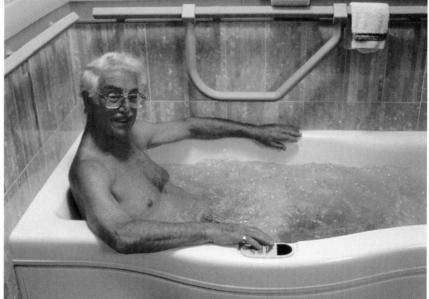

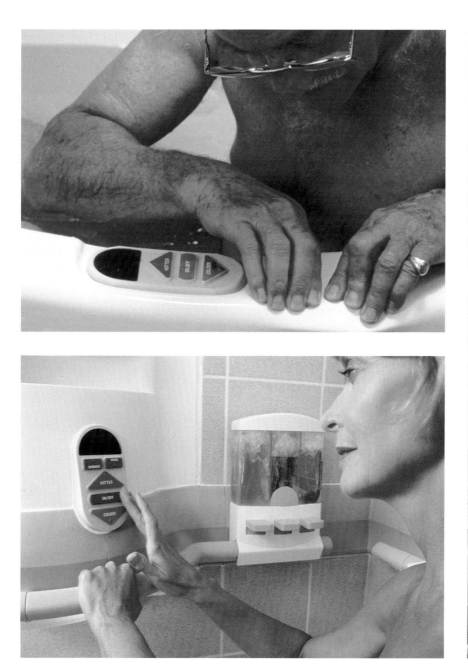

▶**Hearing**

A speaker phone and radio, integrated into the system's water column, also serves as an emergency call-for-help station.

▶Mobility

A patent-pending drain system that is flush with the floor makes the shower totally barrier-free. The toilet features fold-down arms for easier transfers and its height is adjustable. The rail system accepts a fold-down shower chair and/or a hydraulic transfer chair to facilitate safe transfer and more comfortable bathing.

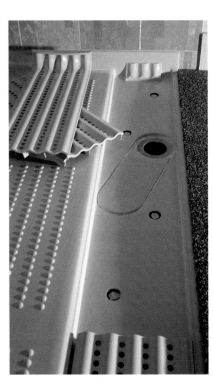

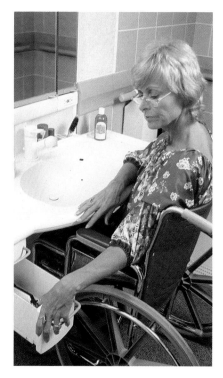

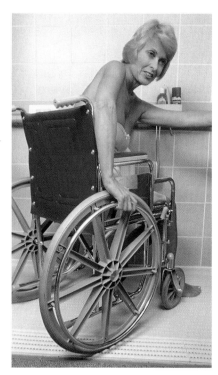

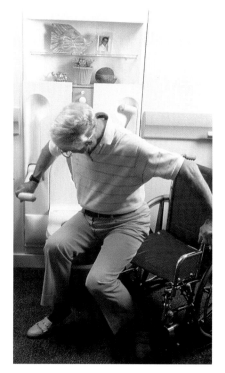

CASE STUDY

A Bathroom for the Elderly

Aging Factors, Design Evaluation Criteria, and a Design Proposal

Prepared for American Standard and the Center for Innovative Technology

Robert F. Graeff, principal investigator and program director

Len D. Singer, editor

Center for Product and Environmental Design

College of Architecture and Urban Studies
Virginia Polytechnic Institute and State University
Blacksburg, Virginia

Summary of Design Problems

As the elderly population in the United States continues to grow, the number of independently living elderly proportionately increases. Yet many of the most important facilities in the home environment have not been adequately resolved in terms of equipment and space to reflect this trend. These problems have received far too little attention, due in large part to the common minimum-cost approach to bathroom design. While today's bathrooms are, of course, a vast improvement over the "outhouse" of the past, they remain in many ways a place of unpleasant, if not harmful, experiences. Tiled wall and floor surfaces are cold and damp; dirt and bacteria collect in corners; floors are often slippery with few hand supports; there is usually no place to sit except on the toilet cover; and little or no provisions exist for removed clothing. These are but a few of the many problems in the bathroom today. In Alexander Kira's words, the average bathroom is "hopelessly antiquated and inadequate, and still consists of a miscellaneous assortment of oddly sized, unrelated and minimally equipped fixtures, with inadequate storage, counter space, lighting and ventilation" (Kira 1976).

Especially in the interests of the elderly and mildly handicapped, the customary bathroom environment poses crucial problems that need to be resolved. There are many more serious problems to cope with, which affect not only the elderly's comfort, but also their safety. Without adequate provisions for support, using the bathroom may cause slips and falls. Many elderly persons find it difficult to get up from the toilet. And the absence of stabilizing supports in the washbasin area causes problems to people with declining balance. A multitude of protrusions and sharp corners can lead to serious injury in case of falls. Fixture controls are often confusing and difficult to use, especially for those with arthritic hands. The usually overstocked and disorganized medicine cabinet provides insufficient space for the many needed supplies. Lighting is often poor and no provisions are made for emergency calls. Access to the shower/tub unit is not only inconvenient, but also unsafe.

For the elderly, the conventional bathroom presents unique problems unappreciated by the younger population. Older people have difficulty finding their way through corridors at night to the bathroom. Lights must be turned on in the dark, slippers and robe must be found—all of which usually happens several times at night. For those not living alone, privacy is another important consideration. To an older person, the risk of encounters with others in the hallway leading to the bathroom, ungroomed or without dentures, can be most embarrassing. And the usual time pressures of the family's morning rush to the bathroom further add to the problems. Indeed, privacy and safety hazards are too often the chief reason for premature institutionalization of an aged parent.

To design a bathroom to respond to these various needs requires an innovative approach that utilizes new spatial and technological resources. Refurbishments in existing homes, both rural and suburban, usually imply adding space. In urban dwellings it is more often a problem of reallocating the preexisting area to newly defined functions, as space is usually a more serious problem than cost. In any event, if a personalized facility is to be added, it should be a compact integrated facility, requiring a minimum amount of construction change in the home.

The bathroom design, satisfying these conditions and needs, is a modular retrofit unit offering the most spatial flexibility and greatest economy for both present and future needs of the population. The low space and cost requirements of the unit make it possible to install the complete bathroom facility within a modified utility wall closet. Visually and dimensionally it could be integrated into the environment much as a wardrobe closet with separating sliding doors. In this manner, the addition of a personal bathroom facility in the home does not require a separate room. For practical reasons, such a unit should be installed in the bedroom. If this is not possible, the adjacent hallway or closet could be a workable alternative. While this design focused primarily on the needs of the able-bodied and mildly handicapped elderly, it offers excellent application also for the wheelchair-bound population.

The proximity to the soft, dry environment of the bedroom provides the user with the most comfortable setting to towel dry and dress. The user may approach the bathroom facility in any state, undressed and in privacy. This immediacy provides a welcome comfort since the hygiene facility is the first need in the morning and the last before bed. All functions can occur with the least amount of interference in the family unit. From a medical standpoint, incontinence and chronic diseases such as diabetes and urinary system disorders have high prevalence among the elderly and cause frequent urination. With an ill or convalescent user, this proximity of the bathroom is a true asset, especially at night. Since only 20 percent of the elderly suffer from no chronic limitation to their mobility, reducing travel distance from bed to the facility becomes an important design prerequisite (Kleeman 1981).

▶ DESIGN OBJECTIVES

With the overall objective to provide maximum safety, privacy, greater comfort and efficiency in the use of the bathroom, especially for the independently living elderly, the following requirements are incorporated into the final design proposal:

- ▶ Access to the functional units at all times
- ▶ Short distance from the sleeping facility to the fixtures
- ▶ Sanitation facilities accessible in absolute privacy
- ▶ Support guides available throughout the entire space
- ▶ Skidproof flooring material
- ▶ Abundant storage space for medicines and special supplies
- ▶ Enclosed storage and open counter space
- ▶ Shallow, splash-free washbasin with distinct, positive controls
- ▶ Spacious shower booth (with room for an assisting person)
- ▶ Provisions for relaxed seating in the shower/bath
- ▶ Equipment for perineal cleaning
- ▶ Generous space for toweling dry and for dressing
- ▶ Effective lighting and ventilation

Of the user-oriented factors, safety, prompt accessibility, and privacy are the most important. These are design-specific and build on the research findings from the study of the behavioral, physical, and psychological characteristics of the aged which resulted in the following set of primary guidelines:

- ▶ Edges clearly visible
- ▶ Falling hazards minimized
- ▶ Provision for emergency access and escape

▶ Provisions for outside emergency help

▶ Surface temperatures comfortable to touch

▶ Sharp edges and corners minimized

▶ Air temperature comfortable to wet skin

▶ Use of room with minimum acute bending

▶ Equipment instructions explicit

▶ Controls easy and positive to use

▶ Surface glare minimized

▶ Light intensity and quality variable to task

▶ Color and lighting contrast for safety

▶ Cleaning and maintenance effort minimized

▶ Minimum of hazardous protrusions

▶ Circulation pathways unimpeded

▶ Maximum audible privacy

▶ Active storage within normal reach

▶ Visual and tactile distractions minimized

▶ Body supports and guides properly secured

▶ Provisions for seating

▶ Traditional/cultural features preserved

▶ Special attention to female needs

▶ Avoidance of spatial distortions

The above factors clearly point to the necessity to consider the hygiene facilities as a functional entity, rather than, as Kira so aptly put it, "a collection of pieces, the assembly of which is left to the whim of a first-cost conscious builder."

▶ SOLUTION PROPOSAL

The following is a narrative description of the design proposal. Refer to the assembly drawing for dimensional and spatial reference.

Toilet, wash basin, and shower are the three traditional sanitary fixtures to be integrated in the new sanitation facility. It is important that

Functional Variations of Concept V

these fixtures maintain their basic conventional features to enable the elderly to encounter minimum difficulties in adapting to new technologies. On condition that the toilet seat and the lavatory are installed at proper height, these fixtures serve their functions adequately well. Thus, a development effort based on careful attention to the spatial relationship between products and user, with the inclusion of distinctive formal adjustments where required, appeared to be a promising approach for design.

The use and the service area around the sanitary fixtures and storage spaces determined the overall dimensions of the facility. Consequently, the sphere of movements of the user and the functional relationship of the fixtures, added to the necessary dimensions required for the plumbing wall, determined the inner dimensions of the enclosures.

The toilet/sink enclosure and the shower enclosure, when arranged in line, result in an overall interior length of 129 1/2 inches (10 feet 9 1/2 inches) and require an inner width of 39 inches (3 feet 3 inches). The two enclosures are too large, however, to be transported through standard doors and hallways in the home, and must therefore be assembled as a modular component system on site. The modular approach permits more flexibility, so that both units may be installed along a bedroom wall, or they may also be positioned separately, depending on the spatial constraints of the home. As the examples demonstrate, the facility's length may be extended to fit

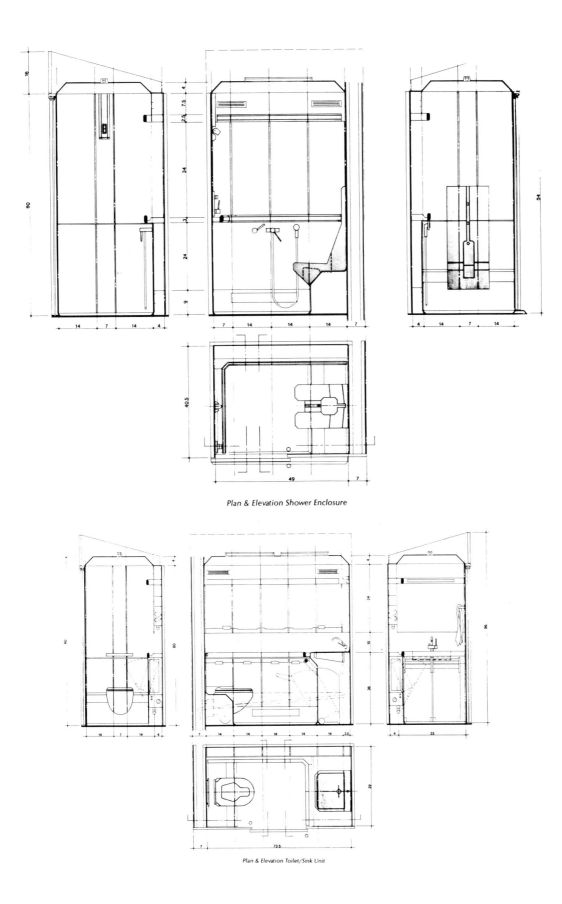

Plan & Elevation Shower Enclosure

Plan & Elevation Toilet/Sink Unit

Figure A–1 Front view of facility with entrance sliding-doors opened. The fixtures remain unexposed. Photo: Courtesy of Robert F. Graeff.

Figure A–2 Full scale appearance model of bathroom facility. This utility closet can be retrofitted in bedrooms for immediate access. (Facility with sliding doors removed.) Photo: Courtesy of Robert F. Graeff.

the room by incorporating a clothing closet with identical sliding door modules where space permits. Minor room length adjustments can be accommodated in changing the width of the plumbing wall module. The resulting space in the enclosures has been divided to form a number of equally sized modular panels for both units. Prefabrication and coordinated modularity of all parts determined the desired arrangements of the interior space, storage units, fittings, plumbing, electric and air-duct connections. This prefabricated, integrated facility achieves a rationalization and precision unmatched by the customary "minimum-first-cost" approach in custom building.

To summarize, the problem statement formulated for the design of a bathroom for the elderly was

> A modular bathroom facility with carefully planned, task-oriented arrangements of fixtures and spaces, integrated body support equipment, storage, lighting and ventilation, requiring least amount of change in the home. This facility was designed to meet the particular spatial and user needs of the aged.

▶ LIMITATIONS

In considering the disadvantages of such a design concept, users may feel some discomfort in the awareness of sleeping in the same room with the toilet, the drains, and associated possible odors. This could be disturbing and must be considered. If, however, the fixtures are not visible, even with open access doors, this would alleviate much of the problem. Consequently, it is important that the front wall panels of the bathroom unit appear neutral and attractive, as they are fully exposed and form one wall surface of the bedroom. An effective ventilation system, planned to serve the entire bedroom to create and maintain the desired air quality, must be integrated within the facility. The installation of the 3- or 4-inch drain pipes from the toilet syphon through the house into the central plumbing core and vents can be difficult and costly. In order to be independent of these large pipe gravity flow plumbing installations, the inclusion of a toilet waste disposal grinder, such as a recent introduction in Sweden and the United Kingdom, is recommended. This toilet disposal system pumps the waste water through 3/4-inch discharge pipework, which consequently allows for a much greater freedom in placing (retrofitting) the bathroom unit at any location and level in the home. The combined facility requires only one fresh water and one waste water access line, which is far more economical than other choices of custom retrofitting individual pieces.

Figure A–3 The front ledge aids to pull oneself up and facilitates posture support. Photo: Courtesy of Robert F. Graeff.

▶ SUPPORT BARS AND GUIDES (TOILET/SINK UNIT)

On entering the proposed closet-bathroom facility, the natural response is to first steady oneself before opening the sliding door. To that end, a vertical grab-pole is positioned to the right, directly in front of the sliding door into the enclosure. Moving the door requires a stable position. The user can step into the facility while holding on to the pole and stands now at the toilet, or, after one further step, directly at the lavatory. For the removal or adjustment of clothing, and for lowering and raising of the body weight from the toilet seat, an identical grab-pole is positioned inside the enclosure next to the toilet. A continuous horizontal body support guide in the form of a wooden ledge in front of the counter shelf runs inside both enclosures from one end to the other at a height of 36 inches, and visually combines the two units. A finger space gap of 1 1/2 inches permits the hand to comfortably hold on to the ledge.

The portion of the ledge in front of the lavatory is within reach from a seated position and encourages the toilet user to stretch forward and hold on without fear of falling over in front. Stretching of the upper body helps many users in the elimination process while they assume a comfortable semisquat position. This ledge also aids the seated user to pull himself up and forward, back into standing position at the lavatory. It further provides support to lean against with minimum risk of wetting the clothing at the sink while the hands are under the water stream. It is a safe and comforting provision for aging individuals who experience loss of equilibrium and balance.

An additional support guide is installed overhead at 70 inches within easy reach, above the medicine cabinet. The least amount of energy is expended by holding on from above. This is especially helpful when reaching up to find and identify medicines. These two-level body guides offer stability and firm support in any position.

The ledge along the counter level also serves as a protecting barrier to prevent objects from tipping off the free access shelf. This minimizes the risk of falling hazards and dizziness from bending over. The support bars are warm to the touch and do not protrude into the normal range of movements. Special care was taken to prevent any prosthetic or institutional appearance. Pronounced stainless steel grab bars such as seen in convalescence homes promote a sense of incapacity which is embarrassing in one's home and constantly refers to one's gradual aging. Both the body guides and the support poles have been integrated into the design with great care as a natural and unobtrusive part of the entire facility.

► SUPPORT BARS (SHOWER UNIT)

A variety of different body positions with off balance washing motions must be supported and secured in the shower enclosure. The two wooden horizontal support guides of the toilet/sink unit continue in the shower enclosure at the same height levels, 36 inches and 70 inches, as exemplified elsewhere. Two vertical grab poles, similar to the ones positioned at the entrance in the toilet/sink unit, are installed at the inside and outside of the sliding door of the enclosure.

► STORAGE

To sustain adequate, organized storage of one's supplies is as difficult as it is desirable. More classified storage space is required to facilitate better product arrangement.

The primary complaint among the elderly in a case study was lack of storage space in the bathroom. In fact, there is an overwhelming need for functional storage especially for the elderly, because of their decreasing

health and increased need for medications and related supplies. Similarly, Kira (1976) states that proper storage is an item of major concern, and "probably represents the single greatest shortcoming in present-day bathrooms." Most conventional bathrooms have only one medicine cabinet which is normally overstocked and completely inadequate to accommodate the great variety of prescription medicines, drugs, personal care appliances, grooming items, and sanitary supplies which accumulate, and are for practical reasons stored in the bathroom.

In considering the criteria for appropriate access to the stored items four primary guidelines for design were established.

▶ Optimal visibility and reach of contents

▶ Avoidance of storage density

▶ Avoidance of need for acute bending

▶ Proper place for support (especially when hand is raised)

The proposed solution incorporates four different kinds of storage, with both open and enclosed access space for a large variety of product items which must be accommodated and organized strategically.

Figure A–4 Wide wall cabinets for superior visibility. (Magnifying provision not yet installed). Both counter top and overhead support ledge (grab bars) are unobtrusively integrated to prevent prosthetic appearance. Photo: Courtesy of Robert F. Graeff.

▶ WALL CABINETS (ENCLOSED STORAGE)

For prescription medicines, drugs, dentures, grooming supplies, etc. Items in densely packed medicine cabinets are difficult to see and are in constant danger of falling, when touched by a searching hand. Broken glass and cut hands and the need to bend over to retrieve the items often result. For maximum visibility and access, the contents of the proposed cabinets are spread in full length of the enclosure on shallow shelves over five 14-inch module cabinets.

A major safety problem confronting elderly users is the proper recognition of medicine labels. Often print is so fine that even young adults have trouble reading it. For the elderly, this is of particular aggravation because of poor eyesight and frequently misplaced glasses. It is an alarming and dangerous reality that taking medicine is often based on memorizing a container's shape, color, or its storage place.

To solve this potentially dangerous problem, a Plexiglas magnifying bar in front of the cabinet shelves protects contents from falling and most importantly renders obscure print readable. This magnifying shield is suspended by two height adjustable levers for adaptation to different labels.

Dimensions: 14 inches wide (modular axis), 24 inches high, 4 inches deep.

Figure A–5 Inner container of base cabinet brings contents within visibility and reach without the need to bend over. Photo: Courtesy of Robert E. Graeff.

▶ BASE CABINETS (ENCLOSED STORAGE)

To accommodate sickroom supplies, bedpan, sanitary supplies, heating pad tissues, soaps, and cleaning equipment.

Traditionally, base cabinets such as in kitchens require the user to bend over or stoop to see and reach the stored items. However, these motions are difficult for the elderly, often causing imbalance or attacks of dizziness. The proposed base storage cabinets make the contents easily accessible, so that the prime storage space under the counter top can be brought to practical application.

Storage cabinets below the counter top are fitted with opening doors hinged at the bottom. They additionally provide upward protruding integrated containers for conveniently accessible contents without requiring the users to bend over.

Dimensions: 14 inches wide (modular axis) doors 24 inches high, 6 inches deep.

A special base-storage cabinet, comfortably accessible from a seated position is provided next to the toilet for items such as ointments, rubber gloves, suppositories, etc.

These storage facilities encourage organized placement of one's medications and supplies in this concentrated bathroom facility, rather than having them spread widely over the house.

Figure A–6 Inner container within base cabinet brings contents within easy reach. Photo: Courtesy of Robert F. Graeff.

▶ COUNTER TOP SHELVES (OPEN ACCESS)

An adequate, well-lit counter space is provided at 36 inches height for items of daily use such as lotions and perfumes, deodorants and tissues. The adjacent "wet deposit" area around the sink extends directly from the counter top.

Dimensions: 73 1/2 inches long and 4 inches deep (excluding the open space to the ledge).

▶ REMOVABLE BINS

Located under the lavatory are two receptacles for dry trash and for soiled laundry. Both containers can be tipped out for access and wheeled out of the unit to avoid having to carry the contents to the washing machine or garbage cans.

▶ MOTION OF CABINET DOORS

Wall cabinets: the two cabinet doors at the end of the enclosure are hinged sideways and open without risk to the user to bump the head when washing hair or rising from the toilet. The three cabinets in the center have upward-sliding tambour doors to avoid interference with the normal range of movements.

▶ PULLS AND HANDLES

The pulls and handles are designed to visually inform the user of the direction in which to move the door. The pulls above the countertop suggest to bend the finger downward, while the pulls below the counter suggest to turn the hand with the fingers bent upward to open the cabinet doors.

While secured or locked storage space is important for items one wishes to keep private, especially in family households with children and occasional guests, it is not essential for the independently living elderly. The possibility of misplaced keys in an emergency could have serious implications. Secured storage is therefore not recommended for this bathroom facility.

▶ TOILET

Seat Height

Accepting the concept of the conventional water closet as we know it, the aspect of seat height, steady support, and safe transfer from a standing position onto and off the seat, posed two main design considerations. The most significant difference in seat height requirement is between men and women. However, since there are more than four times as many older women than men who live alone, and older people of both genders are shorter than younger people, the suggested seat height is below the common geriatric level. Even though it is generally recommended to elevate the toilet seat by 2 or 3 inches for the elderly populations because of their difficulties in coping with low seating, it is desirable from a physiological standpoint to design the seat to encourage a tendency to lean forward and draw one's feet back to facilitate the elimination functions. As physicians agree, the natural posture to encourage defecation is the squatting position. An ideal seat would place the body in the position naturally assumed. While a very low seat cannot seriously be recommended for older people who have difficulties bending their knees, it is nevertheless suggested (with some exceptions) to keep the toilet seat below the 16 inch level. "Sedentary living habits, changes in diet and diminished muscle strength frequently result in constipation" (Kira 1976). For the aged, this problem often requires prolonged sitting. If the toilet seat is higher than 16 inches it will exert pressure under the thighs, impede blood circulation and ultimately result in legs "falling asleep." A lower seat helps avoid these circulation problems while encouraging a posture to aid the body's natural mechanisms.

To maximize the support area under the thighs, a slightly concave cross section of the seat is suggested. Also, for better comfort and easier hand access to the perineal region, a longer seat aperture would be a clear improvement above the common 10- to 12-inch longitudinal apertures.

Conclusion: As the research findings of I. McClelland (1982) also support, the suggested seat height above floor is 15 3/4 inches or 40 cm.

Body Support

The central challenge in designing the water closet was to find ways for a safe and comfortable transfer from the seat to a standing position. Instead of simply providing a higher seat for reasons mentioned earlier, different means are offered to aid the user in lowering and raising himself or herself safely. It is worth noting that a moderate degree of physical activity is beneficial for all users, especially for the independent living elderly whose life styles tend to be sedentary. The ledge in front of the lavatory functions as an integral part of the toilet, supporting the user to pull himself or herself up. It also encourages the user to assume a healthier posture. In addition, the immediacy of the body guide along the countertop, the vertical pole next to the toilet and the flat surfaces on the sides of the seat, all induce steadiness and facilitate safe transfer.

Special Features

The control bar of the flush mechanism is placed at shoulder height above the toilet and can be operated from a seated or standing position. A long and shallow water flush tank is mounted high inside the plumbing wall.

Next to the toilet seat, a special provision dispenses toilet paper or moist tissues. The mechanism is mounted within the bench-like container which supports the porcelain bowl and seat.

Ventilation

Apart from the general ventilation of both enclosures by means of a central fan unit placed in the plumbing wall, there is a separate air intake inside the toilet bowl. The same pipework which serves the water flush into the bowl also serves to draw air out. This negative airflow at the source prevents odors from escaping into the environment. The air is driven into the central fan unit to continue its way by separate ducts into the vent system of the house.

Cleanability

Strict avoidance of "dirt corners" and creases greatly facilitates the unpleasant task of cleaning the toilet. Access under the toilet bowl, bench, and floor is possible from a seated position. All surfaces and transitions can be wiped without effort, preferably with a sponge soaked in a disinfectant solution.

Lavatory

The washbasin is the most frequently used fixture in any traditional bathroom. It should be accessible for recurring use and it should be much more comfortable than the norm we have accepted. Almost without exception, lavatories are mounted too low, so that the body is forced to bend over lightly. This causes a tiresome posture which cannot be sustained at length. As tests have indicated, the body should stand erect in a relaxed position with the upper arms vertical and with the forearms extended horizontally (Kira 1976). During the wetting and rinsing process, the hands are generally held slightly lower to prevent the water from running toward the elbows. It has been determined that the most comfortable working height of the hands for the average population is at 38 inches with the water source approximately 4 inches above, at 42 inches. For the preferable counter top installation, the lavatory and its related surfaces should be mounted in the 34- to 38-inch range. This height is particularly beneficial for the elderly, helping to prevent dizzy spells when bending over. The basin itself should be shallow in order to keep the height of the working surface and the surrounding counter top in a natural relationship to the user's arms.

The proposed lavatory is integrated into the counter top facing the toilet at a height of 36 inches. The opening of the basin is 18 inches wide; it is 15 inches from front to back, and only 4 inches deep. The water source is 42 inches above the floor level with the arc reaching well into the center part of the basin.

To prevent the water from splattering, a nose-shaped rim was integrated along the water path of the shallow lavatory to direct the spray into the basin. This self-rinsing action provides a continuously washed sink surface, reducing the need for deliberate cleaning of residue from make-up, toothpaste, and the like. The countertop surrounding the sink serves as wet deposit area for dental hygiene items, shaving equipment, brushes, wet washcloths, etc. The distinction between "dry" and "wet" allocation of grooming items is real, helping to keep supplies better organized while facilitating upkeep.

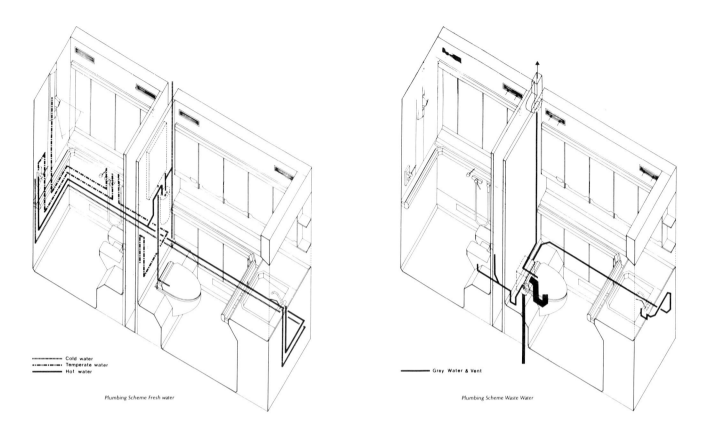

Cold water
Temperate water
Hot water

Plumbing Scheme Fresh water

Grey Water & Vent

Plumbing Scheme Waste Water

Water Controls

Although beyond the scope of this project, water supply controls must be designed to be safe and self-explanatory, simple and direct to use. For the wash basin it would be desirable to provide a fixture that would be operated by one hand only. Lever like controls are easier to grasp and more comfortable to operate with soapy hands than wheel-type faucets. However, a single lever, dual-control for temperature and water pressure such as is now common, tends to complicate the operative motions, requiring temperature adjustments while in use. A proposed solution is a device requiring one single movement to control water pressure only, while the temperature is determined by a preset thermostat. A second, smaller lever with a distinct temperature display would link to the thermostat. The two levers may be operated by one hand sequentially, or with both hands simultaneously, depending on which side of the fixture the levers connect. The larger water pressure lever extends at the side of the spout forward, to prevent having to reach through the water stream. The drain of the sink could be equipped with a removable strainer to eliminate the traditional stopper, as it is rarely ever used and would complicate the fixture.

These suggestions make it clear that a separate study is needed to analyze, research, and design new contemporary water supply controls, for use especially by the aged.

Special Features

Another suggestion is to provide a liquid soap supply to avoid the hazard of having to bend over to retrieve a slippery, wet soap bar from the floor. An integrated soap dispenser should squirt the soap in front of the lavatory into the sink cavity to prevent soap drops from remaining on the countertop.

An electrically heated towel bar, capable of suspending at least two medium-sized hand or face towels, shall be placed above the lavatory on the right, for immediate access.

Lighting and Mirror

A warm, incandescent task light above the mirror illuminates the entire lavatory module. It would be desirable to equip this light source with a dimmer to avoid blinding the eyes at night. This lavatory light, however, must also be adjustable to provide appropriate illumination to serve the make-up functions and for shaving.

Shower Enclosure

The showering process is the most common and the safest form of body cleansing for elderly people. Regrettably, a common problem with the shower is a lack of comfort due to prolonged standing, inadequate clearance for the various washing operations, and absence of support. Another problem the elderly encounter with the shower is lack of sufficient deposit areas for soaps, shampoos, lotions, and washcloths. Poor lighting and ventilation also contribute to an unpleasant environment for the undressed user. Further complications include inoperable water controls, especially for the wet arthritic hand, which introduces the risk of scalding oneself or slipping on a wet soapy floor. This design proposal addresses these problems and introduces some integrated unique features for improved comfort and safety.

The dimensions of the proposed shower enclosure are based on the required space for the essential washing motions, such as wetting, soaping, massaging, and rinsing. This includes the comfortable washing of the feet, and space for an assisting person.

Aspects of safety and comfort were of prime concern. Since the main orientation of the user is toward the water source and the shower enclosure has a rectangular configuration, the water source and the shower seat are positioned along the axis of the water stream. The inner dimensions of the shower enclosure are 3 1/2 modules × 2 1/2 modules, or 49 inches × 35 inches. The width above the open access shelve (36 inches above floor) extends by 4 more inches to 39 inches. A low barrier 3 inches in height is provided at the entrance to contain the water of the shower spray. An effective drain is placed under the shower seat, equipped with an angular overflow aperture to prevent water spillage, insofar as soap, residue, and hair collect at the drain.

Remote Control Shower Head

In traditional units shower users must move in and out from under the water stream to expose different parts of the body to the spray. These actions require additional access space into which the user can move to get out of the water stream.

To minimize the gross movements of the aged user, a new concept of a remote control shower head has been introduced. Rather than requiring the user to move in and out of the water flow, the angle of the water stream can be changed during operation without touching the shower head. For example, this allows a user to instantly redirect a cold or scalding stream away from himself or herself, which is a much safer maneuver than jumping out of the stream, and much faster and safer than readjusting the water controls to stop or moderate the flow. It also allows a more comfortable testing of the water temperature, if no separate spout is provided. This provision helps to reach selected body parts, leaving the hair dry if desired. It also allows the user to move the spray in an alternate swinging motion up and down the back. The addition of a vigorously pulsating water spray offers means for wholesome therapeutic massage. The control lever to move the shower head is located just under the support guide within comfortable reach from a standing or seated position.

The water pressure and temperature control for the shower head, located at the entry, can easily be reached from the inside and outside of the enclosure for adjustments. A reliable thermostat, capable of presetting a desired temperature, can govern all water sources in the shower enclosure.

Shower and Bidet Seat

Though showering is a more efficient, faster, and safer activity than bathing, it cannot offer the same relaxing comfort of the tub bath which unfortunately creates serious problems for the aged when getting in and out of the tub. This proposal offers an intermediate solution, combining the comfort of the bathtub with the accessibility of the standing shower. It provides a restful shower seat which allows one to sit in a passive and relaxed position, leaning on a contoured back support, while letting the water stream flow down the body. This shower seat also offers a therapeutic back massage by means of three water nozzles installed to spray at the nape of the neck, the center shoulder part and the lumbar area. The control of

Figure A–7 Contoured shower seat with provision for perineal cleaning and hand spray for washing selected body parts. Photo: Courtesy of Robert F. Graeff.

the water pressure can be governed by a lever positioned to the right of the seated user. This lever can also activate a supplemental hand spray to reach selected body parts. Feet washing can thus be performed from a seated position, rather than lifting one foot on a stool while standing on the other.

Perineal Cleansing

The shower seat incorporates a provision for perineal cleaning in the form of a cavity for manual access, and a douche spray to rinse the anal-genital region. A special advantage of this shower seat is the convenience by which this cleansing process can be accomplished, in one "sitting." For the many people afflicted with hemorrhoids, it is especially important to ac-commodate these hygiene functions. Some toilet fixtures have integrated provisions for a water spray, but they have limited washing capabilities for use by the elderly. However, in cases where the shower and the sink/toilet unit have to be separated for spatial reasons (i.e., retrofitting), a toilet facility with incorporated provisions for washing and drying is recom-mended. The sitting posture of the proposed shower seat differs signifi-cantly from the conventional bidet, which must be straddled facing the wall, and which does not provide proper support for elderly users. The proposed shower-bidet seat provides wide support under the thighs when the user leans forward and extra support for the buttocks when he or she leans against the back. A shallow cavity for hand access in front, and a small 6 inch × 6 inch × 6 inch-basin with drain in the back provide sufficiently convenient access for cleansing the anal-genital area.

It is necessary to conduct further study to analyze and test a population of elderly people to determine the particular support points and the proper seat angle for final recommendations and dimensions. The douche spray nozzle is governed by the control lever (mentioned earlier) under the horizontal support ledge, which alternately regulates the water pressure of the back jets or the bidet nozzle. The temperature can be preset at the main water control at the entry. It is recommended to introduce a liquid soap dispenser in the shower to avoid risking the imbalance of trying to retrieve a dropped soap bar (and slipping on it).

Material

This new sanitary fixture could be effectively constructed of reinforced metacrylate, possibly with a padded support area to ease the moment of contact when the surface is dry.

Heat Lamp and Hot Air Blower

An infrared heat lamp with parabolic reflector is integrated into the ceiling of the shower enclosure to assist in the dry-toweling functions. Toweling motions are usually difficult for the elderly. As a result, their exposed bodies remain wet for longer periods of time, risking chills, colds, or rheumatism. To accelerate the drying-up time, a warm air blower with an adjustable nozzle may be activated. The blower mechanism is installed within the plumbing wall. A special advantage of this facility is that it allows the user to step out of the enclosure into the dry, warm, and comforting environment of the bedroom with adequate space for dressing in clean, dry clothing.

Sliding Doors

Even though the bathroom facility is designed to be installed in an existing room, the toilet/sink unit and the shower unit must be enclosed for visual privacy. The combined wall surface of both enclosures is divided into five panels: three are stationary and two are entries, fitted with well-engineered, dependable sliding doors. When the doors are closed, the 11-foot front of the facility turns into an interior wall of the bedroom. The two sliding doors have a light surface texture to inform the touching hand in the dark of the entry's location. The two doors have 3-inch-wide openings so that the interior floor nightlights remain visible in the dark and serve for orientation. These floor lights and the counter top task light grow bright when the sliding doors are opened to clearly expose all bathroom equipment. The three stationary panels are each 26 inches wide and the two door panels are 29 inches wide and 77 inches high. Adaptive panels must be provided to bridge and fit the spatial difference between the facility and the ceiling and between the facility and the walls. All visible surfaces and connections are to maintain identical outward appearance to visually integrate the facility in the room. It is suggested to extend available space by incorporating a linen closet or a wardrobe if space permits.

Floor

A primary safety consideration of any bathroom is the floor. The proposed flooring material for both sections, the sink/toilet unit and shower, consists of a slip-resistant, dark commercial sheet vinyl with slightly raised square pegs which facilitate sweeping and washing in linear directions at right angles with much greater effectiveness than is possible with round pegs. The floor is heat sealed along the edges and has a 3 inch, 45-transition band into the vertical planes. This results in a tray-like appearance for both floor sections. Instead of prominent dividers or raised or lowered planes, the shower enclosure employs a 3-inch barrier to contain water at the entry. The user should not have to step down when entering the facility, but both legs should remain at the same level when stepping in. The flooring material extends 2 feet past the sliding doors to connect with the flooring material of the bedroom. This extension visually joins the two enclosures into one cohesive facility. Another reason for extending the floor beyond the enclosures is to provide a tactile indicator that the facility has been reached, a special advantage in the dark and to those with limited vision.

Lighting

Both enclosures are well illuminated by two warm, ambient fluorescent lights mounted in the ceiling of the enclosures. Additional lights are placed at the ground level to illuminate the floor surface, and to assure safe footing. These same floor lights also function as night lights, helping the user orient himself or herself in the dark. In the case of the usually insufficient lighting of the shower unit, this design remedies not only the safety problem, but provides a more pleasant psychological alternative to the dark enclosure of present systems. The toilet sink/ unit has a recessed light above the open access shelves to illuminate the counter top, the toiletries, and miscellaneous hygiene items. It also illuminates the body guide just in front of it, and delineates the dimensions of the enclosure.

Special Benefits

While this bathroom facility is designed to serve primarily the ambulatory to mildly impaired elderly, it is a facility with multiple applications. Its special features can benefit users of all ages, including younger and able-bodied populations. In addition, it can be easily modified to meet the special needs of those with more pronounced limitations. Prospective users could include the wheelchair bound, as well as those whose capabilities progressively decline in the natural course of aging.

For the elderly user, this facility preserves physical independence—privacy and comfort—which in turn ensures psychological well-being. Its availability would improve the quality of life for thousands who would otherwise be consigned to the personal indignity and financial calamity of institutionalization.

The greater economic implications are also worth noting. This facility could postpone institutionalization on an average of 10 to 15 years. Not only would it help alleviate the financial burden of the individual family, but applied to the population at large, it could affect this country's entire health care economy.

▶ REFERENCES

Kira, Alexander. 1976. *The Bathroom.* New York: Viking Press.

Kleeman, Walter B. 1981. *The Challenge of Interior Design.* New York: Van Nostrand Reinhold.

McClelland, Ian L. 1982. *The Ergonomics of Toilet Seats.* Human Factors Society.

A Glossary on Transgenerational Design[18]

► AGING

age segregation

The separation of people on age—as in retirement communities or senior citizen's centers.

aged
(ā' jid)

The state of being old. A person may be defined as aged on the basis of having reached a specific age—for example, 65 is often used for social or legislative policies while 75 is used for physiological evaluations.

ageism
(āj' ism)

Prejudice against people because they are old. Ageism implies a broader meaning than gerontophobia, the unreasonable fear and hatred of older persons. The term was coined by Robert N. Butler, M.D., first director of the National Institute on Aging.

aging
(ā-jing)

The changes that occur normally in plants and animals as they grow older. Some age changes begin at birth and continue until death; other changes begin at maturity and end at death. Also see *aging research* under Research on Aging, below.)

centenarian
(sen-tnar' ē-un)

A person who is 100 years or older. In 1989, 61,000 centenarians were identified by the U.S. Bureau of the Census.

chronological age
(kron-o-loj' i-kal)

An individual's numerical age dating from the time of his or her birth. (Compare with *functional age.*)

competence

An individual's ability, skill, and fitness to deal with the demand character of the environment.

elderly or elder

Generally referring to individuals over age 60. Other terms used to describe certain groups of older people are

frail elderly. Elderly persons whose physical and emotional abilities or social support system is so reduced that maintaining a household or social contacts is difficult and sometimes impossible, without regular assistance from others. Healthy persons are usually not in this group until after age 75, and even then many are not frail until they reach very late years, such as beyond age 90.

18. This appendix was developed in part from material in National Institute on Aging. 1986. *Age Words: A Glossary on Health and Aging.* Bethesda, MD: Department of Health and Human Services, National Institutes of Health (NIH) Publication No. 86-1849.

functional dependent elderly. Individuals whose illnesses, disabilities, or social problems have reduced their ability to perform self-care and household tasks in an independent manner.

functional age

An assessment of age based on physical or mental performance rather than on the number of years since birth. (Compare with *chronological age.*)

geriatric medicine

Also called geriatrics. The medical knowledge of physical disability in older persons—including the diagnosis, treatment, and prevention of disorders. Geriatric medicine recognizes aging as a normal process, not a disease state.

geriatrician
(jer-ē-a-tri' shun)

Physicians with special training in geriatric medicine. In earlier years this training was self-taught through the special attention physicians gave their older patients. Now, 1- to 3-year training programs, which follow the regular medical curriculum, are established in a number of teaching medical centers.

geriatrics
(jer-ē-a' triks)

Refers to geriatric medicine. The term was originally coined in 1909 by the American physician Ingnaz L. Nascher when he recognized a similarity between the fields of aging and pediatrics. Nascher is the founder of modern geriatrics in the United States.

gerontology
(jer-un-tol' ō-je)

The study of aging from the broadest perspective. Gerontologists examine not only the clinical and biological aspects of aging but also psychosocial, economic, and historical conditions. Elie Metchnikoff, of the Pasteur Institute in Paris, first used the term in 1903 to describe the biological study of senescence.

senescence
(se-nes' sens)

Aging. The normal process of growing old, a process that occurs continually at every biological level (chemical, cellular, tissue, organ systems, and organism).

activities of daily living (ADL)

▶ RESEARCH ON AGING

Normally refers to the six basic activities of daily living on the Index of Independence in Activities of Daily Living developed by Katz (1970). They include bathing, dressing, toileting, transferring, continence, and feeding. Additional ADLs include communication, grooming, visual capability, walking, and use of the upper extremities (Ham 1991).

aging research

The study of the interrelating factors that affect aging—clinical medicine, social and psychological relations, and environmental conditions. Aging research attempts to distinguish the changes occurring normally during aging from changes caused by illness, heredity, or the environment.

behavioral sciences	The study of human development, values, and interpersonal relations. The behavioral sciences encompass such fields as psychiatry, psychology, cultural anthropology, sociology, and political science.
biometry *(bi-om′ i-trē)*	The mathematical study of biological facts about a subject. A statistical examination of biological data—e.g., the calculation of life expectancy.
cohort *(kō-′hort)*	A group of people who are born at the same period of time or who enter a system, such as a nursing home, at the same time. One type of research design compares cohorts to see if there are differences in the way they grow old.
demography *(di-mog′ re-fē)*	The study of a population and those variables bring about change in that population. Variables studied by demographers are age, sex, race, education, income, geographic trends, birth, and death. (See *biometry* and *epidemiology.*)
dependency ratio	A comparison between those individuals whom society considers economically productive and those it considers economically unproductive. Since many people over 65 are retired from the workforce, this group is usually classified as economically unproductive (others in this category are children and nonworking individuals between 18 and 64).
epidemiology *(ep-a-dē-mē-ol′o-jē)*	The study of the frequency and distribution of illness in a population. Terms used by epidemiologists include *endemic* (en-dem′ ik). Found in a particular geographic area or among a particular group of people. *epidemic* (ep-a-dem′ ik). Spreading rapidly among many individuals in an area, especially a contagious disease. *pandemic* (pan-dem′ ik). Occurring over a large geographic area—universal or worldwide.
incidence	How frequently a disease occurs. The rate of new cases occurring in a population during a given period of time. (Compare with *prevalence.*)
life cycle	The entire course of a person's life—from infancy to old age. Health, social roles and expectations, and socioeconomic status tend to change as an individual moves from one phase of life to the next.
life expectancy	A statistical projection of the number of years an individual is expected to live. Life expectancy can be calculated from birth (e.g., a person born in 1984 could be expected to live to age 74), or it can be calculated from some other point (such as the number of years a person could expect to live after reaching a given age). Persons of the same age can have different life expectancies depending on their race, sex, or socioeconomic circumstance.

life span	The years a human being could live if negative variables, such as disease or accidents, did not shorten the number. An ideal number, probably approaching 110 years.
longevity *(lon-jev' i-tē)*	The condition or quality of being long-lived.
longitudinal *research*	Studies that examine one group of individuals over a long period of time—as they grow, develop, and age. This is in contrast to cross-sectional research in which individuals of different ages are compared with one another at one point in time.
minority group	A small number of people within a society. Members of racial minority groups who are elderly bear a double burden of discrimination based on both race and age.
morbidity rate *(mor-bid' i-tē)*	The ratio of individuals who are ill or disabled to the total number within a population.
mortality rate	Death rate. The ratio of individuals who have died to the total number of individuals in the population during a given period of time. The deaths of 100 individuals in a population of 1000 would result in a mortality rate of 100.
National Institute *on Aging (NIA)*	One of the National Institutes of Health, the NIA was established by Congress on May 31, 1974 (Public Law 93-296), as a federal agency, the NIA supports research on conditions that affect the aging process. Institute activities range from investigations on biological, social, and psychological issues to training personnel for related research.
prevalence *(prev' a-lenz)*	The total number of individuals in a given population who have a specific disorder at one period in time. (Compare with *incidence*.)
psychosocial *research on aging*	The scientific investigation of individual characteristics (intellectual ability, personality, attitudes, and behaviors) and social environments (family relationships and work situations) as they influence the way people age.

▶ THE BODY

Bones

contracture *(kon'trak-tur)*	Progressive stiffening in the muscles, tendons, and ligaments that surround the joints. Contractures tend to develop after a stroke or an injury when prolonged immobility has limited the movement of joints.
orthopedics *(or-thō-pē' diks)*	The medical knowledge, diagnosis, and treatment of the skeletal system (the bones, joints, muscles, ligaments, and tendons).

osteoporosis
(os′ te-ō-po-rō′ sis)

A decrease in density of the bones causing structural weakness throughout the skeleton. Fractures can result from even a minor injury or fall. Some bone loss occurs normally in older adults, but osteoporosis develops most often in white women after menopause. (See *menopause.*)

▶ BRAIN

Alzheimer's disease
(altz′ hī-mer)

A form of dementia first described in 1906 by German neurologist Alois Alzheimer. Alzheimer's disease produces severe intellectual deterioration in older persons and is currently considered an irreversible disease. (See *dementia.*)

central nervous system

The brain and spinal cord.

cognitive
(kog′ ni-tv)

Refers to the mental processes of comprehension, memory, judgment, and reasoning—as opposed to emotional processes.

dementia
(di-men′ sha)

The severe impairment of cognitive functions (thinking, memory, and personality). Of our elderly population, 5 to 6 percent have dementia. Alzheimer's disease causes approximately one half of these cases, vascular disorders (multiple strokes) cause one fourth, and the other dementias are caused by alcoholism, heart disease, infections, endocrine disorders, toxic reactions to medicines, and other rarer conditions. While impairment from Alzheimer's disease and vascular disorders is permanent, dementia caused by other conditions can usually be corrected.

plaques

Certain areas of the brain that have undergone a specific form of degeneration. Plaques are usually found in patients with Alzheimer's disease, although they are also found in a lesser extent in older persons who are normal.

senile dementia
(sē′ nīl
di-men′ sha)

An outdated term for dementia. Years ago dementia was thought to be part of normal aging, but now we know that most people do not become demented as they grow older and that dementia, when it occurs, is due to some specific disease process. (See *dementia.*)

senility
(si-nil′ i-tē)

An outdated term referring to abnormal deterioration in the mental functions of old people. (See *dementia.*)

stroke

Also called cerebrovascular accident. Disruption in the supply of blood to some part of the brain causing sudden damage to the brain. The outcome of a stroke can vary depending on the cause. Possible outcomes are paralysis, loss of sensation, incontinence, impaired speech and thinking, and sometimes death. Rehabilitation therapy can help stroke patients regain their ability to move and function.

Ears

presbycusis
(prez-bē' kū' sis)

The most common type of hearing loss in people over 65. Presbycusis results in a gradual decline in the ability to hear high-pitched sounds or to distinguish consonants in speech, which sometimes causes an older person to misinterpret what is being said.

Eyes

cataract
(kat' a-rakt)

A cloudiness or opacity that develops in the lens of the eye and results in poorer vision. Previously one of the leading causes of blindness in persons over 60, cataracts can now be surgically removed.

diabetic retinopathy
(dī-ah-be' tik ret-i-nop' ah-thē)

A disorder of the blood vessels in the retina (tissue that transmits visual impulses to the brain). The condition develops most often in older diabetics who have had the condition for many years. Diabetic retinopathy causes blurred vision or it can block vision (from broken blood vessels leaking into the retina) or it can lead to blindness—though blindness can sometimes be averted through early detection. (See *diabetes.*)

glaucoma
(glaw-kō ma)

A disease in which pressure builds up within the eye and causes internal damage, gradually destroying vision. Often hereditary, glaucoma usually affects persons after age 40. Symptoms may be blurred vision, difficulty in focusing, loss of peripheral vision, or slow adaptation to dark. Often there are no symptoms until severe and irreversible loss of vision has occurred. While no method exists for preventing glaucoma, diagnosing the disease in its earliest stages can prevent further damage.

macular degeneration
(mak' u-lar di-jen-er-ā' shun)

Progressive, irreversible damage to the macula (part of the retina) which results in a gradual loss of fine, reading vision and eventually blindness. The use of lasers, a new form of therapy, can in some instances halt the degeneration.

myopia
(mī-o' pē-a)

Nearsightedness.

presbyopia
(prez-bē-ō' pē-a)

Reduction in the ability to see at close range. This is due to the gradual loss of elasticity in the lens of the eye which occurs throughout life, but does not become apparent until the mid-forties.

▶ MEDICAL PROBLEMS

arthritis
(arth-rī' tis)

A general term referring to disease of the joints. Arthritis includes over 1000 different diseases, often involving aches and pains in the joints and connective tissues throughout the body. Most forms of arthritis are chronic, but proper treatment can frequently reduce symptoms substantially. The most common types of arthritis in older persons are osteoarthritis, rheumatoid arthritis, and gout.

gout. An inherited condition, gout usually develops in men between the ages of 40 and 60. The condition results from an excess of uric acid in the blood that accumulates in the joints to produce severe inflammation. Years ago, chronic pain and deformity were common characteristics of gout; now medical treatment almost always controls the disease.

inflammation (in-fla-mā' shun). The reaction of the body tissues to injury. Heat, swelling, redness, and pain in the affected area characterize inflammation.

osteoarthritis (ahs-tē-ō-arth-rī' tis). A degenerative joint disease, osteoarthritis usually produces stiffness or pain in the fingers or in the weightbearing joints (knees, hips, and spine). Inflammation is rare. While the cause of osteoarthritis is unknown, recent research shows that the cartilage in persons without symptoms; also, wear and tear on joint surfaces appears to contribute to the condition. Most people over 60 have this type of arthritis but to varying degrees; only about half experience symptoms.

rheumatism (ru' ma-tiz-um). A term used more often in Great Britain. Rheumatism refers to disease in the joints, muscles, bones, and ligaments and includes most forms of arthritis.

rheumatoid arthritis (ru' ma-toyd). The most common form of arthritis after osteoarthritis. It also has the potential for causing the greatest damage since early, mild symptoms can worsen over the years to produce serious deformity. No cause or cure is known. Common symptoms are inflammation in the hands, arms, hips, legs, and feet. The disease affects women more frequently than men.

hyperthermia
(hī-per-thur' mē-a)

A condition in which the body temperature is so far above normal (e.g., above 104°F or 40°C) that irreversible damage or even death may result. Hyperthermia sometimes appears as heat stroke or heat exhaustion.

hypoglycemia
(hī-pō-glī-sē' mē-a)

Low blood sugar. An uncommon condition in which glucose (sugar) in the blood is below a normal level. Onset can be sudden and if left untreated, it can lead to confusion, sleepiness, or even unconsciousness. Hypoglycemia is sometimes caused by the overuse of an antidiabetic medicine such as insulin or oral antidiabetic drugs.

hypothermia
(hī-pō-thur' mē-a)

A condition in which the body temperature drops so far below normal (e.g., below 95°F or 35°C) that irreversible damage or death may result. Anyone exposed to severe cold can develop accidental hypothermia; however, those at greatest risk are older persons who have chronic illnesses, suffer from temperature regulation defects, or who cannot afford heating fuel.

influenza

Also called the "flu." A contagious viral infection that spreads rapidly from person to person. Symptoms include fever, headache, aching muscles, chills, and coughing. Influenza threatens older persons because it lowers their resistance to serious infections like pneumonia.

insomnia
(in-som' nē-a)

The inability to sleep or unusual wakefulness. Insomnia in the elderly is frequently a manifestation of depression.

Parkinson's disease
(par' kin-sunz)

A neurological disorder characterized by involuntary muscle tremor and rigid movements. In advanced stages the individual develops a shuffling gait with stooped posture and loses facial expression. The disease occurs most frequently in persons over age 60, striking approximately 1 in 100 persons. The cause of Parkinson's disease is unknown, yet scientists have learned it has to do with a disorder in brain cells that results in the loss of dopamine, a substance regulating normal body movement.

L-dopa. Also called levodopa. L-dopa is a medication used for alleviating symptoms of Parkinson's disease by compensating for the loss of dopamine in the brain.

pneumonia
(nū-mōn' ya)

Pneumonia is an inflammation of the lungs caused by bacterial infection. Symptoms are similar to influenza but more severe—with fever, coughing, and shaking chills. Pneumonia is one of the five leading causes of death among people over 65.

progeria
(prō-jer' i-a)

Premature aging. Progeria is a rare condition known also by the name Hutchinson-Gilford progeria syndrome. Signs begin to appear in the individual soon after birth, and the average life expectancy is approximately 12 years.

syncope
(sing' kō-pē)

Fainting. In older people this is a common cause of falling. (See *falling,* under Related Terms, below.)

▶ RELATED TERMS

acute
(a-kūt')

Developing rapidly with pronounced symptoms and lasting a short time. One example of an acute illness is the flu (influenza). (Compare with *chronic.*)

atrophy
(a' trō-fē)

The wasting away of an organ or body part. Atrophy can result when part of the body is not used or, to a lesser extent, in the normal course of aging.

chronic
(kron' ik)

Continuing over a long period of time or recurring frequently. Chronic conditions often begin inconspicuously and symptoms are less pronounced than in acute conditions. (Compare with *acute.*)

disability

A restriction or lack of ability to perform an activity in the manner or within the range considered normal for a human being. (Compare with *handicap* and *impairment.*)

dysmobility (*dis-mō-bil' a-tē*)	Limitations in one's ability to perform bodily movements (e.g., walking, sitting, lifting, reaching, grasping, stooping, bending, etc.), whether produced by disease or injury. Dysmobility is a critical factor affecting one's ability to remain independent.
etiology (*ē-tē-ol' a-jē*)	The study of the cause or origin of a disease.
falling	A common problem experienced among older people, due to any number of underlying causes. Evaluating people who have falls involves assessing the injuries sustained in the fall and the cause for the fall. In older people, falling frequently results in broken bones and other serious injuries that may lead to disability and sometimes death.
handicap	A disadvantage for a given individual resulting from an impairment or a disability, that limits or prevents the fulfillment of a role that is normal (depending on age, sex, and social and cultural factors) for that individual. (Compare with *disability* and *impairment.*)
impairment	Loss or abnormality of psychological, physiological, or anatomical structure or function. (Compare with *disability* and *handicap.*)
implant	Transplanted or inserted material—e.g., artificial joints used in reconstructive surgery. (See *prosthetic device.*)
infection	An illness caused by an organism such as a virus, bacterium, or fungus.
nonspecific presentation of illness	Symptoms appearing in an individual that do not clearly point to a single disease or single organ system. Older persons, more than those in other age groups, come to the attention of health care providers due to nonspecific reasons.
prosthetic device (*pros-thet' ick*)	Sometimes called a prosthesis. Artificial limbs, false teeth, and hearing aids are examples of prostheses—all of which augment or replace lost functions of the body. (See *implant.*)
symptom (*sim' tum*)	The subjective evidence of a patient's condition (pain, shortness of breath, and fainting spells) as opposed to a sign, which is the objective evidence of disease (high blood pressure, a heart murmur, and swollen joints).
syndrome (*sin' drōm*)	A group of symptoms that, together, characterize a particular disease.

▶ SOCIAL PROGRAMS AND SERVICES

ADA	See *Americans with Disabilities Act.*
adult day care	The social, recreational, and rehabilitation services provided for persons who require daytime supervision. An alternative between care in the home and in an institution.

allied health professionals	Persons with special training in fields related to medicine such as medical social work and physical or occupational therapy. Allied health professionals work with physicians or other health professionals.
Americans with Disabilities Act (ADA)	Civil rights legislation enacted on July 26, 1990, which became effective January 26, 1992. The Americans with Disabilities Act, Public Law 101-336, prohibits discrimination on the basis of disability by private entities in places of public accommodation.
congregate housing (kong' gra-gāt)	Apartment houses or group accommodations that provide health care and other support services to functionally impaired older persons who do not need routine nursing care.
grey lobby	An advocacy movement whose members are concerned with the needs of the elderly. These individuals come from the general public, organizations of older people (e.g., American Association of Retired Persons, Grey Panthers), and health and welfare professions.
home health care	Health services provided in the homes of the elderly, disabled, sick, or convalescent. The types of services provided include nursing care, social services, home health aide and homemaker services, and various rehabilitation therapies (e.g., speech, physical, and occupational therapy).
homemaker or home health aide	A person who is paid to help in the home with personal care, light housekeeping, meal preparation, and shopping. Some states and agencies make a distinction between homemaking (or housekeeping) services and personal services.
hospice (hos' pis)	A concept that refers to enhancing the dying person's quality of life. Hospice care can be given in the home, a special hospice facility, or a combination of both.
institutionalization	Admission of an individual to an institution, such as a nursing home, where he or she will reside for an extended period of time or indefinitely.
long-term care	The medical and social care given to individuals who have severe, chronic impairments. Long-term care can consist of care in homes, by family members, assistance through voluntary or employed help (e.g., as provided by established home care agencies), or care in institutions. Various types of long-term care facilities exist throughout the country which frequently differ in their available staff, reimbursements, and services.
	domiciliary care facility. A nonmedical institution providing room, board, laundry, some forms of personal care, and usually recreational and social services. Licensed by state departments of social services, these facilities are not eligible for Medicare or Medicaid reimbursement.
	intermediate care facility. Provides health-related care and services to individuals who do not require the degree of care or treatment normally given

by a hospital or skilled nursing facility but who do require health-related institutional care above the level of room and board. Eligible for Medicaid reimbursement.

skilled nursing facility. Provides the greatest degree of medical care. Every patient is under the supervision of a physician, and the facility has a transfer agreement with a nearby hospital. Twenty-four-hour nursing is provided with a physician on call to furnish medical care in case of emergency. May be covered under both Medicare and Medicaid.

Medicaid   A national medical assistance program administered by the individual states. Medicaid provides reimbursement for medical and health-related services to persons who are medically indigent. Nursing home care for needy older persons is also covered by Medicaid.

Medicare   A national health insurance plan for people over 65 and for some people under 65 who are disabled. It includes two parts: Part A covers hospital costs and some skilled nursing care, and Part B is the supplemental portion (for which the insured pays premiums) covering a portion of the physician's fee as well as various types of therapy.

Older Americans Act   Enacted in 1965, the Older Americans Act (Public Law 89-73), gives elderly citizens more opportunity to participate in and receive the benefits of modern society—e.g., adequate housing, income, employment, nutrition, and health care.

physical therapy   The treatment of disease or impaired motion through a physical method such as heat, hydrotherapy, massage, exercise, or mechanical devices. (See *rehabilitation therapy.*)

rehabilitation therapy   Therapy aimed at restoring or maintaining the greatest possible function and independence. Rehabilitation therapy is especially useful to persons who have suffered from stroke, and injury, or disease by helping them recover the maximum use of the affected area(s) of the body.

retirement   The act of leaving paid employment. The retiree, on reaching a predetermined age, is usually provided with some regular payment such as a pension and/or a Social Security payment.

flexible retirement. An employment option allowing an individual to retire at an age of his or her choice.

mandatory retirement. The policy of requiring persons to leave employment on reaching a designated age. This designated age "ceiling" was recently raised by law in the United States from age 65 to 70.

self-help, self-care   A concept of health care stressing that individuals can manage many of their own health problems when given sufficient instruction and appropriate medications. It teaches how and when to use self-treatment techniques and when to seek professional help.

senior center	A community facility for the elderly. Senior centers provide a variety of activities for their members—including any combination of recreational, educational, cultural, or social events. Also, some centers offer nutritious meals and limited health care services.
Social Security	A national insurance program that provides income to workers when they retire or are disabled and to dependent survivors when a worker dies. Retirement payments are based on worker's earnings during employment.
social services	Services designed to help individuals with problems that concern housing, transportation, meals, recreation, and family support and relations. These services are provided by professional social workers.
Supplemental Security Income	This national program provides supplemental payments to older persons who already receive public assistance. The program's aim is to raise the incomes of these individuals to the poverty threshold.

▶ DESIGN

accessible design	Products and environments designed and constructed so as to be readily accessible to and usable by persons with disabilities (e.g., providing such access to places of public accommodation, commercial facilities, and transportation systems through the installation of ramps, curb cuts, grab bars, braille signs, etc.). Also referred to as barrier-free design normally associated with architecture, landscape architecture, and interior design.
adaptive design	Products and environments originally designed for use by the general public that have been modified or "adapted" to the special needs of those with disabilities (e.g., slip-on grips for eating utensils and writing instruments, jar and bottle openers, raised toilet seats, add-on handles and grab bars, etc.).
aesthetic design	Products and environments designed and marketed on the basis of their appearance or aesthetic appeal. Such designs normally offer the user little, if any, physical accommodation or functional utility. Much of what is considered "fashionable" falls within the aesthetic design category.
barrier-free design	See *accessible design.*
ergonomics (*er-ga-nō′ miks*)	An applied science concerned with the characteristics of people that need to be considered in designing and arranging things that they use in order that people and things will interact most effectively and safely—called also *human engineering* (*Webster's Ninth New Collegiate Dictionary*).
functional design	Products and environments designed primarily for their functional utility. Such designs normally offer the user little, if any, physical accommodation or aesthetic appeal. Instead, such factors as cost reduction and ease of manufacture and assembly determine the resulting appearance and usability.

human factors	See *ergonomics*.
humanistic design	Products and environments designed to serve the needs of people, focusing on such factors as safety, comfort, convenience, ease of use, and bodily fit.
industrial design	*Industrial design,* as defined by the Industrial Designers Society of America (IDSA), is the professional service of creating and developing concepts and specifications that optimize the function, value, and appearance of products and systems for the mutual benefit of both user and manufacturer.
transgenerational design	The practice of making products and environments compatible with those physical and sensory impairments associated with human aging and which limit major life activities. It rejects as discriminatory and stigmatizing, specialized products or devices targeted directly at older consumers. Rather, it insists that products and environments be designed at the outset to accommodate a "transgenerational" population, which includes the young, the middle-aged, and the elderly—without penalty to any group.
universal design	A generic "umbrella" term that embraces *accessible* design, *adaptive* design, and *transgenerational* design. This unreachable design ideal seeks "universal" environmental access and support for people of all ages, physical and sensory capabilities, and cognitive skills. Its goal is to close the environmental gap that separates those who are functionally impaired or disabled from those who are well and able-bodied.

Gerontology and Aging-Related Programs and Centers[19]

Boston University
53 Bay State Road
Boston, MA 02215
Boston University Gerontology Center
(617) 353-5045

Brandeis University
Florence Heller Graduate School
P.O. Box 9110
Waltham, MA 02254
Program in Aging
(617) 736-3800

California State University
5151 State University Drive
Los Angeles, CA 90032
Roybal Center for Applied Gerontology
(213) 343-4724

Duke University Medical Center
Box 3003
Durham, NC 27706
*Center for the Study of Aging and Human
  Development*
(919) 624-2248

Miami University
396 Upham Hall
Oxford, OH 45056
Scripps Gerontology Center
(513) 529-2914

New Mexico State University
Box 30001, Dept. 3TG
Las Cruces, NM 88003-0001
*The Institute for Gerontological Research and
  Education (TIGRE)*
(505) 646-3426

Oregon State University
School of Home Economics and Education
Corvallis, OR 97331
Program on Gerontology
(503) 737-1084

Pennsylvania State University
S-210 Henderson Building
University Park, PA 16802
Gerontology Center
(814) 865-1710

Portland State University
P.O. Box 751
Portland, OR 97207
Institute on Aging
(503) 725-3952

Syracuse University
Maxwell School
Syracuse, NY 13244-1090
All-University Gerontology Center
(315) 443-9043

19. For an extensive listing of programs contact the Association for Gerontology in Higher Education, 1001 Connecticut Avenue, Suite 410, Washington, DC 20036 (202) 429-9277.

University of Akron
Akron, OH 44325-4307
Institute for Life Span Development and Gerontology
(216) 972-7243

University of Alabama
386 Nott Hall
Box 870326
Tuscaloosa, AL 35487
Center for the Study of Aging
(205) 348-1345

University of Michigan
300 N. Ingalls
Ann Arbor, MI 48109-2007
Institute of Gerontology
(313) 764-3493

University of Minnesota
330 Humphrey Center
301 19th Avenue South
Minneapolis, MN 55455-0421
All-University Council on Aging
(612) 625-9099

University of Nebraska
School of Public Affairs and Community Service
Annex 24
Omaha, NE 68182
Gerontology Department
(402) 554-2272

University of New Mexico
Nursing/Pharmacy Bldg. 179-A
Albuquerque, NM 87131
Center for Aging, Research, Education and Service
 (UNM CARES)
(505) 277-0860

University of North Carolina at Chapel Hill
School of Social Work
CB# 3550, 223 E. Franklin Street
Chapel Hill, NC 27599
Program on Aging
(919) 966-5945

University of North Texas
P.O. Box 13438
Denton, TX 76203
Center for Studies in Aging
(817) 565-2765

University of South Florida
College of Arts and Sciences
4202 East Fowler Avenue SOC 107
Tampa, FL 33620-8100
Department of Gerontology
(813) 974-2414

University of Southern California
University Park
Los Angeles, CA 90089
Gerontology Center
(213) 740-6060

University of Utah
316 Nursing Building
25 South Medical Drive
Salt Lake City, UT 84112
Gerontology Center
(801) 581-8198

University of Wisconsin–Madison
425 Henry Mall, Room 330
Madison, WI 53706
Institute on Aging and Adult Life
(608) 262-1818

National Association of State Units on Aging (NASUA)

Membership Directory as of November 1992

▶ **ALABAMA**

Commission on Aging
770 Washington Avenue, Suite 470
Montgomery, AL 36130
(205) 242-5743

▶ **ALASKA**

Older Alaskans Commission
Department of Administration
Pouch C-Mail Station 0209
Juneau, AK 99811-0209
(907) 465-3250

▶ **ARIZONA**

Aging and Adult Administration
Department of Economic Security
1400 West Washington Street
Phoenix, AZ 85007
(602) 542-4446

▶ **ARKANSAS**

Division of Aging and Adult Services
Arkansas Department of Human Services
P.O. Box 1437, Slot 1412
7th and Main Streets
Little Rock, AR 72201
(501) 682-2441

▶ **CALIFORNIA**

Department of Aging
1600 K Street
Sacramento, CA 95814
(916) 322-5290

▶ **COLORADO**

Aging and Adult Service
Department of Social Services
1575 Sherman Street, 4th Floor
Denver, CO 80203-1714
(303) 866-3851

▶ **CONNECTICUT**

Department on Aging
175 Main Street
Hartford, CT 06106
(203) 566-3238

▶ **DELAWARE**

Division on Aging
Department of Health and Social Services
Administration Bldg., Annex 2nd Floor
1901 North DuPont Highway
New Castle, DE 19720
(302) 577-4791

▶ **DISTRICT OF COLUMBIA**

Office on Aging
1424 K Street, NW, 2nd Floor
Washington, DC 20005
(202) 724-5626

▶ **FLORIDA**

Department of Elder Affairs
Building I, Room 317
1317 Winewood Boulevard
Tallahassee, FL 32301
(904) 922-5297

▶ GEORGIA

Office of Aging
878 Peachtree Street, N.E., Room 632
Atlanta, GA 30309
(404) 894-5333

▶ GUAM

Division of Senior Citizens
Department of Public Health and Social Services
Government of Guam
Post Office Box 2816
Agana, GU 96910
011 (671) 734-4361

▶ HAWAII

Executive Office on Aging
Office of the Governor
335 Merchant St., Room 241
Honolulu, HI 96813
(808) 586-0100

▶ IDAHO

Office on Aging
Statehouse, Rm. 108
Boise, ID 83720
(208) 334-3833

▶ ILLINOIS

Department on Aging
421 East Capitol Avenue
Springfield, IL 62701
(217) 785-2870

▶ INDIANA

Bureau of Aging/In Home Services
402 W. Washington Street, Room E-431
Indianapolis, IN 46207-7083
(317) 232-7020

▶ IOWA

Department of Elder Affairs
Suite 236, Jewett Building
914 Grand Avenue
Des Moines, IA 50319
(515) 281-5187

▶ KANSAS

Department of Aging
Docking State Office Building, 122-S
915 S.W. Harrison
Topeka, KS 66612-1500
(913) 296-4986

▶ KENTUCKY

Division of Aging Services
Cabinet for Human Resources
CHR Building–6th West
275 East Main Street
Frankfort, KY 40621
(502) 564-6930

▶ LOUISIANA

Office of Elderly Affairs
4550 N. Boulevard, 2nd Floor
P.O. Box 80374
Baton Rouge, LA 70806
(504) 925-1700

▶ MAINE

Bureau of Elder and Adult Services
Department of Human Services
State House—Station #11
Augusta, ME 04333
(207) 624-5335

▶ MARYLAND

Office on Aging
State Office Building
301 West Preston Street, Room 1004
Baltimore, MD 21201
(410) 225-1100

▶ MASSACHUSETTS

Executive Office of Elder Affairs
1 Ashburton Place, 5th Floor
Boston, MA 02108
(617) 727-7750

▶ MICHIGAN

Office of Services to the Aging
P.O. Box 30026
Lansing, MI 48909
(517) 373-8230

▶ MINNESOTA

Board on Aging
444 Lafayette Road
St. Paul, MN 55155-3843
(612) 296-2770

▶ MISSISSIPPI

Council on Aging
Division of Aging and Adult Services
421 West Pascagoula Street
Jackson, MS 39203-3524
(601) 949-2070

▶ MISSOURI

Division on Aging
Department of Social Services
P.O. Box 1337—615 Howerton Court
Jefferson City, MO 65102-1337
(314) 751-3082

▶ MONTANA

The Governors Office on Aging
State Capitol Building
Capitol Station, Room 219
Helena, MT 59620
(406) 444-3111

▶ NEBRASKA

Department on Aging
P.O. Box 95044
301 Centennial Mall—South
Lincoln, NE 68509
(402) 471-2306

▶ NEVADA

Division for Aging Services
Department of Human Resources
340 North 11th Street, Suite 114
Las Vegas, NV 89101
(702) 486-3545

▶ NEW HAMPSHIRE

Division of Elderly and Adult Services
6 Hazen Drive
Concord, NH 03301-6501
(603) 271-4680

▶ NEW JERSEY

Division on Aging
Department of Community Affairs
CN807
South Broad and Front Streets
Trenton, NJ 08625-0807
(609) 292-4833

▶ NEW MEXICO

State Agency on Aging
224 East Palace Avenue, 4th Floor
La Villa Rivera Building
Santa Fe, NM 87501
(505) 827-7640

▶ NEW YORK

Office for the Aging
New York State Plaza
Agency Building #2
Albany, NY 12223
(518) 474-4425

▶ **NORTH CAROLINA**

Division of Aging
CB 29531
693 Palmer Drive
Raleigh, NC 27626-0531
(919) 733-3983

▶ **NORTH DAKOTA**

Aging Services Division
Department of Human Services
Box 7070
1929 North Washington Street
Bismarck, ND 58507-7070
(701) 224-2577

▶ **NORTHERN MARIANA ISLANDS**

Division of Veterans Affairs
Office of the Governors
Commonwealth of the Northern Mariana Islands
Saipan, MP 96950
Tel. Nos. 9411 or 9732

▶ **OHIO**

Department of Aging
50 West Broad Street, 9th Floor
Columbus, OH 43266-0501
(614) 466-5500

▶ **OKLAHOMA**

Aging Services Division
Department of Human Services
P.O. Box 25352
Oklahoma City, OK 73125
(405) 521-2327

▶ **OREGON**

Senior and Disabled Services Division
313 Public Service Building
Salem, OR 97310
(503) 378-4728

▶ **PENNSYLVANIA**

Department of Aging
231 State Street
Harrisburg, PA 17101-1195
(717) 783-1550

▶ **PUERTO RICO**

Governors Office for Elderly Affairs
Corbian Plaza Stop 23
Ponce De Leon Avenue #1603
U.M. Office C
San Ture, PR 00908
(809) 721-5710

▶ **RHODE ISLAND**

Department of Elderly Affairs
160 Pine Street
Providence, RI 02903-3708
(401) 277-2858

▶ **(AMERICAN) SAMOA**

Territorial Administration on Aging
Office of the Governor
Pago Pago, AS 96799
011 (684) 633-1252

▶ **SOUTH CAROLINA**

Commission on Aging
Suite B-500
400 Arbor Lake Drive
Columbia, SC 29223
(803) 735-0210

▶ **SOUTH DAKOTA**

Office of Adult Services and Aging
700 North Illinois Street
Kneip Building
Pierre, SD 57501
(605) 773-3656

▶ TENNESSEE

Commission on Aging
706 Church Street, Suite 201
Nashville, TN 37243-0860
(615) 741-2056

▶ TEXAS

Department on Aging
P.O. Box 12786 Capitol Station
1949 IH 35, South
Austin, TX 78741-3702
(512) 444-2727

▶ REPUBLIC OF PALAU

Agency on Aging
P.O. Box 100
Koror, PW 96940

▶ UTAH

Division of Aging and Adult Services
Department of Social Services
120 North—200 West
Box 45500
Salt Lake City, UT 84145-0500
(801) 538-3910

▶ VERMONT

Aging and Disabilities
103 South Main Street
Waterbury, VT 05676
(802) 241-2400

▶ VIRGINIA

Department for the Aging
700 Centre, 10th Floor
700 East Franklin St.
Richmond, VA 23219-2327
(804) 225-2271

▶ VIRGIN ISLANDS

Senior Citizen Affairs
Department of Human Services
#19 Estate Diamond Fredericksted
St. Croix, VI 00840
(809) 772-4950 ext. 46

▶ WASHINGTON

Aging and Adult Services Administration
Department of Social and Health Services
P.O. Box 45050
Olympia, WA 98504-5050
(206) 586-3768

▶ WEST VIRGINIA

Commission on Aging
Holly Grove—State Capitol
Charleston, WV 25305
(304) 558-3317

▶ WISCONSIN

Bureau of Aging
Division of Community Services
217 South Hamilton Street, Suite 300
Madison, WI 53707
(608) 266-2536

▶ WYOMING

Commission on Aging
Hathaway Building, Room 139
Cheyenne, WY 82002-0710
(307) 777-7986

Related Professional and Nonprofit Organizations and Resources

American Association of Homes for the Aging
1050 17th Street NW, Suite 770
Washington, DC 20045
(202) 783-2242

American Association of Retired Persons
1909 K Street NW
Washington, DC 20049
(202) 424-2277

American Council of the Blind
1155 15th Street NW, Suite 720
Washington, DC 20005
(202) 467-5081

American Foundation for the Blind
15 West 16th Street
New York, NY 10011
(212) 620-2172

American Industrial Hygiene Association
P.O. Box 8390
245 White Pond Drive
Akron, OH 44320
(216) 873-2442

American Institute of Architects
1735 New York Avenue
Washington, DC 20006
(202) 626-7300

American Nurses Association
600 Maryland Avenue, SW
West Wing 100
Washington, DC 20024
(202) 554-4444

American Occupational Therapy Association
1383 Piccard Drive, Suite 301
Rockville, MD 20850
(301) 948-9626

American Physical Therapy Association
1111 North Fairfax Street
Alexandria, VA 22314
(703) 684-2782

American Society of Interior Designers
1430 Broadway
New York, NY 10018
(212) 944-9220

American Speech-Language-Hearing
  Association
c/o ASHA
10801 Rockville Pike
Rockville, MD 20852
(800) 638-TALK (voice/TTY,[20] toll-free)
(301) 879-5700 (voice/TTY)

---

20. *Voice* refers to the traditional telephone system, *TTY* indicates that teletypewriters can be used to send and receive typed messages through the phone system.

Americans with Disabilities Act
Civil Rights Division
U.S. Department of Justice
P.O. Box 66118
Washington, DC 20035-6118
(202) 514-0301 (voice)
(202) 514-3081 (TDD)[21]
(202) 514-0383 (TDD)

Architectural and Transportation
Barriers Compliance Board
1331 F Street NW, Suite 1000
Washington, DC 20004
(202) 272-5447

Arthritis Foundation
Department of Public Education
1314 Spring Street, N.W.
Atlanta, GA 30308
(404) 872-7100

Association for Gerontology in Higher
  Education
1001 Connecticut Avenue, Suite 410
Washington, DC 20036
(202) 429-9277

Better Hearing Institute
5021-B Backlick Road
Annandale, VA 22003
(800) 424-8576
Cooper-Hewitt National Museum of Design
Smithsonian Institution
2 East 91st Street
New York, NY 10128
(212) 860-6868

FDA Office of Consumer Affairs
HFE-88
5600 Fishers Lane
Rockville, MD 20857

Gerontological Society
1 DuPont Circle
Washington, DC 20036
(202) 842-1275

Human Factors and Ergonomics Society
P.O. Box 1369
Santa Monica, CA 90406
(310) 394-1811

Industrial Designers Society of America (IDSA)
1142-E Walker Road
Great Falls, VA 22066
(703) 759-0100

Institute of Industrial Engineers
25 Technology Park/Atlanta
Norcross, GA 30092
(404) 449-0460

International Council of Societies of Industrial
  Design (ICSID)
ICSID Secretariat
Klunvikatu I.D.
SF-00100 Helsinki, Finland
+358 06 26 661

National Association of Area Agencies on Aging
1112 16th Street NW, Suite 100
Washington, DC 20036
(202) 296-8130

National Association of Social Workers
750 1st Street NE
No. 700
Washington, DC 20002
(202) 408-8600

21. Telecommunications device for the deaf. A typewriter-like device that attaches easily to a standard telephone handset used to communicate with a hearing impaired person.

National Association of State Units on Aging
  (NASUA)
1225 I Street NW, Suite 725
Washington, DC 20005
(202) 898-2578

National Association of the Deaf
814 Thayer Avenue
Silver Spring, MD 20910
(301) 587-1788 (voice/TTY)

National Captioning Institute
5203 Leesburg Pike, Suite 1500
Falls Church, VA 22041
(703) 998-2462 (voice/TTY)

National Center for Vision and Aging
Division of The Lighthouse
111 East 59th Street
New York, NY 10022
(212) 355-2200

National Council on the Aging
409 3rd Street SW, 2nd Floor
Washington, DC 20024
(202) 479-1200

National Information Center on Deafness
Gallaudet College, Kendall Green
800 Florida Avenue, NE
Washington, DC 20002
(202) 651-5051 (voice/TTY)

National Institute of Aging
Information Office
90000 Rockville Pike
Building 31, Room 5C 27
Bethesda, MD 20892
(301) 496-1752

Rehabilitation Engineering Society of North
  America (RESNA)
1101 Connecticut Avenue NW
Suite 700
Washington, DC 20036
(202) 657-1199

Self Help for Hard of Hearing People, Inc.
7800 Wisconsin Avenue
Bethesda, MD 20814
(301) 657-2249 (TTY)

Society for Environmental Graphics (SEGD)
1 Story Street
Cambridge, MA 02138
(617) 868-3381

U.S. Department of Health and Human Services
Administration on Aging
330 Independence Avenue SW
Washington, DC 20201
(202) 619-0724

U.S. Department of Associated Dental and
  Health Professionals
Bureau of Health Professionals
Park Lawn Building, Rm. 8-103
5600 Fishers Lane
Rockville, MD 20857
(301) 443-6887

Geriatric Education Centers (GEC)[22]

Appalachian Geriatric Education Center*
Bowman Gray School of Medicine
Medical Center Boulevard
Winston-Salem, NC 27157-1051
(919) 716-4284

California Geriatric Education Center
Department of Medicine
University of California, Los Angeles
32-144 CHS
10833 Le Conte Avenue
Los Angeles, CA 90024-1687
(310) 825-8255

Colorado Geriatric Education Center
Health Sciences Center
Office of Academic Affairs
Box A094, 4200 E. 9th Avenue
Denver, CO 80262
(303) 270-8974

Creighton Regional Geriatric Education Center*
Creighton University School of Medicine
3615 Burt Street
Omaha, NE 68131
(402) 551-3772

Dakota Plains Geriatric Education Center*
University of North Dakota
501 North Columbia Road
Grand Forks, ND 58203
(701) 777-3200

Delaware Valley Mid-Atlantic Geriatric
  Education Center
Institute on Aging
3615 Chestnut Street

Philadelphia, PA 19104
(215) 898-3174

Duke University Geriatric Education Center*
Center for the Study of Aging and Human
  Development
Box 3003
Duke University Medical Center
Durham, NC 27710
(919) 684-5149

Geriatric Education Center of Michigan*
B-544 West Fee Hall
Michigan State University
East Lansing, MI 48824
(517) 353-7780

22. A nationwide network of GECs funded by the Department of Human Services offering education and training opportunities for health professionals to enhance the availability and equality of primary health care for older adults. As of October 1992, 27 GECs were assisted by grants from the department's Bureau of Health Professions, Division of Associated, Dental, and Public Health Professionals. GECs assisted previously are indicated by an asterisk (*). GECs provide education and training experiences to physicians, nurses, dentists, social workers, pharmacists, occupational and physical therapists, optometrists, podiatrists, dieticians, and other allied health and public health faculty, practitioners, and students. Centers provide resource clearinghouses, including the development of audiovisual and other curriculum materials and information.

Geriatric Education Center of Pennsylvania
University of Pittsburgh
121 University Place
Pittsburgh, PA 15260
(412) 624-9190

Geriatric Education Center of University of
  Puerto Rico*
School of Medicine
Medical Sciences Campus
G.P.O. Box 5067
San Juan, PR 00936
(809) 751-2478

Great Lakes Geriatric Education Center*
Chicago College of Osteopathic Medicine
5200 South Ellis Avenue
Chicago, IL 60615
(312) 947-2708

Harvard Geriatric Education Center
Division on Aging
Harvard Medical School
643 Huntington Avenue
Boston, MA 02115
(617) 432-1463

Hunter/Mt. Sinai Geriatric Education Center
425 East 25th Street
New York, NY 10010-2590
(212) 481-5142

Illinois Geriatric Education Center
University of Illinois at Chicago
College of Associated Health Professionals
808 S. Wood Street (M/C 778), Room 166 CME
Chicago, IL 60612
(312) 996-6698

Indiana Geriatric Education Center
Indiana University School of Medicine
Coleman Hall 120
1140 West Michigan Street
Indianapolis, IN 46202-5119
(317) 274-4702

Intermountain West Geriatric Education
  Center*
College of Nursing
University of Utah
25 South Medical Drive
Salt Lake City, UT 84112
(801) 581-4064

Iowa Geriatric Education Center*
Department of Internal Medicine
University of Iowa Hospitals and Clinics
Iowa City, IA 52242
(319) 356-1027

Louisiana Geriatric Education Center*
Louisiana State University
School of Medicine
1542 Tulane Avenue
New Orleans, LA 70112
(504) 568-5842

Meharry Consortium Geriatric Education Center
1005 D.B. Todd Boulevard
Nashville, TN 37208
(615) 327-6947

Miami Area Geriatric Education Center
University of Miami
1425 N.W. 10th Avenue (D 303)
Sieron Building, 2nd Floor
Miami, FL 33136
(305) 545-0949

Minnesota Area Geriatric Education Center
Box 197 Mayo
420 Delaware Street, SE
University of Minnesota
Minneapolis, MN 55455
(612) 624-3904

Mississippi Geriatric Education Center
University of Mississippi Medical Center
2500 North State Street
Jackson, MS 39216-4505
(601) 984-6190

Missouri Gateway Geriatric Education Center
St. Louis University
School of Medicine
1402 S. Grand Boulevard, Room M238
St. Louis, MO 63104
(314) 577-8462

Nevada Geriatric Education Center
University of Nevada at Reno
Sarah Fleishman Building—146
5FB 100D
Reno, NV 89557
(702) 784-1689

New Jersey Geriatric Education Center
University of Medicine and Dentistry of New
 Jersey
School of Osteopathic Medicine
301 S. Central Plaza, Suite 3200
Stratford, NJ 08084-1504
(609) 346-7141

New Mexico Geriatric Education Center*
University of New Mexico
Center for Aging, Research and Services
1836 Lomas Boulevard, NE
Albuquerque, NM 87131-6086
(505) 277-5134

Northwest Geriatric Education Center
University of Washington, HL-23
Seattle, WA 98195
(206) 685-7478

Ohio Valley Appalachia Regional
Geriatric Education Center
University of Kentucky
20 Chandler Medical Center, Annex 1
Lexington, KY 40536-0079
(606) 233-5156

Oklahoma Geriatric Education Center
University of Oklahoma
O'Donoghue Rehabilitation Institute
1122 N.E. 13th Street, Room C4201

Oklahoma City, OK 73117
(405) 271-8558

Oregon Geriatric Education Center
Oregon Health Sciences University
3710 S.W. U.S. Veterans Road (140)
Portland, OR 97201
(503) 721-7821

Pacific Geriatric Education Center*
Los Angeles Caregiver Resource Center
University of Southern California, Los Angeles
3715 McClintock
Los Angeles, CA 90089-0191

Pacific Islands Geriatric Education Center*
University of Hawaii at Manoa
347 W. Kuakini Street
Honolulu, HI 96817
(808) 523-8461

San Diego Geriatric Education Center*
School of Medicine, M-038
University of California, San Diego
La Jolla, CA 92093
(619) 543-6275

South Texas Geriatric Education Center
Department of Dental Diagnostic Science
7703 Floyd Curl Drive
San Antonio, TX 78284-7921
(512) 567-3370

Stanford Geriatric Education Center
Stanford University
703 Welch Road, Suite H-1
Stanford, CA 94305-0151
(415) 723-7063

Texas Consortium of Geriatric Education
  Centers
Baylor College of Medicine
One Baylor Plaza, Room M320
Houston, TX 77030
(713) 798-6470

University of Alabama at Birmingham
Geriatric Education Center
CH-19, Suite 201
933 19th Street South

Birmingham, AL 35294-2041
(205) 934-1094

University of Connecticut*
Geriatric Education Center
Travelers Center on Aging
School of Medicine, MC 5215
Farmington, CT 06030
(203) 679-3956

University of Florida*
Geriatric Education Center
P.O. Box 100277
University of Florida
Gainsville, FL 32610-0277
(904) 395-0651

University of South Florida*
Geriatric Education Center
Suncoast Gerontology Center
University of South Florida Medical Center,
  Box 50
12901 Bruce B. Downs Boulevard
Tampa, FL 33612
(813) 974-4355

Virginia Geriatric Education Center
Virginia Commonwealth University
520 W. 12th Street
The Lyons Building
Richmond, VA 23298-0228
(804) 786-9060

Western New York Geriatric Education Center
State University of New York at Buffalo
Beck Hall
3435 Main Street
Buffalo, NY 14214
(716) 829-3176

Western Reserve Geriatric Education Center
12200 Fairhill Road
Cleveland, OH 44120
(216) 368-5433

Wisconsin Geriatric Education Center
Marquette University
Academic Support Facility, Room 160
735 W. 17th Street
Milwaukee, WI 53233
(414) 288-3712

Americans with Disabilities Act (ADA)[23]

▶ TITLE III HIGHLIGHTS[24]

23. For additional information, contact:

Office on the Americans with Disabilities Act
Civil Rights Division
U.S. Department of Justice
P.O. Box 66118
Washington, DC 20035-6118
(202) 514-0301 (voice)
(202) 514-0383 (TDD)
(202) 514-6193 (electronic bulletin board)

24. For specific ADA guidelines for providing accessibility to places of public accommodation and commercial facilities by individuals with disabilities, see ADA Accessibility Guidelines for Buildings and Facilities; Appendix A to Part 36—Standards for Accessible Design, obtainable from the Department of Justice, Office on the Americans with Disabilities Act.

▶ I. WHO IS COVERED BY TITLE III OF THE ADA

▶ The Title III regulation covers

Public accommodations (i.e., private entities that own, operate, lease, or lease to places of public accommodation),

Commercial facilities

Private entities that offer certain examinations and courses related to educational and occupational certification

▶ Places of public accommodation include over five million private establishments, such as restaurants, hotels, theaters, convention centers, retail stores, shopping centers, dry cleaners, laundromats, pharmacies, doctors' offices, hospitals, museums, libraries, parks, zoos, amusement parks, private schools, day care centers, health spas, and bowling alleys.

▶ Commercial facilities are nonresidential facilities, including office buildings, factories, and warehouses, whose operations affect commerce.

▶ Entities controlled by religious organizations, including places of worship, are not covered.

▶ Private clubs are not covered, except to the extent that the facilities of the private club are made available to customers or patrons of a place of public accommodation.

▶ State and local governments are not covered by the Title III regulation, but rather by the Department of Justice's Title II regulation.

▶ II. OVERVIEW OF REQUIREMENTS

▶ Public accommodations must

Provide goods and services in an integrated setting, unless separate or different measures are necessary to ensure equal opportunity.

Eliminate unnecessary eligibility standards or rules that deny individuals with disabilities an equal opportunity to enjoy the goods and services of a place of public accommodation.

Make reasonable modifications in policies, practices, and procedures that deny equal access to individuals with disabilities, unless a fundamental alteration would result in the nature of the goods and services provided.

Furnish auxiliary aids when necessary to ensure effective communication, unless an undue burden or fundamental alteration would result.

Remove architectural and structural communication barriers in existing facilities where readily achievable.

Provide readily achievable alternative measures when removal of barriers is not readily achievable.

Provide equivalent transportation services and purchase accessible vehicles in certain circumstances.

Maintain accessible features of facilities and equipment.

Design and construct new facilities and, when undertaking alterations, alter existing facilities in accordance with the ADA Accessibility Guidelines issued by the Architectural and Transportation Barriers Compliance Board and incorporated in the final Department of Justice Title III regulation.

▶ A public accommodation is not required to provide personal devices such as wheelchairs; individually prescribed devices (e.g., prescription eyeglasses or hearing aids); or services of a personal nature including assistance in eating, toileting, or dressing.

▶ A public accommodation may not discriminate against an individual or entity because of the known disability of a person with whom the individual or entity is known to associate.

▶ Commercial facilities are only subject to the requirement that new construction and alterations conform to the ADA Accessibility Guidelines. The other requirements applicable to public accommodations listed above do not apply to commercial facilities.

▶ Private entities offering certain examinations or courses (i.e., those related to applications, licensing, certification, or credentialing for secondary or postsecondary education, professional, or trade purposes) must offer them in an accessible place and manner or offer alternative accessible arrangements.

▶ III. "INDIVIDUALS WITH DISABILITIES"

▶ The Americans with Disabilities Act provides comprehensive civil rights protections for "individuals with disabilities."

▶ An individual with a disability is a person who

Has a physical or mental impairment with substantially limits one or more "major life activities," or

Has a record of such an impairment, or

Is regarded as having such an impairment

▶ Examples of physical or mental impairments include, but are not limited to, such contagious and noncontagious diseases and conditions as orthopedic, visual, speech, and hearing impairments; cerebral palsy, epilepsy, muscular dystrophy, multiple sclerosis, cancer, heart disease, diabetes, mental retardation emotional illness, specific learning disabilities, human immunodeficiency virus (HIV) disease (whether symptomatic or asymptomatic), tuberculosis, drug addiction, and alcoholism. Homosexuality and bisexuality are not physical or mental impairments under the ADA.

▶ "Major life activities" include functions such as caring for oneself, performing manual tasks, walking, seeing, hearing, speaking, breathing, learning, and working.

▶ Individuals who currently engage in the illegal use of drugs are not protected by the ADA when an action is taken on the basis of their current illegal use of drugs.

▶ IV. ELIGIBILITY FOR GOODS AND SERVICES

▶ In providing goods and services, a public accommodation may not use eligibility requirements that exclude or segregate individuals with disabilities, unless the requirements are "necessary" for the operation of the public accommodation.

For example, excluding individuals with cerebral palsy from a movie theater or restricting individuals with Down's syndrome to only certain areas of a restaurant would violate the regulation.

▶ Requirements that tend to screen our individuals with disabilities, such as requiring a blind person to produce a driver's license as the sole means of identification for cashing a check, are also prohibited.

▶ Safety requirements may be imposed only if they are necessary for the safe operation of a place of public accommodation. They must be based on actual risks and not on mere speculation, stereotypes, or generalizations about individuals with disabilities.

For example, an amusement park may impose height requirements for certain rides when required for safety.

▶ Extra charges may not be imposed on individuals with disabilities to cover the costs of measures necessary to ensure nondiscriminatory treatment, such as removing barriers or providing qualified interpreters.

▶ V. MODIFICATIONS IN POLICIES, PRACTICES, AND PROCEDURES

▶ A public accommodation must make reasonable modifications in its policies, practices, and procedures in order to accommodate individuals with disabilities.

▶ A modification is not required if it would "fundamentally alter" the goods, services, or operations of the public accommodation.

For example, a department story may need to modify a policy of only permitting one person at a time in a dressing room if an individual with mental retardation needs the assistance of a companion in dressing.

▶ Modifications in existing practices generally must be made to permit the use of guide dogs and other service animals.

▶ Specialists are not required to provide services outside of their legitimate areas of specialization.

For example, a doctor who specializes exclusively in burn treatment may refer an individual with a disability, who is not seeking burn treatment, to another provider. A burn specialist, however, could not refuse to provide burn treatment to, for example, an individual with HIV disease.

▶ VI. AUXILIARY AIDS

▶ A public accommodation must provide auxiliary aids and services when they are necessary to ensure effective communication with individuals with hearing, vision, or speech impairments.

▶ "Auxiliary aids" include such services or devices as qualified interpreters, assistive listening headsets, television captioning and decoders, telecommunications devices for deaf persons (TDDs), videotext displays, readers, taped texts, brailled materials, and large-print materials.

▶ The auxiliary aid requirement is flexible. For example, a brailled menu is not required, if waiters are instructed to read the menu to blind customers.

▶ Auxiliary aids that would result in an undue burden, (i.e., "significant difficulty or expense") or in a fundamental alteration in the nature of the goods or services are not required by the regulation. However, a public accommodation must still furnish another auxiliary aid, if available, that does not result in a fundamental alteration or an undue burden.

▶ VII. EXISTING FACILITIES: REMOVAL OF BARRIERS

▶ Physical barriers to entering and using existing facilities must be removed when "readily achievable."

▶ Readily achievable means "easily accomplishable and able to be carried out without much difficulty or expense."

▶ What is readily achievable will be determined on a case-by-case basis in light of the resources available.

The regulation does not require the rearrangement of temporary or movable structures, such as furniture, equipment, and display racks to the extent that it would result in a significant loss of selling or serving space.

Legitimate safety requirements may be considered in determining what is readily achievable so long as they are based on actual risks and are necessary for safe operation.

▶ Examples of barrier removal measures include

Installing ramps

Making curb cuts at sidewalks and entrances

Rearranging tables, chairs, vending machines, display racks, and other furniture

Widening doorways

Installing grab bars in toilet stalls

Adding raised letters or braille to elevator control buttons

▶ First priority should be given to measures that will enable individuals with disabilities to "get in the front door," followed by measures to provide access to areas providing goods and services.

▶ Barrier removal measures must comply, when readily achievable, with the alterations requirements of the ADA Accessibility Guidelines. If compliance with the Guidelines is not readily achievable, other safe, readily achievable measures must be taken, such as installations of a slightly narrow door than would be required by the guidelines.

▶ VIII. EXISTING FACILITIES: ALTERNATIVES TO BARRIER REMOVAL

▶ The ADA requires the removal of physical barriers, such as stairs, if it is "readily achievable." However, if removal is not readily achievable, alternative steps must be taken to make goods and services accessible.

Examples of alternative measures include

Providing goods and services at the door, sidewalk, or curb

Providing home delivery

Retrieving merchandise from inaccessible shelves or racks

Relocating activities to accessible locations

▶ Extra charges may not be imposed on individuals with disabilities to cover the costs of measures used as alternatives to barrier removal. For example, a restaurant may not charge a wheelchair user extra for home delivery when it is provided as the alternative to barrier removal.

▶ IX. NEW CONSTRUCTION

▶ All newly constructed places of public accommodation and commercial facilities must be accessible to individuals with disabilities to the extent that it is not structurally impracticable.

▶ The new construction requirements apply to any facility occupied after January 26, 1993, for which the last application for a building permit or permit extension is certified as complete after January 26, 1992.

▶ Full compliance will be considered "structurally impracticable" only in those rare circumstances when the unique characteristics of terrain prevent the incorporation of accessibility features (e.g., marshland that requires construction on stilts).

▶ The architectural standards for accessibility in new construction are contained in the ADA Accessiblity Guidelines issued by the Architectural and Transportation Barriers Compliance Board, an independent federal agency. These standards are incorporated in the final Department of Justice Title III regulation.

▶ Elevators are not required in facilities under three stories or with fewer than 3,000 square feet per floor, unless the building is a shopping center, shopping mall, professional office of a health care provider, or station used for public transportation.

▶ X. ALTERATIONS

▶ Alterations after January 26, 1992, to existing places of public accommodation and commercial facilities must be accessible to the maximum extent feasible.

▶ The architectural standards for accessibility in alterations are contained in the ADA Accessibility Guidelines issued by the Architectural and Transportation Barriers Compliance Board. These standards are incorporated in the final Department of Justice Title III regulation.

▶ An alteration is a change that affects usability of a facility. For example, if during remodeling, renovation, or restoration, a doorway is being relocated, the new doorway must be wide enough to meet the requirements of the ADA Accessibility Guidelines.

▶ When alterations are made to a "primary function area," such as the lobby or work areas of a bank, an accessible path of travel to the altered area, and the bathrooms, telephones, and drinking fountains serving that area, must be made accessible to the extent that the added accessibility costs are not disproportionate to the overall cost of the original alteration.

Alterations to windows, hardware, controls, electrical outlets, and signage in primary function areas do not trigger the path of travel requirement.
The added accessibility costs are disproportionate if they exceed 20 pecent of the original alteration.

▶ Elevators are not required in facilities under three stories or with fewer than 3,000 square feet per floor, unless the building is a shopping center, shopping mall, professional office of a health care provider, or station used for public transportation.

▶ XI. OVERVIEW OF AMERICANS WITH DISABILITIES ACT ACCESSIBILITY GUIDELINES FOR NEW CONSTRUCTION AND ALTERATIONS

▶ New construction and alterations must be accessible in compliance with the ADA Accessibility Guidelines.

▶ The Guidelines contain general design ("technical") standards for building and site elements, such as parking, accessible routes, ramps, stairs, elevators, doors, entrances, drinking fountains, bathrooms, controls and operating mechanisms, storage areas, alarms, signage, telephones, fixed seating and tables, assembly areas, automated teller machines, and dressing rooms. They also have specific technical standards for restaurants, medical care facilities, mercantile facilities, libraries, and transient lodging (such as hotels and shelters).

▶ The guidelines also contain "scoping" requirements for various elements (i.e., it specifies how many, and under what circumstances, accessibility features must be incorporated).

▶ Following are examples of scoping requirements in new construction.

At least 50 percent of all public entrances must be accessible. In addition, there must be accessible entrances to enclosed parking, pedestrian tunnels, and elevated walkways.

An accessible route must connect accessible public transportation stops, parking spaces, passenger loading zones, and public streets or sidewalks to all accessible features and spaces within a building.

Every public and common use bathroom must be accessible. Only one stall must be accessible, unless there are six or more stalls, in which case two stalls must be accessible (one of which must be of an alternate, narrow-style design).

Each floor in a building without a supervised sprinkler system must contain an "area of rescue assistance" (i.e., an area with direct access to an exit stairway where people unable to use stairs may await assistance during an emergency evacuation).

One TDD must be provided inside any building that has four or more public pay telephones, counting both interior and exterior phones. In addition, one TDD must be provided whenever there is an interior public pay phone in a stadium or arena; convention center; hotel with a convention center; covered shopping mall; or hospital emergency, recovery, or waiting room.

One accessible public phone must be provided for each floor, unless the floor has two or more banks of phones, in which case there must be one accessible phone for each bank.

Fixed seating assembly areas that accommodate 50 or more people or have audio-amplification systems must have a permanently installed assistive listening system.

Dispersal of wheelchair seating in theaters is required where there are more than 300 seats. In addition, at least 1 percent of all fixed seats must be aisle seats without armrests (or with movable armrests). Fixed seating for companions must be located adjacent to each wheelchair location.

Where automated teller machines are provided, at least one must be accessible.

Five percent of fitting and dressing rooms (but never less than 1 percent) must be accessible.

▶ Following are examples of specific scoping requirements for new construction of special types of facilities, such as restaurants, medical care facilities, mercantile establishments, libraries, and hotels.

In restaurants, generally all dining areas and 5 percent of fixed tables (but not less than 1 percent) must be accessible.

In medical care facilities, all public and common use areas must be accessible. In general-purpose hospitals and in psychiatric and detoxification facilities, 10 percent of patient bedrooms and toilets must be accessible. The required percentage is 100 percent for special facilities treating conditions that affect mobility, and 50 percent for long-term facilities and nursing homes.

In mercantile establishments, at least one of each type of counter containing a cash register and at least one of each design of checkout aisle must be accessible. In some cases, additional checkout aisles are required to be accessible (i.e., from 20 to 40 percent) depending on the number of checkout aisles and the size of the facility.

In libraries, all public areas must be accessible. In addition, 5 percent of fixed tables or study carrels (or at least 1 percent) must be accessible. At least one lane at the checkout area and aisles between card catalogs, magazine displays, and stacks must be accessible.

In hotels, 4 percent of the first 100 rooms and approximately 2 percent of rooms in excess of 100 must be accessible to persons with hearing impairments (i.e., must contain visual alarms, visual notification devices, volume-control telephones, and an accessible electrical outlet for a TDD) and to persons with mobility impairments. Moreover, an identical percentage of additional rooms must be accessible to persons with hearing impairments.

Technical and scoping requirements for alterations are sometimes less stringent than those for new construction. For example, when compliance with the new construction requirements would be technically infeasible, one accessible unisex bathroom per floor is acceptable.

► XII. EXAMINATIONS AND COURSES

► Certain examinations or courses offered by a private entity (i.e., those that are related to applications, licensing, certification, or credentialing for secondary or postsecondary education, professional, or trade purposes) must either be given in a place and manner accessible to persons with disabilities, or be made accessible through alternative means.

► In order to provide an examination in an accessible place and manner, a private entity must

Assure that the examination measures what it is intended to measure, rather than reflecting the individuals's impaired sensory, manual, or speaking skills.

Modify the examination format when necessary (e.g., permit additional time).

Provide auxiliary aids (e.g., taped examinations, interpreters, large-print answer sheets, or qualified readers), unless they would fundamentally alter the measurement of the skills or knowledge that the examination is intended to test or would result in an undue burden.

Offer any modified examination at an equally convenient location, as often, and in as timely a manner as are other examinations.

Administer examinations in a facility that is accessible or provide alternative comparable arrangements, such as providing the examination at an individual's home with a proctor.

▶ In order to provide a course in an accessible place and manner, a private entity may need to

Modify the course format or requirements (e.g., permit additional time for completion of the course).

Provide auxiliary aids, unless a fundamental alteration or undue burden would result.

Administer the course in a facility that is accessible or provide alternative comparable arrangements, such as provision of the course through videotape, audiocassettes, or prepared notes.

▶ XIII. ENFORCEMENT OF THE ADA AND ITS REGULATION

▶ Private parties may bring lawsuits to obtain court orders to stop discrimination. No monetary damages will be available in such suits. A reasonable attorney's fee, however, may be awarded.

▶ Individuals may also file complaints with the Attorney General who is authorized to bring lawsuits in cases of general public importance or where a "pattern or practice" of discrimination is alleged.

▶ In suits brought by the Attorney General, monetary damages (not including punitive damages) and civil penalties may be awarded. Civil penalties may not exceed $50,000 for a first violation or $100,000 for any subsequent violation.

▶ XIV. TECHNICAL ASSISTANCE

▶ The ADA requires that the federal agencies responsible for issuing ADA regulations provide "technical assistance."

▶ Technical assistance is the dissemination of information (either directly by the Department of Justice or through grants and contracts) to assist the public, including individuals protected by the ADA and entities covered by the ADA, in understanding the new law.

▶ Methods of providing information include, e.g., audiovisual materials, pamphlets, manuals, electronic bulletin boards, checklists, and training.

▶ The Department of Justice issued for public comment on December 5, 1990, a government-wide plan for the provision of technical assistance.

The Department of Justice's efforts focus on raising public awareness of the ADA by providing

Fact sheets and pamphlets in accessible formats

Speakers for workshops, seminars, classes, and conferences

An ADA telephone information line

Access to ADA documents through an electronic bulletin board for users of personal computers

▶ The department has established a comprehensive program of technical assistance relating to public accommodations and state and local governments

Grants will be awarded for projects to inform individuals with disabilities and covered entities about their rights and responsibilities under the ADA and to facilitate voluntary compliance.

The Department of Justice will issue a technical assistance manual by January 26, 1992, for individuals or entities with rights or duties under the ADA.

Index